ST. MARY'S UNIVERSITY COLLEGE LIBRARY
A COLLEGE OF THE QUEENS UNIVERSITY OF BELFAST

Tel. 028 90268237
Web site www.stmarys-belfast.ac.uk
email: library@stmarys-belfast.ac.uk

Fines are charged for overdue and recalled books not returned by notified date.
You will be notified by email of the new date for Recalled books.

Date Due	Date Due	Date Due
2 6 JAN 2015		
1 8 DEC 2018		

CHRIST IN ETERNITY AND TIME:
MODERN ANGLICAN PERSPECTIVES

To my mother and father,

Kathleen and Willie Coll

CHRIST IN ETERNITY AND TIME

Modern Anglican Perspectives

NIALL COLL

With a foreword by John Macquarrie

FOUR COURTS PRESS

Set in 10.5 on 12.5 point Ehrhardt for
FOUR COURTS PRESS LTD
Fumbally Lane, Dublin 8, Ireland
e-mail: info@four-courts-press-ie
http//www.four-courts-press.ie
and in North America for
FOUR COURTS PRESS
c/o ISBS, 5824 N.E. Hassalo Street, Portland, OR 97213.

A catalogue record for this title
is available from the British Library.

ISBN 1–85182–599–1

Printed in Great Britain
by MPG Books, Bodmin, Cornwall

Foreword

It is a privilege to be invited to write a foreword commending Dr Coll's book. It is a work which deserves to be read in its own right, as a thoughtful contribution toward a clearer understanding of one of the most important topics in Christian theology, namely, the doctrine of the Person of Christ. Based on the author's doctoral thesis submitted to the Gregorian University, the book is distinguished by the high qualities of scholarship which we associate with that eminent institution.

But the work is to be welcomed not only as a significant piece of theological reflection, but in addition as a new voice in the current dialogue between Roman Catholics and Anglicans. Not many years ago, theologians of these two communions went their separate ways without bothering to read one another's writings, or were perhaps even discouraged from doing so. Fortunately, that time has now passed, and something like a genuine dialogue is now going on.

In such a dialogue, there will sometimes come about the discovery that there is already a surprising extent of agreement between the two communions, as happened in the case of the 'agreed statements' on the eucharist and ministry, but the dialogue will also focus on areas of disagreement, which will call for further study. Much of this work will be done by individual theologians, and Dr Coll's book is a notable example of how deeper and better understanding may be built up.

He confines his study to the topic of the pre-existence of Christ, as expounded by four Anglican theologians of the twentieth century. His interpretation of these writers is both sympathetic and critical. It will be a very good experience for Anglicans and Roman Catholics alike to read these pages.

John Macquarrie

Contents

Preface

This book studies the interpretations of the doctrine of Christ's pre-existence to be found in the writings of four twentieth-century Anglican authors: Lionel S. Thornton, Eric L. Mascall, John A.T. Robinson and John Macquarrie. The work began life as a doctoral thesis submitted to the Gregorian University, Rome in 1995. I should like to take this opportunity to thank Professor Gerald O'Collins SJ for his careful supervision during my research. He gave me the benefit of his wide learning and enormous application to the field of christology, for which I am most grateful. Professor Jacques Dupuis SJ examined my thesis and I would like to thank him for his critical comments.

At all stages of my research I was shown much kindness by Professor John Macquarrie, one of the authors whose work is examined here. When I visited him in Oxford to discuss his christology he received me with the courtesy and respect that are his hallmarks. I should like to take this opportunity to thank him for placing his great erudition at my disposal. Later, I sent him a copy of my dissertation. Having read it, he kindly urged me to publish it, even though it offered some criticisms of his work. I thank him most sincerely for contributing the generous foreword to this volume.

In preparing the thesis for presentation and this book for publication, I had access to many sources. In particular, I am grateful for the use of library facilities at the following: the Gregorian University, Rome; the Anglican Centre, Rome; the Pontifical Irish College, Rome; Pusey College, Oxford; Campion Hall, Oxford; St Patrick's College, Carlow; St Patrick's College, Maynooth; the Milltown Institute of Theology and Philosophy, Dublin; Trinity College, Dublin; the Dublin Diocesan Library; the Representative Church Body Library, Dublin.

I would also like to acknowledge my indebtedness to the staff and students of both of the colleges in Rome where I resided during my time of research: the Pontifical Irish College and the Collegio di Santa Maria dell'Anima.

A special word of thanks is also due to my former colleagues and students at St Patrick's College, Carlow, and to my former and present bishops, Dr Seamus Hegarty and Dr Philip Boyce, respectively, for their encouragement.

Thanks is also due to my family and friends for their support, and to Helen Wynne and Graham Harrison for their eagle-eyed copy-editing and for their invaluable suggestions. Finally, I am also indebted to Michael Adams and his colleagues at Four Courts Press.

List of abbreviations

ABD   D.N. Freedman (ed. in chief), *The Anchor Bible Dictionary*, 6 vols. (New York, 1992).

CCCH   E.L. Mascall, *Christ, the Christian and the Church: A Study of the Incarnation and its Consequences* (London, 1946).

CLBC   L.S. Thornton, *The Common Life in the Body of Christ*, 4th ed. (London, 1963).

CTNS   E.L. Mascall, *Christian Theology and Natural Sciences: Some Questions in Their Relation*, The Bampton Lectures of 1956, (London, 1956).

DS   H. Denzinger & A. Schönmetzer (eds), *Enchiridion Symbolorum, definitionum et declarationum de rebus fidei et morum*, 25th ed. (Freiburg, 1973).

HFG   J.A.T. Robinson, *The Human Face of God* (London, 1973).

IL   L.S. Thornton, *The Incarnate Lord* (London, 1928).

JCMT   J. Macquarrie, *Jesus Christ in Modern Thought* (London, 1990).

Jesus   E.L. Mascall, *Jesus: He Who Is And How We Know Him* (London, 1985).

NJBC   R. Brown et al. (eds), *The New Jerome Biblical Commentary* (Englewood Cliffs, New Jersey, 1990).

ODCC   F.L. Cross & E.A. Livingstone (eds), *The Oxford Dictionary of the Christian Church*, 3rd ed. (Oxford, 1997).

PJ   J.A.T. Robinson, *The Priority of John* (London, 1985).

RR   J.A.T. Robinson, *The Roots of a Radical* (London, 1980).

TCM   J. Macquarrie, *Theology, Church and Ministry* (London, 1986).

TGC   E.L. Mascall, *Theology and the Gospel of Christ: An Essay in Reorientation* (London, 1977).

WHHM   E.L. Mascall, *Whatever Happened to the Human Mind?* (London, 1980).

I

Introduction

PRE-EXISTENCE UNDER FIRE

Christology is a vital concern of Christian theology, and the twentieth century has witnessed much activity in the christological field. In the West the accounts of christology, both Catholic and Protestant, whatever their differences, strikingly converge in their firm insistence that the christological enterprise take utterly seriously the full humanity and human history of Jesus Christ.[1] In holding resolutely to this position, these contemporary christologies have felt it necessary to break with centuries of high classical christology which characteristically focused on metaphysical reflection concerning the divine sonship of Jesus Christ.[2] This break has been so comprehensive in many quarters, and the urge to emphasise the humanity of Christ so complete, that many feel compelled to revise drastically, others to reject completely, a doctrine which figured prominently in the classical christological formulations: Christ's pre-existence as the eternal Son of God.[3] Talk of such pre-existence – the belief that Jesus Christ somehow had a personal history with God prior to his human life – is judged to jeopardise Jesus' true and full humanity.[4]

1 See, for example, the writings of such Protestant scholars as as G. Ebeling, J. Hick, E. Jüngel, J. Moltmann W. Pannenberg, and such Catholic scholars as J. Dupuis, W. Kasper, D. Lane, H. Küng, K-J. Kuschel, G. O'Collins, K. Rahner, E. Schillebeeckx, J. Sobrino. For an introduction to the salient characteristics of twentieth-century christology, see A. Schilson, 'Christologie', *Lexikon für Theologie und Kirche*, vol. 2, 3rd ed. (Freiburg etc., 1994), 1164-74.   2 This is not to infer that they all necessarily deny what Karl-Josef Kuschel has termed 'the abiding validity of classical christology'. See his *Born before All Time? The Dispute over Christ's Origin* (London: 1992), 424. The most outstanding exception to this trend in contemporary christology is arguably the work of the Swiss, Catholic theologian, Hans Urs von Balthasar. He resolutely chooses a method 'from above'. His christology draws heavily from the Johannine theology of the Word become flesh. For a concise introduction to his christology, see J. O'Donnell, *Hans Urs von Balthasar* (London, 1992), 44-53.   3 Brendan Byrne, citing what he characterises as 'Kuschel's massive survey of the question from Barth to Schilllebeeckx', claims that for many contemporary scholars the doctrine is the cause of 'a grave embarrassment'. See his 'Christ's Pre-Existence in Pauline Soteriology', *Theological Studies*, 58 (1997) 309.   4 A striking articulation of this viewpoint is to be found in the writings of Roger Haight when he claims that

These contemporary accounts of christology which are cautious about, if not downright hostile towards, pre-existence target a doctrine which has deep roots in the formulations of classical christology. Even before we consider whether the New Testament *in fact* upholds Christ's pre-existence and whether the doctrine *really* threatens the fullness of Christ's humanity, it is evident that the conciliar teachings of the early Church, framed as they are in a language of ontology, uphold, or at least obviously imply, the doctrine. These teachings are based on the firm presupposition, often disputed today, that the New Testament itself clearly teaches the doctrine.[5] The First Council of Nicea (325 AD), in rebutting the claims of Arius, refers to the only-begotten consubstantial Son of the (eternal) Father and mediator of creation: 'begotten, not made, one in being (*homoousios*) with the Father, through whom all things were made' (*DS* 125). Any suggestion that there was a time when he was not is flatly rejected (*DS* 126). The First Council of Constantinople (381 AD) repeats and develops this theme: he was born of the Father 'before all time' (*DS* 150). The Council of Chalcedon (451 AD) speaks of the two births of the one Son: 'the same one in being (*homoousios*) with the Father as to the divinity and one in being with us as to the humanity ... begotten from the Father before the ages as to the divinity ...' (*DS* 301).

For conciliar orthodoxy, then, the Son shares in the divine attribute of eternity: he exists timelessly, since eternity is itself timeless. An explicit trinitarian doctrine of God is taking shape and it is seen that belief in a triune God implies belief in the incarnation of the eternal, pre-existent Son of God, consubstantial with the Father. In finding the language to express this conviction, the christology of the early Councils, and indeed later christological speculations, drew upon some of the philosophical insights and categories concerning the questions of time and eternity then in vogue in the Greco-Roman world, especially in Neoplatonic circles. Reflection on the concepts of time and eternity would continue in the wake of these great christological Councils. Eternity would find its classical formulation in the writings of the philosopher Boethius (*c*.480–*c*.524); echoing much of the Neoplatonism of Plotinus and Proclus, he commented that 'Eternity is the complete and total possession of unending life all at once'.[6] Thomas Aquinas' teaching on time and eternity is heavily influenced by Boethius: he argues that God is eternal in the sense of being distinct from time.[7] The importance of a

'The problem with a notion of the pre-existence of Jesus is that it is incompatible with the doctrine of Chalcedon that Jesus is consubstantial with us'. See his *Jesus Symbol of God* (Maryknoll, New York, 1999), 459, n.67. 5 For christological orthodoxy the doctrine of Christ's pre-existence does not depend on any particular philosophical frame of reference: it arose not as a consequence of philosophical speculation but as the inevitable outcome of inquiry into the personal identity of the risen One. 6 *'Aeternitas est interminabilis vitae tota simul et perfecta possessio.'* See Boethius, *Consolatio Philosophiae*, Book V, Prose 6. For text see E.K. Rand (ed.), in H.F. Stewart, E.K. Rand, & S.J. Tester (eds), *Boethius: The Theological Tractates and the Consolation of Philosophy* (London, 1973). 7 See B. Davies, *The Thought of Thomas Aquinas*

careful philosophical analysis of time and eternity for the modern debate concerning Christ's pre-existence will become apparent below.

The aim of this book is to explore critically how four twentieth-century Anglican theologians understand the doctrine of Christ's pre-existence: Lionel S. Thornton, Eric L. Mascall, John A.T. Robinson and John Macquarrie.[8] An examination of these authors should furnish us with a fairly representative overview of the general shape of thought concerning Christ's pre-existence in certain Anglican circles in England during this period. This study does not set out to deal with the whole modern discussion about pre-existence – that would have be impossible if it were to be kept within bounds.[9] Nor does it deal with the incarnation as such. Nevertheless, it must be said that we cannot have a doctrine of pre-existence without also having a doctrine of the incarnation: the pre-existent, eternal Son of God took flesh from his human mother; the historical Christ is at once fully God and fully human.[10]

Given the intimate relationship between an author's approach to christology in general and his interpretation of the doctrine of Christ's pre-existence in particular, this study in its treatment of each author first sets out his overarching approach to christology before focusing in detail on his interpretation of Christ's pre-existence. It takes the writers in chronological sequence, summarises the relevant biographical material, indicates the sources on which they drew and the notable influences they manifest, sketches their overall christologies, and then focuses in detail on their specific treatments of Christ's pre-existence.

The final chapter, entitled 'Critical issues', explores the parallels between each writer's treatment of pre-existence and his interpretations of other key issues like resurrection and divine identity. It then investigates what precisely is meant by the term pre-existence and acknowledge that there is a certain ambiguity about the very term 'pre-existence' which might lead one to conclude mistakenly that it implies temporal succession, as though Christ merely anteceded or antedated everything that later began in or with time. The final two 'critical issues' discuss the significance for christology of a debate among Anglo–American philosophers of religion on the concept of eternity, and asks whether we can speak of a single, distinctive Anglican approach to the question of Christ's pre-existence.

(Oxford, 1992), 104.   8 No specific studies of any of the four authors' treatments of Christ's pre-existence had previously been made. The overall christologies of two of these writers have been the subjects of doctoral research: P.S.Y. Shen, *The Christology of L.S. Thornton* (Chicago, 1969) and E.L. Piotrowski, *The Christology of E.L. Mascall* (Rome, 1987). No systematic studies of the christological perspectives of Robinson and Macquarrie have yet appeared.   9 A good introduction to this modern discussion and to exegetical considerations is Kuschel's aforementioned *Born before All Time*?   10 Balthasar gets to the heart of this matter when he writes that the 'Word, which is one with God's wisdom, was in the beginning with God and was God; God 'sends' it into the world as a Word-made-flesh, there to manifest his 'glory' in the fullness of 'grace and truth'. See his *Theo-Drama*, vol. 3 (San Francisco, 1992), 255.

GENERAL CHARACTERISTICS AND MAJOR PREOCCUPATIONS OF
ANGLICAN THEOLOGY BETWEEN WORLD WAR ONE AND THE 1960S

The four Anglican authors whose interpretations of Christ's pre-existence form
the subject of this study were all born within a thirty-five year period between
1884 and 1919. The earliest of them, Thornton, was still a youth when the twentieth century began, and the other three are clearly children of that new century.
It is appropriate then at the outset to dwell briefly on the general shape of Anglican theology in the decades between the Great War and the 1960s.[11] But just
before that, a word is necessary on Anglican self-understanding and theological
method, of which no criticism will be offered until the final chapter.

H.R. McAdoo has commented that what is distinctive about Anglicanism from
the Reformation in the sixteenth century to the present day, by contrast with
Roman Catholicism and some forms of Calvinism, is its refusal to affirm as *de fide*
any doctrine not clearly held by Scripture or the primitive Church.[12] He concurs with the classic formulation of Anglican theological heritage by Lancelot
Andrewes: 'One canon ..., two testaments, three creeds, four general councils, five
centuries and the series of the Fathers in that period ... determine the boundary of
our faith.'[13] For McAdoo Anglicanism is not a theological system but a particular
method; its distinctiveness 'proceeds not from systematic theology but from the
spirit in which theological questions are handled'.[14] In this judgement he is in
agreement with Michael Ramsey who has written that Anglican theology is
neither a system nor a confession, 'but a method, a use and a direction, it cannot
be defined or even perceived as a 'thing in itself' ...'[15] William Temple has commented that the special character and the peculiar contribution of Anglicanism to
the universal Church arise from the fact, that it has been enabled

> to combine in [its] one fellowship the traditional Faith and Order of the
> Catholic church with the immediacy of approach to God through Christ
> to which the Evangelical Churches especially bear witness, and freedom of

11 We begin with the immediate post-World War One theology since it was to be of such decisive importance for Thornton, the first of our authors. The 1960s limit is explained by the
conviction here that the general direction of each one's overall theological outlook was firmly in
place by then (indeed as that decade began Thornton was already a very old man).   12 H.R.
McAdoo (1916-98), the former Anglican Archbishop of Dublin and Anglican co-chairman of
the first Anglican-Roman Catholic International Commission, draws attention to Anglicanism's refusal to make essential, for example, the Marian dogmas or Calvinist teaching on
election and reprobation. See his *Anglican Heritage: Theology and Spirituality* (Norwich, 1991),
2.   13 L. Andrewes, *Opuscula Quadem Posthuma* (Oxford, 1852), 3. Bishop successively of
Chichester, Ely and Winchester, Andrewes (1555-1626) is regarded as one of the principal
influences in the formation of Anglican theology.   14 H.R. McAdoo, *The Spirit of Anglicanism:
A Survey of Anglican Theological Method in the Seventeenth Century* (London, 1965), 5.   15
A.M. Ramsey, as quoted in S.W. Sykes, *The Integrity of Anglicanism* (London, 1978), 63.

intellectual inquiry whereby the correlation of the Christian revelation and advancing knowledge is constantly effected.[16]

Thus Anglicanism maintains that its doctrine is both catholic and reformed. It is catholic because it holds to the faith of Christ, as professed by the early Church and expressed in the Nicene-Constantinople Creed and in the early Church Fathers, and because it retains many of the traditions associated with the Catholic Church in terms of liturgy and order. Anglicanism is reformed because it affirms the primacy of Scripture in determining doctrine, rejects the authority of the pope, and places salvation by faith at the centre of its thinking.[17]

Following the First World War and across the decades down to the 1960s, there was much intellectual ferment, sharp debate and bitter disagreement in Anglican theology concerning christological matters. The thrust of the interpretation of Christ's pre-existence in each of our theologians respectively was deeply influenced by their differing reactions, both positive and negative, to the various, often conflicting, streams of orthodox and heterodox christological thought which ebbed and flowed during that period.

We can begin, then, by noting that, in the years leading up to the outbreak of the First World War, Anglican theology was greatly influenced by Continental Liberal Protestantism. Many Anglican scholars, known as 'Modernists', imbibed a great number of ideas from the works of such continental theologians as Albrecht Ritschl, Adolf Harnack, Albert Schweitzer and Alfred Firmin Loisy.[18] So strong was the German influence on liberal English theology at this time, that W. Stählin could be quoted as saying: 'what Germany thinks today, Britain will begin to think tomorrow'.[19] The Churchman's Union, founded in 1898 (renamed the Modern Churchman's Union in 1928), was dedicated to the task of advancing liberal religious thought within the Church of England. Among those especially associated with this group, Alister McGrath notes the following: Kirsopp Lake (1872-1946), E.W. Barnes (1874-1953), Hastings Rashdall (1858-1924), H.D.A. Major (1871-1961) and William R. Inge (1860-1954).[20]

Following the First World War there was a resurgence in the fortunes of the orthodox, Anglo-Catholic wing of the Church of England. (Evangelicalism, however, within the Church 'was never weaker than in the 1920s'.)[21] The publication of *Essays Catholic and Critical* (1926), to which such scholars as Lionel S.

---

16 W. Temple, *Lambeth Conferences* (1867-1930) (London, 1948), 113-4. Temple (1881-1944) is a former Archbishop of Canterbury.   17 G. L. Carey, 'Anglicanism' in R.P. McBrien (general ed.), *The HarperCollins Encyclopedia of Catholicism* (New York, 1995), 49.   18 A.M. Ramsey, *From Gore to Temple* (London: 1950), 61.   19 Quoted in B. Leeming, 'Reflections on English Christology', in A. Grillmeier & H. Bacht (eds), Das Konzil von Chalkedon, vol. 3 (Würzburg, 1954), 703.   20 A. McGrath, *The Renewal of Anglicanism* (London, 1993), 127.   21 A. Hastings, *A History of English Christianity, 1920-1985* (London, 1986), 234.

Thornton, John K. Mozley and Edwyn C. Hoskyns contributed, signalled the emergence of a significant new theological school whose most salient characteristic was the repudiation of liberal presuppositions in theology.[22] In the first preface to the book, the editor, E.G. Selwyn, claimed that the volume was in the succession, as well as the tradition, of the *Lux Mundi* essays.[23] In due course it came to constitute what J.M. Creed has termed 'the most vigorous theological movement' of post-First World War England.[24] It was characterised in particular by a rejection of the general heterodox tendencies that characterised christology in the previous century, and Bernard Leeming could thus approvingly claim that in England 'the twenties of our century saw a growing appreciation of the failure of "Liberal Theology"'.[25] Although this volume of essays made no reference to Karl Barth and his *Römerbrief* (1918), much of it clearly recalls the Swiss theologian's devastating critique of nineteenth-century (Continental) liberal theologies.[26] (An English translation of the second edition of Barth's work appeared in 1933 as *The Epistle to the Romans*.) Anglo-Catholicism grew in strength in the 1930s, attracting such famous converts as T.S. Eliot (1888-1965) and W.H. Auden (1907-73).

In the immediate wake of the Second World War, the main impetus in Anglican theology passed to the field of biblical studies. Fundamental matters, such as belief in God or in Christ, were seldom discussed: it was as if they were secure and might be taken for granted.[27] This period was to be a particularly

---

22 The prominent theologian and historian, Adrian Hastings, has spoken of it as a school of theological thought which was 'at once more roundly Catholic than anything going before it but also far more critically liberal than any of its orthodox predecessors. Effectively it gave back to the Church of England a viable theology of the supernatural, modifying the crudities of earlier Anglo-Catholic attitudes and producing a corpus of scholarship, at once creative and essentially orthodox ...' See his *A History of English Christianity, 1920-1985*, 234.   23 E.G. Selwyn, *Essays Catholic and Critical*, 3rd ed. (London, 1931), xxvii. *Lux Mundi* (1890), a volume under the editorship of the prominent Anglo-Catholic, Charles Gore (1853-1932), arose as an attempt to accommodate the orthodox faith of the Oxford Movement to the best insights of the liberal, nineteenth-century mind on science, criticism, and philosophy. Its aim was to recover, on the one hand, the balance that had been lost in the neglect of tradition by rationalists and evangelicals, and, on the other, the need to redress the Tractarian tendency to emphasise tradition at the expense of reason. See R. Morgan, 'Preface', in R. Morgan (ed.), *The Religion of the Incarnation: Anglican Essays in memory of Lux Mundi* (Bristol, 1991), xvii-xviii. *Lux Mundi* is regarded as 'the founding document of liberal Catholicism in the Church of England'; see C. Welch, *Protestant Thought in the Nineteenth Century* (New Haven, 1985), 168.   24 J.M. Creed, *The Divinity of Christ: A Study in the History of Christian Doctrine since Kant* (Cambridge, 1938), 10.   25 Leeming., 'Reflections on English Christology', 712.   26 Barth's message in this book was strengthened in a second (completely revised) edition and several subsequent editions. He argued that the liberal theologies had been so anxious to adjust Christianity to the culture of the age that its genuine content had been submerged. He then went on to argue that liberal theology was responsible in a large measure for the spiritual plight of Europe and for the dreadful events of the First World War and what followed it.   27 P.A. Welsby, *A History of the Church of*

happy one for the Evangelical wing of English Anglicanism.[28] Meanwhile, as David Edwards notes, English popular culture was marked by an accelerated 'process of dechristianization'.[29] Central theological concerns, however, were to return very much to centre stage in the face of the storm which broke out in Church of England academic circles in the 1960s with a radical questioning of the traditional understanding of God and of Christ. This development was occasioned by the publication of two books, the first of which was a volume of essays published by a group of Cambridge academics under the title, *Soundings: Essays concerning Christian Understanding* (1962)[30] and the second, the popularly written *Honest to God* (1963) by John Robinson.

Having sketched the principal contours of the Anglican theological terrain between the Great War and the 1960s, and hinted at the ebb and flow in the successive tides of liberalism and orthodoxy in its theology, we can now examine the christological ideas of four leading Anglican theologians of the twentieth century. In the chapters which follow, it will be seen that the two earlier writers, Thornton and Mascall, were firmly convinced of the need to recover a solidly orthodox understanding of Christ. In the two later authors, Robinson and Macquarrie, greater openness to the tide carrying heterodox ideas will become apparent.

England (Oxford, 1984), 67.   28 The Evangelicals drew most of their theology from Dutch Calvinism.   29 D. Edwards, *Leaders of the Church of England, 1828-1978* (London, 1978), 343. We should note that this process did not, of course, begin at this time. Discussing the 1920s, Adrian Hastings judges that even if the Church of England was the Established Church and most of the English people at least nominal members, the principal intellectual (as opposed to social) orthodoxy of the time was 'a confident agnosticism'. Orthodox Christianity, he argues, appeared increasingly implausible to the intelligent person; only the clergy, Roman Catholics and a few eccentric medievalists were believed to be exempt from this state of affairs. Hastings goes on: 'To believe meant standing out against every single one of the giants of modernity, the prophets who had established the framework of understanding wherein which intellectual discourse, the whole modern civilisation of the mind, seemed now established. Ever since the middle of the Victorian age a climate of unbelief had been building up ... Religious thinking was more and more simply abandoned among the wise as essentially primitive and, in the modern world, redundant - it would be eliminated on the principle of Occam's razor, the law of parsimony. It was simply no longer needed'. Hence Hastings can echo the sentiments of A.E. Taylor the Anglican Platonist, when he declared at the Anglo-Catholic Congress of 1920: 'The fate of our Christianity is visibly hanging in the balance'. See Hastings, *A History of English Christianity, 1920-1985*, 221-2.   30 It was edited by Alec Vidler, Dean of King's College, and published by Cambridge University Press.

2

Lionel S. Thornton's interpretation of Christ's pre-existence

INTRODUCTION

Lionel Spencer Thornton was born in 1884, the son of an evangelical Church of England country rector. He attended Malvern College and Emmanuel College, Cambridge. In 1907 he obtained his BA, with a first class in theology, winning the Carus Greek New Testament Prize. In 1913 he was awarded the Norrisian Prize for an essay which later became his first book, *Conduct and the Supernatural* (1915). In 1928 he published *The Incarnate Lord* for which he received his BD. In 1943 he was awarded a DD from Cambridge after the publication of *The Common Life in the Body of Christ* (1942). A year later in 1944, he was the recipient of an honorary doctorate from the University of Durham.

Thornton was ordained into the Anglican priesthood in 1909, and served as curate at both St. Paul's, Lorrimore Square, London, and at Lingfield. In 1913 he entered the religious life when he joined the Community of the Resurrection, Mirfield, Yorkshire. He was professed in 1915. From 1914 to 1944 he served as tutor and lecturer at the College of the Resurrection and it was in that office that he wrote most of his books. In 1944 he left Mirfield and spent some years at the London Priory of the Community. From there he returned to Mirfield in 1959 and resumed his lectures at the College of the Resurrection.

In 1922 he was appointed by the Archbishops of Canterbury and York to the Commission on Christian Doctrine. He submitted various memoranda to the Commission before it finally published its report in 1938. Alan Wilkinson, who has written a history of the Community of the Resurrection, has claimed that Thornton gained much from his membership of this Commission. When it finished its work, Thornton became increasingly isolated, at least in terms of the breadth of intellectual ideas to which he was exposed; he was never a member of a university faculty.[1]

---

1 A. Wilkinson, *The Community of the Resurrection: A Centenary History* (London, 1992), 188. Wilkinson hints that this relative seclusion contributed to Thornton's movement away from interest in contemporary philosophical issues in theology.

Thornton was naturally shy and abstracted in temperament. It is said that he required a good deal of private explanation for any but the most unsubtle jokes. But then as E.L. Mascall (who knew him well) remarked: 'although this was in many ways a handicap, it had the compensating advantage that he found it natural and easy to take everybody seriously'.[2] He was also, except in theological controversy, notoriously silent. This is well illustrated by Wilkinson when he recalls the story about how a guest at Mirfield, on seeing Thornton sitting isolated from the others at tea, asked his name. A *confrère* immediately quipped: 'That is Fr Thornton. He is writing a book on the Common Life!'.

Thornton's main publications

As was noted above, his first book was *Conduct and the Supernatural* (1915) an essay concerning the supremacy of the Christian ethic. Then came *Richard Hooker* (1924), a study of the thought of the influential sixteenth-century Anglican theologian. Thornton saw Hooker as significant in that he marked the divide between Anglican and Reformed theology. He also turned his attention to the question of the atonement with his *The Doctrine of the Atonement* (1937). In 1926 Thornton contributed to the influential Anglo-Catholic *Essays Catholic and Critical*[3] with an essay on 'The Doctrine of God'. He emphasised the utter dependence of the created world upon God, and the sacramental significance of that world. His most significant work, *The Incarnate Lord* (1928), saw him expound the doctrine of the incarnation in terms of the contemporary philosophy of organism, as enunciated by the philosopher, A.N. Whitehead, as we shall see below. Thornton's next book, *The Common Life in the Body of Christ* (1942), marked a turning-point in his thought and the beginning of the second and final phase of his career. In the preface to this book, the scope of Thornton's shift was evident from the question that he posed: 'What if the Gospel became obscured by our presuppositions and preoccupations, so that we neither see the scope of its application nor suffer it to speak for itself?'[4] In this work the interplay of biblical and philosophical categories had disappeared and there was no critical analysis of the stages of biblical thought. Whitehead's name does not even appear in the index. Scripture was now interpreted by scripture. More and more, in the works that followed upon this, Thornton immersed himself in the typological study of the bible. He recognised connections that had never before been seen. In doing so, however, he failed to clarify the principles by which he drew these conclusions. Thus Michael Ramsey (as Archbishop of York), in an appreciation of Thornton published after his death in 1960, commented: 'I was one of those rarely convinced [by his typological exegesis], ready to say that eccentricity had crept into the working of his mind, and suspecting that he was not always quite serious.'[5]

2 E.L. Mascall, *Saraband* (Leominster, 1992), 174-5.   3 Published under the editorship of E.G. Selwyn.   4 *The Common Life in the Body of Christ*, 1st ed. (London, 1942), xiii; hereafter CLBC.   5 A.M. Ramsey, 'Lionel Thornton: Theologian' in *CLBC*, 4th ed., 1963, ix.

Notwithstanding, these vagaries, Ramsey acknowledges that Thornton was saying much else besides: about the wholeness of the bible in its witness to Christ, the unity of creation and redemption, and the essence of revelation in its forms. These convictions emerged in *Revelation and the Modern World* (1950), *The Dominion of Christ* (1952) and *Christ and the Church* (1956). In these books, which formed a trilogy called *The Form of the Servant*, Thornton advanced the conviction that revelation does not merely transcend the cultural environment; it masters and transforms it by a process of condescension. Interpolated into the series was the volume *Confirmation: Its Place in the Baptismal Mystery* (1954).

In the opinion of the great majority of commentators, Thornton's best contributions to theology came in the earlier stage of his career when he attempted to relate the revelation of God in Christ to a school of philosophical thought then current. This study accepts this basic presupposition and is mainly directed towards an exposition of the *early* Thornton's interpretation of the pre-existence of Christ, since in the second phase of his career Thornton's attentions had shifted from a primarily incarnational focus to one which viewed the incarnation in its relation to the Church (this is not to suggest, however, that he left the incarnation aside). This study, in attempting to come to terms with the earlier strains of his thought, is arguably meeting Thornton at his very best. (After all, as Bernard Leeming has commented, in tones of understatement: 'Thornton's later books, though interesting, are somewhat subtle').[6] Thornton's obituarist claimed that his interest in Whiteheadian philosophy returned towards the end of his life, stimulated to some extent by the thought of Teilhard de Chardin, which he found *sympathique*.[7] In the next section an attempt will be made to identify the forces, intellectual and cultural, which shaped the thought of the early Thornton.

A critical thinker
In the first chapter we said something about the uncertain state of religious belief in England after the First World War, characterising the general tone as being one of 'a confident agnosticism'. It was in this religious and intellectual matrix of increasing agnosticism, if not downright atheism, that the younger Thornton would have to apply his intellectual energies. From the outset Thornton's commitment to theological orthodoxy was clear:[8] he was a member of the theologically orthodox Anglo-Catholic wing of the Church of England.[9] If he was to be successful, however, in his aim of articulating a theology which was at once faithful to

6 B. Leeming, 'Reflections on English Christology' in A. Grillmeier & H. Bacht (eds), *Das Konzil von Chalkedon*, vol. 3 (Würzburg, 1954), 715.   7 Anon., 'Lionel Thornton, CR: A Distinguished Theologian', *Church Times*, 148 (1960) 11.   8 This is the judgement of E.L. Mascall in his *Christ, the Christian and the Church* (London, 1946), 45.   9 During the period between the two World Wars, the Anglo-Catholics were at the centre of Anglican theology and life, providing some bishops and university professors. See K. Hylson-Smith, *High Churchmanship in the Church of England* (Edinburgh, 1993), 268.

the Scriptures and the Fathers and yet acceptable to the demands of contemporary thought, Thornton would first have to show that he was familiar with the pieces with which the contemporary challenge to faith was constructed. This forced him to appraise critically what he termed 'the dispersive tendencies of thought and life which lie at the root of our modern world [and which have] received stable form in the course of the seventeenth and eighteenth centuries'.[10]

We shall now undertake a more precise examination of Thornton's criticism of post-Enlightenment thought. It will illustrate the wide range of Thornton's philosophical interest, see him posit reasons for the crisis of faith and suggest the means by which these difficulties may be overcome. He will do this by indicating the basis upon which he finds himself attracted to the philosophy of organism as a vehicle by which the doctrine of the incarnation, the central Christian doctrine, can be made more accessible to the contemporary age.

A critic of post-Enlightenment ideas
By way of introduction here it must be said that we are not intending to write a history of modern philosophy, still less a history of modern ideas. The aim is much less ambitious: we are attempting to come to terms with Thornton's assessment of certain movements of thought which he considered important to the understanding of the then contemporary mind and the predicament in which Christian theism in England found itself.[11] In this way we shall see Thornton, the orthodox and critical philosopher and theologian, at work as he attempts to see how the assumptions of these currents of thought had, by the nineteenth century, served to

> bring about situations of the gravest danger for Christian thought. Time-honoured traditions and classic systems of interpretation lose their appeal and are dethroned to make way for new experiments. Landmarks disappear and lines of continuity become exceedingly tenuous. Cohesion of thought gives place to dispersiveness. Rival traditions grow up and become stabilised. Specialised studies lead to bifurcation of interests and mental habits. Theology follows in the general track and is affected by both the advances and the limitations of the age. Consequently in a period of disintegration a clear synoptic view of religious truth becomes exceedingly difficult.[12]

The challenge to Christian theism
Thornton acknowledges that the nineteenth century was a time of particular challenge to Christian theism and that: 'it must have seemed to many minds

10 *The Incarnate Lord* (London, 1928), 17; hereafter *IL*.   11 Not least among the thinkers of interest here would be Descartes, Kant, Hobbes, Newton, Green, Darwin and Spencer.   12 *IL*, 16.

that Christian theism was fighting a losing battle. It suffered a double attrition between the monistic tendencies of idealism on the one side and the dissecting analysis of science and historical criticism on the other'.[13] While acknowledging the contribution of such thinkers as Descartes, Kant, Locke, Berkeley, Hume and Newton and others to the development of these differing movements of thought, he singles out for particular attention the varying contributions of two thinkers, Hegel and Darwin. He identifies the 'watchwords' of their contrasting intellectual movements as development (*à la* Hegel) and evolution (*à la* Darwin):[14] concepts which radically challenged the traditional theistic concepts of transcendence and which are worthy of further treatment here. Firstly, the Hegelian contribution.

Thornton recognises the profound influence of the German philosopher Georg Wilhelm Friedrich Hegel (1770-1831) on Continental and English thought.[15] The starting-point of Hegel's philosophy was his wish to overcome the sentence 'God himself is dead', which he considered to be the expression of the culture of his age and the feeling upon which the religion of his day was based. Hans Küng succinctly encapsulates Hegel's project when he states:

> His concern, in which specifically theological factors intersect with Christological ones, is the dynamic unity of the living Godhead. The living God is for him the one who moves, changes and undergoes a history, who does not rigidly *remain* what he is, but *becomes* what he is. And he is the God who does not stubbornly remain within himself in a lofty posture of splendid isolation above the world, but comes out of himself and externalises himself in the beginning of the world, a movement which comes to a climax when God himself becomes man. According to Hegel, this God is the true, the Christian God.[16]

Hegel's intention, therefore, was to rediscover the living God: the God in the world. But he does not want knowledge of God as an object: that is to say, it is not knowledge of God as something or someone other than me which I can finally

---

13 He goes on: 'According to the one the transcendence of God and the particularity of His action in history were irrational. On the other side mechanism could find no place for the soul and its claim to religious experience, whilst the abstracting principles of analysis and a naïve conception of causation taken over from the natural sciences seemed in the hands of historical critics and anthropologists to evacuate the spiritual content and significance of sacred literature and religious history.' Ibid., 20. 14 *The Doctrine of the Atonement* (London, 1937), 32-3. It is somewhat surprising that Thornton pays no attention to the ideas of such prominent British Christian apologists of the day as C.S. Lewis, Hilaire Belloc and G.K. Chesterton. 15 For fuller treatments of Hegel's thought, see, for example: K. Barth, *Protestant Thought in the Nineteenth Century* (London, 1972), 384-421; H. Küng, *The Incarnation of God: An Introduction to Hegel's Theological Thought as Prolegomena to a Future Christology* (Edinburgh, 1987). 16 Küng, *The Incarnation of God*, 433.

describe quite accurately. He wants knowledge of God as a subject, that is a kind of knowledge which a subject has of itself when it is no longer alienated or estranged from itself.[17] Walter Kasper cautions, however, that 'despite the sublimity of the ideas involved, Hegel's effort to eliminate atheism dialectically was marked by ambiguity ... [and] that as far as its historical influence was concerned, Hegel's philosophy turned into the atheism that has shaped our situation down to the present time'.[18]

Now to return to Thornton. His primary interest in Hegel is in relation to the Hegelian concept of development which, according to Thornton, holds that

> continuity and rationality are to be found in history, because the historical process is the developing expression of the Hegelian Idea. Thus history is to be interpreted teleologically and explanations are to be sought in ends not origins. For the full expression of the Idea is to be sought at the end and not at the beginning of the process. Thus the process of history has a logical structure like the process of thought.[19]

Whatever the details of the Hegelian system and we can only just touch on them in passing, Thornton judges its primary importance in terms of its contribution of a sense of the idea of historical development to philosophy[20] and hence to theology, since philosophy forms a special part of the human culture with which theology must dialogue.[21] Having familiarised ourselves with the Hegelian turn, we shall now direct our attention in the opposite direction, to what Thornton regards as the other great moulder of the contemporary mind: the Darwinian theory of evolution.

Charles Darwin (1809-82) in his works *The Origin of Species* (1859) and *The Descent of Man* (1870) held that species of living beings evolve by natural selection, the fittest for their biological purpose in each generation alone surviving and propagating. While the detail of this argument cannot delay us here,[22] Thornton notes its contrast with Hegelian idealism in that 'it suggested a type of continuity whose explanation must be sought not in ends [as with Hegel]

---

17 James Mackey summarises the Hegelian project in the following terms: 'it was the aim of Hegel's philosophy to make man at home in this world, *zu Hause*. So [much so that] in the end he had no place for a divinity which would be other than man and his universe. Divinity rather was a state of development of spirit, embodied always in human spirit, now fully aware of itself ... Hegel was the supreme rationalist ... Beyond the universe and Man's awareness of it there was nothing.' See Mackey, *The Problem of Religious Faith* (Dublin, 1972), 43.   18 W. Kasper, *The God of Jesus Christ* (London, 1984), 27-8. This ambiguity became even more apparent after his death when his disciples split up into what are known as right-wing and left-wing Hegelians. 19 *IL*, 21.   20 Ibid., 25.   21 See G. O'Collins, *Fundamental Theology* (London, 1981), 25.   22 It is worth noting, however, these words of Darwin: 'It may be said that natural selection is daily and hourly scrutinising throughout the world, every variation, even the slightest; rejecting that

but in origins'.[23] Thornton notes that Darwin's scientific theory was made the instrument of a new philosophy of evolution by Herbert Spencer (1820-1903) and others.[24] The consequence of this, as Thornton observes, was that

> great confusions were introduced. For such a philosophy must necessarily find explanations in origins, and must therefore represent all developments as 'preformed' out of an original source and thus predetermined by its original character. This was to erect the traditional scientific concept of causation into a universal philosophical dogma. The concept of causation had been supremely successful in the sphere of physical science with its mechanistic methodology. Consequently Spencer's philosophy involved a mechanistic interpretation of evolution as a metaphysical explanation of the universe. It yielded, in fact, nothing but an empty formula which left no room for the appearance of new facts.[25]

Having briefly surveyed, with Thornton, the Hegelian conception of an inner, logical structure of teleological development and the Darwinian (Spencerian) understanding of a mechanistic evolution or unfolding from origins, we have touched upon two quite different explanations of continuity which were influential at that time in England. Regardless of the tremendous gulf that separated these two intellectual movements, they had at least one very clear, shared consequence: the Christian emphasis on the incarnation with its centre of reference in a divine entry into history in the past seemed to be out of keeping with the thought of the age. Thus Thornton can comment: 'Neither the immanent development of the Hegelian Idea nor the mechanistic conception of evolution left room for such past action of divine transcendence upon the field of history as the doctrine of the Incarnation asserted.'[26]

When the focus of inquiry turns from past action to that aspect which faces towards the goal of the historical process, the picture is no more encouraging. For according to the Hegelian view, Thornton goes on, 'the Idea of history is to

which is bad, preserving and adding up all that is good, silently and insensibly working, whenever and wherever opportunity offers at the improvement of each organic being in relation to its organic and inorganic condition of life.' See his *On the Origin of the Species by Means of Natural Selection* (London, 1859), 84. In his later years Darwin modified his theory in some measure, and was prepared to take more account of the impact of environment upon evolution. See O. Chadwick, *The Victorian Church*, vol. 2 (Oxford, 1970), 1-23. **23** *IL*, 21. **24** Thornton also mentions Henri Bergson and William James. See *IL*, 25. Spencer was the leading exponent of agnosticism in nineteenth century England. Anthony Quinton has noted that Darwin's theory of evolution 'was the most important event in British intellectual history in the nineteenth century' and that the most sustained and penetrating' of its proponents was 'the indefatigably prolix' Spencer. See Quinton, 'British Philosophy', in P. Edwards (ed. in chief), *The Encyclopedia of Philosophy*, vol. 1 (London, 1967), 388. **25** *IL*, 22. **26** Ibid.

be sought, not in a particular event of the past, but in the full development of the process; whilst ... [for the evolutionist school] the ideal end of the human endeavour must be sought in the future, and could not have been revealed once for all in the historical Christ'.[27]

What alternatives then remain for an adequate interpretation of the incarnation? Thornton singles out two other approaches for special mention: one which rejects outright the historical basis of the incarnation ('Jesus as myth') and the other which attempts to penetrate beneath the later dogmatic overlay and discover the authentic picture of the real Jesus (the search for the 'Jesus of history'). Thornton flatly rejects the 'Jesus as myth' approach, noting that those who hold that the figure of Jesus is only a myth have not received the support of serious historians. Nothing more needs to be said! And as to the quest for the 'Jesus of history',[28] which had been such a particular feature of scholarly endeavour from the eighteenth century to the early years of the twentieth century,[29] he is keenly aware of its questionable presuppositions. He cites the judgement of Friedrich Loofs[30] that such a search was bound to fail since it was carried out under naturalistic or purely immanental presuppositions into agreement with which the facts had to be forced.[31] While this is not the place for an analysis of the assumptions and methods of the movement, it will suffice for our purposes to note that, as far as Thornton is concerned, two crucial points are to be kept in mind. Firstly, the philosophy of theism is left in a precarious state when it fails to enlist the support of concrete historical religion. Secondly, that the historical element in Christianity cannot be explained on historical principles alone. It is both historic and 'metahistoric'. In other words, it calls for a metaphysical interpretation.

To conclude: this section has illustrated the wide range of Thornton's analysis of what he regards as the formative intellectual movements in the England of his day. It is debatable whether Hegel and Darwin[32] occupy quite the places Thornton assigns to them in the field of philosophy and even more debatable whether he shows convincingly how they can be said to have shaped the modern mind. It is not our task in this work to make those judgements. What is important to us, however, is to note that it is with these insights into the shape of contemporary theism that Thornton will attempt to find a means for presenting the

---

27 Ibid.   28 He references D.F. Strauss on this point. Ibid., 23.   29 He observes that 'in the opinions of Wrede, Schweitzer, Loofs and many others to-day, this search has ended in failure'. Ibid.   30 Loofs had studied the history of dogma under Harnack at Leipzig and Ritschl at Güttingen. He taught at Leipzig (1882-7) and at Halle (1888-1928).   31 *IL*, 23. Interestingly, Thornton says in relation to Loofs' point here that 'many theologians in this country would say the same'. This rather awkwardly constructed remark, it seems fair to suggest, points to a feature which has often been remarked upon: the rather isolationist attitude that was all too prevalent in English theology.   32 The inclusion of Darwin refers not so much to his own writings as to the philosophies that his ideas engendered in others: most notably perhaps, in the writings of Herbert Spencer.

doctrine of the incarnation. And, as we would expect, this presentation will be committed to an orthodox presentation of Jesus Christ as both a historical and a metaphysical figure.

The prospects for a new synthesis

Having identified what he regards as those elements of contemporary thought in which the greatest challenges to Christian theism have arisen and having indicated their principal weaknesses, Thornton now turns his attention to the constructive aspect of his project. Before attending to this, however, a word of warning! Thornton's style often makes for difficult reading; this is a point to which we shall return.[33] That said, the aim of his constructive endeavour may be summarised as follows: 'The philosophy of theism and the doctrine of the Incarnation must be brought into a new alliance.'[34] He is confident that this can be achieved in the England of the 1920s because of the emergence of a new 'mental mood'[35] which he felt would be more sympathetic to Christian theism.[36] This new intellectual climate which he senses is rooted in the growing doubts about the finality of the Newtonian synthesis, with its mechanical view of the universe, its closed continuum between cause and effect and its rationalist emphasis on the pure objectivity of science, which had been emerging since the 1890s.[37]

---

33 One reviewer of *IL*, F.H. Brabant, while stating that the book was 'a really important piece of work on the frontiers of Science and Theology', went on to say that: 'At times I have been driven to distraction by [Thornton's] difficult style and the intolerable complexity of his argument ... And as to style, if to the intricacies of theological language are to be added by our future instructors the intricacies of biological language, the lay reader will retire altogether, and even the ranks of the experts will become thinned.' *Theology*, 18 (1929) 289. Similar sentiments are expressed by almost all who have commented on Thornton's work.   34 *IL*, 23.   35 This is Hastings' term (not Thornton's) to describe the new situation of 'somewhat complacent optimism' among Christian apologists of the 1920s. Hastings identifies the English philosopher, Whitehead as a prime example of it in its most religiously sympathising form. See Hastings, *A History of English Christianity, 1920-1985*, 231. As we shall see below, Whitehead was to make a very profound contribution to Thornton's thought.   36 Among the characteristics of this new intellectual climate Thornton notes the following factors: i) the steady criticism of evolutionary incursions into philosophy from the standpoint of teleology and values; ii) the realisation among scientists of the limitations of mechanical concepts, especially in the fields of anthropology, biology, psychology and sociology;   iii) the realisation that the concept of evolution is meaningless unless it allows for the idea of a process in which new factors emerge; vi) the entry of the new as giving meaning also to the idea of time; v) the concept of time in turn as the key to a new understanding of the cosmic series which unfolds itself in our minds under the patient analysis of scientists and historians; vi) the general linking up of all departments in the modern hierarchy of knowledge which surveys the cosmic series of the time-process: not least psychology and anthropology; vii) the consequences of the theory of relativity, modern discoveries in physics, and the new philosophy of nature in bringing the world of the inorganic within the same orbit. *IL*, 25-6.   37 This was especially true in the field of physics which, in the early

Thornton is optimistic that, as he puts it, 'the field in which these two elements [the philosophy of Theism and the doctrine of the Incarnation] will be found to meet is that general meeting-place in which all thought to-day is seeking a new synthesis, the field of time and history interpreted on the widest lines'.[38] He argues that the new synthesis can be achieved through an articulation of the incarnation in terms of the philosophy of organism. How successful he will be in this regard remains to be seen.

Thornton and the philosophy of organism

Thornton argues that the new 'mental mood' with its criticisms of the excesses of mechanism and idealism provides fresh opportunities for the advancement of Christian theism. As we shall now see, he identifies in A.N. Whitehead's philosophy of organism a contemporary philosophical system which will be of supreme use to him in the task he has set himself: an articulation of Christian theism adequate to the needs of the England of the 1920s.[39] E.L. Mascall has pithily summarised the scope of Thornton's ambitions when he states that Thornton 'was doing with the philosophy of A.N. Whitehead what St Thomas Aquinas had done with the philosophy of Aristotle'.[40] A comment of Thornton's in the preface to his *The Incarnate Lord* clearly demonstrates the hopes that the young Thornton placed in Whitehead. He writes: 'It was Aristotle's great achievement that, starting from the interests associated with the Ionian tradition, he effected a new synthesis between those interests and elements derived from Eleatic and Platonic sources. Dr Whitehead seems to be engaged in a similar task today.'[41]

years of the new century, was undergoing something of a revolution and was presenting a portrayal of nature different in many respects from the one which had been so dominant during the nineteenth century. The leading figures of this movement included: Max Planck (1858-1947) (he formulated his quantum theory in 1900); Albert Einstein (1879-1955) (he presented his general and special theories of relativity respectively in 1905 and 1916); Werner Heisenberg (1901-76) (he framed his uncertainty principle in 1927). One consequence of these new theories was that it no longer seemed possible to give a complete description of the behaviour of elementary physical entities in the way classical natural science had attempted. Now it was realised that the natural scientist's own method allows him only to make statements pertaining to the sciences. This had consequences for deliberations on the question of the existence of God. As Kasper notes: 'God is by definition not an inner-worldly entity alongside other such entities; neither, therefore is he a hypothesis that can be reliably tested by empirical methods ...' See Kasper, *The God of Jesus Christ*, 25. **38** *IL*, 23-4. **39** We must note that Thornton's understanding of the concept of organism is also influenced by the writings of such thinkers as Smuts, Morgan and Alexander. But, as John Culp points out, 'Whitehead was the dominant factor'. See his 'Modern Thought Challenges Christian Theology: Process Philosophy and Anglican Theologian Lionel Thornton', *Anglican Theological Review*, 76 (1994) 332. **40** Mascall, *Saraband*, 172. **41** *IL*, xi.

Before we can come to terms with the detail of Thornton's use and modifications of Whitehead's system, it will be appropriate to acquaint ourselves with the origin and the basic principles of the philosophy of organism. We shall then proceed to examine its implications for Thornton's christological endeavour.

As we have seen, Thornton was uneasy with the dominant intellectual movements that had shaped the mind of contemporary England. The philosopher, Alfred North Whitehead (1861-1947), was similarly dissatisfied. By the early years of the twentieth century, Whitehead had come to believe that the time was ripe for a new comprehensive synthesis of knowledge.[42] This was to be achieved by a new realistic metaphysics which, like any kind of metaphysics, sets out to give a comprehensive account of reality.[43] In doing so Whitehead developed a philosophy that is far removed from absolute idealism and materialism, though one which keeps closely in touch with the natural sciences

Whitehead uses the word 'organism' not only in a narrow biological sense but also to designate a reality in which all aspects of experience are perceived as interconnected: aesthetic, moral and religious interests as well as those ideas of the world which have their origin in the natural sciences.[44] Whitehead conceives the world in dynamic terms. The world is not to be thought of as being underlaid by a static 'substance', still less is it to be thought of dualistically as two such substances, mind and matter. It is to be thought of rather in terms of 'process'. The world is a fabric of interconnected and interdependent events.[45] The fundamental units of the reality Whitehead calls *actual entities* or *actual occasions*. There are many such *actual entities*, ranging from God at the top of the scale down to the most trivial 'puff of existence'. It is in the *becoming* of these *actual entities* that the world-process exists, and we cannot go behind them to find anything more real. Whitehead rejects the Cartesian legacy of a bifurcation of nature where body and mind are thought of as two ultimate substances which can somehow act on each other. He argues steadfastly that every *actual entity* is bipolar; it has both a physical pole and a mental pole, though the word 'mental' does not necessarily imply consciousness.

Thornton's *The Incarnate Lord* was published in 1928, one year before Whitehead's *Process and Reality* in which Whitehead's argued for the dynamic, temporal character of God's consequent nature. Thornton would part company with Whitehead on this point, since he was determined to retain a dualism between God and the world.[46] Before that landmark, however, Thornton found

---

42 Whitehead's attempts to do just that can be divided into three periods: i) the early philosophy of science, 1919-22; ii) the transition, 1925-7; iii) the mature cosmology, 1929-38. This point is discussed in N. Lawrence, *Alfred North Whitehead: A Primer of His Philosophy* (New York, 1974), xix.   43 See J. Macquarrie, *Twentieth-Century Religious Thought*, 4th ed. (London, 1988), 259.   44 Like Morgan and Alexander, Whitehead conceives of the world in dynamic terms. See Macquarrie, *Twentieth-Century Religious Thought*, 4th ed, 264.   45 Lawrence, *Alfred North Whitehead: A Primer of His Philosophy*, 32.   46 It is appropriate to note that Whitehead

himself attracted to Whitehead's evolutionary conceptions of nature as congenial to theism, and more specifically his dissolution of scientific materialism into organic events. Thornton had closely read *The Concept of Nature* (1920) and *Principles of Natural Knowledge* (2nd ed., 1925), and he tended to interpret *Science and the Modern World* (1925) in line with these earlier works, and was acquainted with *Religion in the Making* (1926).[47] In these writings Whitehead develops a theory of overlapping events characterised by reiterated patterns, showing how sub-events may be organically influenced by the patterns of the events within which they are included. Such influence modifies and transforms simpler organisms, thereby allowing for evolutionary growth. Thornton quotes Whitehead, directly, at length:

> An individual entity, whose own life-history is a part within the life-history of some larger, deeper, more complete pattern, is liable to have aspects of that larger pattern dominating its own being, and to experience modifications of that larger pattern reflected in itself as modifications of its own being. This is the theory of organic mechanism ... The general principle is that in a new environment there is an evolution of the old entities into new forms ... the whole point of the modern doctrine is the evolution of the complex organisms from the antecedent states of less complex organisms. The doctrine thus cries aloud for a conception of organism as fundamental for nature. It also requires an underlying activity – a substantial activity – expressing itself in individual embodiments, and evolving in achievements of organisms.[48]

Whitehead asserts, however, that we cannot account for an ordered universe simply by means of *actual entities*. An aggregate of *actual entities*, each of which was pure creativity, would be formless chaos. There must therefore be a realm of forms or eternal objects which actual entities prehend as well as prehending one another.[49] Out of these actual entities and eternal objects Whitehead proceeds to build up the world in which creativity manifests itself and the universe of our experience emerges.[50]

holds to a unique *actual entity* whose function is to be the non-temporal locus of all the *eternal objects*; and to which he gives the name God. See *IL*, 467. Thornton, in *IL*, was somewhat unsure what to make of Whitehead's doctrine of God and after the publication of *Process and Reality* decidedly rejected Whitehead's God who had turned out to be dependent upon the world.   47 See Appendix C, 'Objects and Events', in *IL*, 456-69.   48 Ibid., 460. Thornton is dwelling here on Whitehead's system as expounded in *Science and the Modern World*, 1st ed. (Cambridge, 1925), 156-8.   49 These are not unlike the 'ideas' of Plato. See Macquarrie, *Twentieth-Century Religious Thought*, 4th ed., 266.   50 Thus Thornton can continue to quote Whitehead: 'The organism is a unit of emergent value, a real fusion of the characters of eternal objects, emerging for its own sake... The emergence of organism depends on a selective activity

THE INCARNATION AND THE PHILOSOPHY OF ORGANISM

As we have noted above Thornton's principal work on the doctrine of the incarnation, *The Incarnate Lord*, a book of over five hundred pages, is heavily and openly indebted to a philosophy of organism. The author defines it as 'an essay concerning the doctrine of the Incarnation in its relations to organic conceptions'.[51] In this section we shall outline Thornton's presentation of this central Christian doctrine. Before doing so it is important that we appreciate the novelty of Thornton's project. He was the first Christian theologian to attempt a fundamental and systematic treatment of Whitehead's philosophy.[52] One reviewer, Francis J. Hall, accorded it a generous welcome in 1929: 'This is, in my judgement the greatest contribution to Christology that has appeared in many a year; ... the book is magnificent, and opens up a new and convincing apologetic.'[53]

Another admirer of Thornton's project was Michael Ramsey who, in a review of another of Thornton's books, *Revelation and the Modern World*, remarked that 'it will not be surprising if the verdict of history puts this work together with *The Incarnate Lord* and *The Common Life in the Body of Christ* as among the most signal contributions which English theology has made towards the understanding of the Christian Faith'.[54]

A decade later, in 1961, as Archbishop of York, Ramsey, in an appreciation of the recently deceased Thornton, described *The Incarnate Lord* as a book which 'towers above other works of the kind by the success with which it avoids assimilating the historical revelation to the demands of the philosophical system'.[55]

The English theologian, Leonard Hodgson,[56] a contemporary of both Thornton and Ramsey, described *The Incarnate Lord* in enthusiastic terms:

> This is in my opinion the greatest theological work that has appeared in my lifetime. I believe that if it had been originally written in German or Russian, British theologians would have been falling over each other in their eagerness to expound it to their fellow countrymen; as it was the work of an Englishman writing in English they could not be bothered to wrestle with its unfamiliar and, at first sight, uncongenial terminology.

akin to purpose ... Enduring things are thus the outcome of a temporal process; whereas eternal things are the elements required for the very being of the process.' See *IL*, 460 which relies on *Science and the Modern World*, 1st ed., 157-8.   **51** This is the subtitle of the *IL*.   **52** Whether Thornton was in fact the first largely depends on how we assess Henry Nelson Wieman's three chapters devoted to Whitehead in *The Wrestle of Religion with Truth* (New York, 1927).   **53** F.J. Hall, review of *IL*, *Anglican Theological Review*, 12 (1929-30) 93.   **54** A.M. Ramsey, review of *Revelation and the Modern World*, *Theology*, 54 (1951) 488.   **55** Ramsey, 'Lionel Thornton: Theologian', viii.   **56** Hodgson held the chair of Christian Apologetics at General Theological Seminary, New York City from 1925 to 1931. He was later the Regius Professor of Divinity at Oxford.

In it Fr Thornton sets out to expound the Christian doctrine of God in terms of the philosophy of A.N. Whitehead. In doing so he never falls into the temptation to assimilate the historic revelation to the demands of the philosophical system, as so many idealistic theologians have done. On the contrary, he brought into the philosophy from the Christian revelation what it needed to make that system work, to save it from the necessity of postulating pan-psychism in order to account for movement in the universe ... I can say no more about this book here beyond expressing my very great indebtedness to it, an indebtedness which speaks from almost every page of these lectures.[57]

Despite such acclaim, we must acknowledge, however, that there is virtually no knowledge of, or interest in, Thornton or his major theological work today.[58] John Macquarrie's extensive treatment of various christologies, ancient and modern, in his recent *Jesus Christ in Modern Thought*, fails even to mention him.[59] Be that as it may, however, Mascall in his memoirs of 1992, could look back over a lifetime's theological endeavour and comment that *The Incarnate Lord*

was potentially an important work and one ahead of its time; and it was certainly significant of its author's basic attitudes and presuppositions. For, when liberal Anglo-Catholics in general were making subtle adjustments to bring the Christian revelation into line with modern thought, Lionel Thornton, in *The Incarnate Lord*, was making drastic modifications in a contemporary philosophical system in order to bring it into line with the Christian revelation.[60]

The incarnation and the philosophy of organism
It must be said that the reader is at a disadvantage in attempting to set out Thornton's complex presentation of the connection between the incarnation and the organic theory, because it is often difficult to find a complete statement of Thornton's argument. It has to be gathered from many incomplete statements in different parts of *The Incarnate Lord*. It is essential from the outset that we grasp, however, that Thornton is not setting out as a faithful disciple dedicated to writing a Whiteheadian christology. His intention is to reaffirm the orthodox doctrine of Jesus Christ in conversation with Whitehead's organic conceptions of

---

57 L. Hodgson, *The Doctrine of the Trinity* (London, 1951), 228-9.   **58** Robert M. Cooper argues that Thornton should be considered as an early process theologian, a forebear of John B. Cobb, Schubert M. Ogden, Charles Hartshorne, and others. He is critical of process theology for not acknowledging this debt. See 'A Note on Lionel S. Thornton: An Early Process Theologian', *Anglican Theological Review*, 55 (1973) 188.   **59** London, 1989.   **60** Mascall, *Saraband*, 171-2.

the relationship between God and the world, and thus present a christology which is accessible to his contemporaries. His ambition, therefore, is more theological than philosophical. He wants 'to reaffirm in terminology relevant to modern ways of thought, precisely that doctrine which was slowly formulated in a succession of ecumenical councils'.[61] It is little wonder then that the process philosopher and leading exponent of Whitehead's philosophy, Lewis S. Ford, in the course of a brief note on Thornton, describes him as 'primarily a church theologian present-ing a high christology in conversation with Whitehead's analysis of experience'.[62] John Culp concurs with Ford's judgement when he comments that 'Thornton's theology offers an Anglican appropriation of Whitehead's philosophy rather than a Process Theology or even a simple Anglican theology'.[63] In examining how Thornton relates this theory of organic development to the unfolding of the Christ-event,[64] it is useful to attend first to the details of the organic universe.

The organic universe

The first section of *The Incarnate Lord* is devoted to an in-depth analysis of the 'organic universe' as the background for the Christ-event. In taking this starting-point, Thornton's desires are twofold: to preserve that conception of the universe as a hierarchically graded and organic whole which was so prominent a theme of medieval thought,[65] while at the same time meeting the demands of modern evolu-tionary theories and avoiding the difficulties inherent in the medieval doctrine of determinate species.[66] Thornton argues that the idea of organism provides a key to the cosmic series as a whole,[67] and that this idea is destined to prove of the utmost

---

61 *IL*, 253.   62 And for this reason he dismisses Robert M. Cooper's claim that Thornton should be considered an early process theologian. See Ford, 'Response: Lionel S. Thornton and Process Christology', *Anglican Theological Review*, 55 (1973) 479.   63 J. Culp, 'Modern Thought Challenges Christian Theology', 330.   64 While the term 'Christ-event' was seldom, if ever used by Thornton (never in *IL*), it will appear from time to time in this study to denote the inclusive reality variously called Jesus Christ, the Incarnate Lord (his favourite term), the *Mysterium Christi* (a term used by Thornton in his later, more biblically focused, writings) and the like. The intention in appealing to this term is to underline the fact that the Incarnate Lord has a reference much wider than the life of an historical figure: Christ's coming is the decisive fact of salvation history and includes his incarnation, life, death, resurrection and the gift of the Spirit. Thus Thornton can speak of 'the Incarnation considered as an event' in the nativity stories and in John's prologue. In the former, 'the new humanity of Christ was the product of the creative activity of [sic] Holy Spirit', while in the latter; 'the Logos, or Word of God, pre-existent and transcendent over creation, becomes incarnate in a human life story ...' See *IL*, 327-8.   65 This insistence on the hierarchy of grades shows Thornton's affinities with classical philosophy. The Schoolmen established the natural hierarchy of things in the universe by means of their theory of the rhythmic evolution of substantial forms, the '*eductio formarum e potentiis materiae*'. See M. de Wulf, *Scholasticism Old and New: An Introduction to Scholastic Philosophy, Medieval and Modern* (Dublin, 1907), 116-8.   66 *IL*, 32.   67 Ibid., 38.

importance for the theology of the incarnation.[68] Thornton views the *Mysterium Christi* [69] as an infinite event, a mystery that reveals the very structure of reality itself as an infinite event. The purpose of appealing to Whitehead's philosophy of organism to describe the Christ-event is that other systems, whether based on contemporary philosophy or scriptural imagery, are less adequate for the task of understanding the unified and unifying character of the Christ-event. To Thornton, the first formal requirement of a christology is that it seeks to address the wholeness of the reality of Christ, whether this is done in philosophical categories or biblical imagery. Thornton justifies this interest in unity by appeal to the interest of reason: 'Reason is always primarily concerned with the unity of experience ... It craves for ordered connexion and system.'[70] Now to the details of Thornton's understanding of the organic nature of the universe.

In terms clearly reminiscent of Whitehead,[71] Thornton recognises in the organic structure of the universe three characteristic features:[72] the manner in which the series is continuously built up out of parts into wholes; the organic unity of the whole as pervading the parts; the *transformation* which occurs at each stage of the process. His 'stodgy and elephantine' elucidation of these themes[73] begins by assuming that the universe, generally, is an ascending series of organisms each level or grade of which possesses its own typical organic structure. All levels in this hierarchical series are organically interconnected. Each level provides the basis for and is included in the level next above it.[74]

A corollary of this is that each of the higher organisms includes within itself and rests upon all the organic levels below it. No single entity in the series is self-explanatory. The organic units are not only connected on a vertical (hierarchical) basis with those of higher and lower levels, but there is also a horizontal reference between similar entities belonging to the same rank in the series. This means that the whole organic series of the universe is bound

---

68 Ibid., 31.   69 This is the term Thornton uses in a book from the second phase of his career: *Revelation and the Modern World* (London, 1952), 298.   70 *IL*, 383.   71 Mascall, in an approving assessment of Thornton's christological endeavour, has commented that he doubts whether Thornton's work really owes as much to Whitehead as Thornton himself 'with the humility of the true scholar is inclined to think'. See his *Christ, the Christian and the Church*, 44-5.   72 *IL*, 38.   73 This is a description of Thornton's literary style in *IL* proffered by Mascall. He then goes on to say that the book has earned 'the adjective "unreadable" as justly as any book that anybody has in fact managed to read ... I read it when I was a schoolmaster at Coventry because it was the only book that I had in my bedroom when I was quarantined with the chicken-pox'. See his *Saraband*, 171.   74 Thus Thornton continues: 'The cell, for example, is the first unit in the series of living entities. The living organism, plant or animal, is a whole built up out of a variety of parts and organs; of these parts the cell is apparently the fundamental unit. Thus the cell provides the foundation of a more complex organism; and such an organism requires and pre-supposes the cell as the unit of its more complex structure. As the cell to the organism, so the atom to the molecule.' *IL*, 36.

together in one, immense, complex, inter-related system in which each part has significance for and influence upon the series taken as a whole.

The series is characterised by increasing complexity of structure as it advances, since each organism includes more organic units within itself as a developing organism. At the same time, Thornton goes on, the more complex an organism's structure, the more marked is its unity. The character of a given organism is determined by its *principle of unity*. This principle is *the highest law of being* of the level in which that organism occurs. As a particular organism is taken up into a higher organic level, its *own principle of unity* is submerged within and transformed by the *principle of unity* which determines the character of the higher organism, though without the *principle of unity* of the lower organism being lost in the process. It is thus assimilated into a higher rhythm or mode of being without, however, losing its own identity. It functions as a unit in a larger whole and its significance depends upon this whole. Thus the organism still has its own *law of being*, but the highest law of being according to which it now functions is that of the higher organic level in which it is now included. The principle of unity of the higher organism causes that organism to be a unified hierarchy of several *principles of unity* functioning as a unit according to its own highest law of being. We have in this representation of the universe an *increasing complexity of structure* through a *progressive unification of structure*.[75]

Man

The highest grade of this ascending series is man.[76] The human individual, like other developing organisms, is a developing whole built out of a multiplicity of parts, extending over all grades of the cosmic series. But what is significant about the human organism is mind developing on the level of spirit.[77] In accordance with the general character of the cosmic series, all the earlier grades are subsumed and transformed into a unity of organic function on the level of spirit.[78] Man, then, so to speak, is typified by the direction towards which he tends to function, the direction of life in the spirit. As spirit is the highest level in the cosmic series, it follows that man stands at the head of the cosmic series, a kind of microcosm in which there is included a hierarchy of all the grades.[79] Thus Thornton argues that in man all the previous grades are taken up and transformed into a unity of organic function on the level of spirit. By this he

---

75 Ibid., 37.   76 Some may find the use of the term 'man' offensive: Thornton, of course, wrote before there was a consciousness of the need for inclusive language.   77 It is necessary to note here, as L.B. Smedes points out, that when Thornton uses the term *spirit* to denote the essential characteristic of man, he is not isolating a certain organ as the root centre of manhood, as the Greeks did with *nous* and as some idealists did with self-consciousness. As Thornton says, 'there is no centre of the human organism distinct from and older than the organism itself'. See *IL*, 56. Neither *nous* nor will nor heart is essential to man. See Smedes, *The Incarnation: Trends in Modern Anglican Thought* (Amsterdam, 1953), 41.   78 *IL*, 46.   79 Ibid., 43.

means that all organic units with their own *principle of unity* become integral parts of a single organism whose characteristics are determined by spirit. They are all, therefore, subordinate to the ends of this organism which exists on this level of spirit and which Thornton terms the *spiritual organism.*[80] It is this fact which constitutes the dominion of man over creation.[81]

Thornton notes that at every stage in the ascending series of the universe 'there is an entry of *creative activity* [italics mine] and an 'emergence' of new factors and conditions which are the products of that activity'.[82] With the arrival of the series at the human level there emerges an organic unity of mind which distinguishes the human being from other living organisms. Thus Thornton can compare and contrast the experience of the human and the animal in the following words:

> The conscious life of the child at first shares with animals this characteristic of absorption in the present, despite the fact that both child and animal are developing units in their life-stories. But as the human organism matures there emerges an organic unity of mind which rises far beyond this stage of experience. For whereas other organisms transcend change and succession, the human organism becomes aware of itself in this relation. The human mind is aware of its own continuity as an enduring entity in contrast to the flow of events.[83]

In the order of reality to which mental life belongs, Thornton proceeds, the human being has capacities for apprehending an order of reality which transcends the cosmic series: 'man finds himself confronted with ultimate values and with standards of reference which transcend all other levels of his experience. They must therefore transcend the series in which he is rooted ...'[84] Thus man has experience of an order of reality different from and other than the organic series of the universe: the *eternal order.*

The eternal order

This is an order of reality whose significance in no way depends upon the conditions of change and development which characterise the series of events in space-time.[85] Thornton emphasises the transcendent 'beyondness' of this order as it is known to our experience, and notes that since 'it is given to our experience ...

---

80 Ibid., 51. 81 Thus it can be said that in man all creation is 'summed up', or recapitulated, and as man is redeemed, so is creation redeemed. Man has therefore a mediatorial function in creation, and the creation, if redeemed, must be redeemed through man. See Thornton, *Revelation and the Modern World*, 41. This, in turn, anticipates the method of atonement according to the doctrine of recapitulation. See Smedes, *The Incarnation*, 41. 82 *IL*, 44. 83 Ibid., 54-5. 84 *IL*, 56. Thornton appeals here to W.R. Sorley, especially to his series of Gifford Lectures, *Moral Values and the Idea of God* (Cambridge, 1921), to support his argument. 85 *IL*, 56.

it has an immanent aspect, as well ...' He sees evidence of this experience of immanence being manifested in our capacity to recognise and approve the manifestations and embodiments in the world of such qualities as beauty, goodness and noble actions.[86] Thus Thornton can draw the following conclusion: 'The individual is no longer merged in the tribe or series as appears to be the case with animals. The individual organism has become a bearer of eternal values and must have a destiny beyond the space-time series in the eternal order.'[87]

How is the continuous emergence of the new to be explained? Thornton dismisses the view that it is derived from the repetitive series of events and goes on to explain the new factors in terms of the eternal order: 'What cannot emerge out of the process of events in the series enters into that series from beyond it, that is from the eternal order. Thus, whilst a bare succession of events points to an activity, the creativeness of the activity which we may discern in the universe through the entry of the new is a creativeness which we must trace to the eternal order.'[88]

While Thornton goes on to develop, at length, his metaphysic, restrictions in space here dictate that we must draw the threads of his argument together insofar as they are of direct relevance to this study. At the heart of the organic conception of the universe is the notion of its ascending order. The tendency of organisms towards greater unity (within complexity) Thornton calls the *principle of individuality*.[89] As an organism advances in the cosmic series, its *principle of individuality* proceeds. It is the product of creative activity. The source of such creative activity,

---

86 Thornton sees a threefold structure in man's relationship to the eternal order: i) He apprehends it in the meaning, beauty or significance of particular objects in the context of the organic universe around him; ii) he comes to recognise the supra-temporal and transcendent character of the order to which these qualities and characteristics belong; iii) he comes to reflect upon his relation to this order as something of which we have direct experience. This threefold apprehension of the eternal order, Thornton continues, in accordance with the general tendency of the organic series, tends to pass into over-flowing activity which incorporates the results of such assimilation. Thus the appreciation of beauty sets up a *nisus* towards expression in the creation of beautiful objects. The appreciation of the good sets up a *nisus* towards moral response and so on. See ibid., 58-9. It is interesting to note that these three movements are reminiscent of Balthasar's *triptych*: i) *Theo-phany* – 'the way we encounter and perceive the phenomenon of divine revelation in the world (in the manifold forms of its 'glory' [*Herr-lichkeit*])'; ii) *Theo-praxy* – where we 'allow the encountering reality to speak in its own tongue or, rather, let ourselves be drawn into its dramatic arena'; iii) *Theo-logy* – where we 'reflect on the way in which this action is expressed in concept and word'. See Balthasar, *Theo-Drama*, vol. 1 (San Francisco, 1988), 15.   87 *IL.*, 59.   88 Ibid., 85-6.   89 The *principle of individuality* has its highest realisation in man. See ibid., 221. This principle means just about the opposite of individualism; it refers to 'integrated wholeness' and occurs perfectly only where the individual and social principles co-exist in perfect harmony. Thornton's argument will later reach a stage where he will identify the only perfect instance of this coexistence of the social and individual principles in terms of the Triune God: 'Three Persons in One Absolute Individuality'. Ibid., 415.

Thornton argues, can be regarded in a manner which is compatible with a religious interpretation of the universe.[90] In doing this Thornton acknowledges that he is not advancing an argument to prove the existence of God.[91] Rather he is demonstrating that the universe as we know it fits readily into a religious interpretation. The consequence of the religious interpretation of the universe proffered by Thornton is that creative activity is envisaged to be 'a Being who embraces all the significance of His creation, whose actuality transcends in concreteness and comprehensiveness all that is to be found in the developing series of His creatures. God is thus Absolute Actuality, not in process of realisation but in concrete unchangeable reality'.[92] God is therefore the ground of the structure of the universe and this process of creative activity, wherein the eternal order is revealed to human experience, can be interpreted as having 'many cross-connexions' with the religious revelation which have been part of human experience all the world over.[93] More particularly, this process of creative activity can be seen to be hinted at in the revelation of God recorded in the bible. Thornton notes that this biblical revelation advanced through various stages from a primitive tribal and anthropomorphic Hebrew religion to its fulfilment in Christ and his Church.[94]

Having briefly spoken about the place God occupies in Thornton's organic theory, we shall return to our discussion of man and the organic series. Despite man's being the highest level in the series, it does not reach its end in man, because he shares the unfinished character of the series.[95] The series according to Thornton comes 'to a dead end in man himself, his unfinished character, his non-attainment, his experience of ethical failure and sinful estrangement'.[96] This means that even though man is the organic summation of the series,[97] he cannot be the final goal of the series.[98] He too needs to be taken up organically into a

90 Ibid., 82, 88.   91 Ibid., 82.   92 Ibid., 86. By means of extremely complex argumentation which need not delay us here, Thornton arrives at the view that his definition of the organism by reference to a *principle of unity* controlling and transcending plurality, enables him to see in the doctrine of the Trinity the complete harmony of the unity and plurality which is partially seen in the various grades of the evolutionary process.   93 Ibid., 134. Hence the first section of *IL* (3-157) is largely an account of the nature of religious experience, without specific Christian reference.   94 Ibid., 134-5.   95 Ibid., 225. This is partially because of sinful individualism (which is a factor in man's experience of 'non-attainment'). More importantly, however, the roots of his inability lie in the structure of the universe.   96 Ibid., 164. Thornton comments: 'An interpretation of the universe which combines the organic conception of development with a recognition of the eternal order and its absolute standards as both the background and the goal of that development is an interpretation which can effectually lay the ghost of an autonomous humanity. When to that interpretation there is added the religious conception of man as a dependent creature who can find fulfilment only in the bosom of his Creator, then we can see the monstrous image of a humanity self-completed and self-sufficing being smitten and broken in pieces by a stone cut without hands. In its place there appears the kingdom of the true Son of Man, a kingdom in which all the unfinished and fragmentary treasures of this world-order are gathered up into the wholeness of a new creation'. Ibid., 238.   97 Ibid., xx.   98 Thus Thornton notes

higher *principle of unity*, the same one which is ever beyond his own reach.[99] Thornton's argument is difficult to follow here but, if I have understood him correctly, he is saying that the individual human spirit is conscious, especially in its religious experience, of its incompleteness. It can only find satisfaction in a spiritual life which is larger than that which, as an individual, it can call its own. Ultimately, Thornton argues, the individual can only find this completion in the infinite and absolute life of God.[100] This issue is resolved for Thornton, as we shall see, in the incarnation.

The incarnation

In turning to an examination of the incarnation, Thornton comments that it marks the final 'incorporation' of creative activity in the world. Man finds the 'integrated wholeness' that all finite organisms innately seek, when *Absolute Individuality* in the person of the Son is incorporated into the finite order. The Incarnate Lord represents the full incorporation of the eternal order in its wholeness into the world process.[101] The Christ-event stands at the apex or goal of the advancing significance which had characterised the organic series. It can thus be spoken of, Thornton states, in more theologically conventional terms as the 'progression of revelation'[102] (a term which seems to pre-figure Teilhard de Chardin's point *Omega*).

To conclude this section, it will suffice to say that Thornton, with the aid of Whitehead's organic philosophy, has outlined an understanding of the universe which sees it culminating in the incarnation. In the section that follows, we shall examine in detail how Thornton's approach comes to terms with the doctrine of the pre-existence of Christ.

that 'whilst historically he is the last term, metaphysically he cannot be the final term in respect of his organic connexion with the series'. Ibid., 116. **99** Ibid., 362. **100** Thornton is clearly reminiscent of Balthasar here: see Balthasar's discussion of 'Infinite and finite freedom' in his *Theo-Drama*, vol. 2 (San Francisco, 1990), 189-304. Smedes claims that there is quite a similarity here between Thornton's thought and that of the orthodox Anglican religious philosopher, C.C.J. Webb (1865-1954). He was a Fellow of Magdalen College, Oxford from 1889 to 1922, and from 1920 to 1930 he was (the first) Oriel (now Nolloth) Professor of the Philosophy of the Christian Religion at Oxford. See his *God and Personality* (1918), 164. See Smedes, *The Incarnation*, 43, n. 228. **101** Thornton adds that in this process the human organism is taken up on to the 'level' of deity and notes that the idea of the deification of man was one of the great themes of patristic thought from St Irenaeus onwards. He draws attention to the well known words of St Athanasius upon this topic: Αὐτὸς γὰρ ἐνηνθρώπησεν ἵνα ἡμεῖς θεωποιηθῶμεν (*De Incarnatione*, ch. 54; *PG* XXV. 192 B.). *IL*, 225 and n. 1. **102** For a fuller examination of Thornton's thinking on this relationship, see *IL*, 143-4.

THORNTON AND THE PRE-EXISTENCE OF CHRIST

Having familiarised ourselves with Thornton's organic system, we shall now attempt to come to terms with its consequences for the understanding of the doctrine of the pre-existence of Christ: the belief that Jesus of Nazareth was/is personally identical with the Son of God, who has existed from all eternity and who enters the world to be revealed in human history. It will emerge that Thornton is fully committed to the doctrine of pre-existence. What will be of interest to us is his conviction that his organic theory sheds light on the process that led the Church to formulate the doctrine of the pre-existence of Jesus Christ. In order to accomplish this task, we shall travel with Thornton through his exegesis of the scriptures and mention writings of various Fathers (especially Origen). We shall begin by examining the doctrine's relationship to Thornton's organic theory.

Pre-existence and the organic theory

There is no place in his writings where Thornton explicitly sets out to justify the doctrine of the pre-existence of Christ. The detail of his writings demonstrates that he presupposes its validity.[103] As he was a member of the Anglo-Catholic school of Anglican theology, committed to doctrinal orthodoxy, this comes as no surprise.[104] His commitment to the doctrine of pre-existence, and to christological orthodoxy in general, means that in his account of the incarnation, in terms of a philosophy of organism, he has to distinguish between the Incarnate Lord and the cosmic series of advancing organisms. Thus as we have seen above, Christ is not to be conceived of as the final point in some evolutionary series. To understand the Christ-event solely in these terms is to overlook the uniqueness and 'finality' (my terms, not Thornton's) of the Christ-event. Thus Thornton comments, in relation to a number of different strains of thought, that

---

103 In saying this it must be acknowledged that Thornton was familiar with the writings of the liberal German theologian, Adolf von Harnack (1851-1930) and made passing reference to his 'reduced text' exegesis of the Q passage on the relation of the Son to the Father (Lk 10; Mt 11). See *IL*, 294-5, 297, n. 2. Harnack was a last great exponent of the programme of historical-critical study of the history of Christianity and was highly critical of the doctrine of the pre-existence of Christ. He regarded anything that stands in the way of a historical consideration of the Lord or seems to make it superfluous as blocking the way to a living faith. He argued that the doctrine of pre-existence should be repudiated since it involved dissolving the Saviour in endless speculations on his person. See K.H. Neufeld, *Adolf von Harnack – Theologie als Suche nach der Kirche* (Paderborn, 1977), 109 and K-J Kuschel, *Born before All Time? The Dispute over Christ's Origins* (London, 1992), 37-41.   104 Thus Mascall could comment: 'in dealing with Christology, Thornton is altogether determined to be orthodox'. See his *Christ, the Christian and the Church*, 45. Ramsey expressed similar sentiments in his: 'Lionel Thornton: Theologian', viii.

whilst the Incarnation is in line with the ascending curve of creative activity, it is not simply a continuation of that curve. The Christ whom Christians worship as God is not a product of creative activity, anymore than He is the product of emergent evolution or of an Idea or Spirit immanent in a developing universe ... The passage of creative activity by 'steps and degrees'... could not bring the stream forward to its end in God, because the incorporation of creative activity was in all its stages only partial and fragmentary.[105]

A new factor, therefore, must be present, one which safeguards the transcendence and guarantees the uniqueness of Christ as the Lord Incarnate. Thornton identifies this factor as the subsumption of the life of Jesus in the Eternal Word, who at this point – and only at this point – 'enters' the world of organic evolution where he takes to himself the human organism which has been prepared by the preceding levels of creation.[106] Thus Thornton adds: 'the Eternal Word is very God. His self-incorporation into the organic series does not, therefore, constitute a new level of the old series. For He is eternally on the level of deity.'[107]

In describing this nexus of the eternal order and its creative activity, Thornton feels justified in appealing to two 'imaginative thought-forms': there has been a *flowing down* into the series and an *ascending* towards the eternal order. He says that theology is normally content to speak of these activities as the Son of God 'coming down from heaven' and becoming man, and on the other hand of 'a taking up of manhood into God'. Thus Thornton, returning to the language of organism, adds: 'the Incarnation was an Incorporation of Absolute Actuality [i.e. the One who transcends completely the developing series][108] into history and of the eternal order in its wholeness into the time-series ... But on the other hand we must also say that it means the taking up of the human organism on to the level of deity'.[109]

At this point it is appropriate that we pause briefly to ensure that we have absorbed the kernel of Thornton's argument about the identity of the Incar-

---

105 *IL*, 227-8.   106 It should be noted here, that this is not to imply that God is obliged to wait upon the preparations made for him through the ascending curve of the organic series. Thornton prefers to say that it is God himself who has prepared, through the whole emergent series, for the appearance of that organism in the incarnation. See N. Pittenger, *The Word Incarnate* (London, 1959), 108.   107 *IL*, 228. Thornton's argument here is very relevant to the traditional Catholic distinction between nature and grace. We can recall the words of the prominent, German Catholic theologian, Matthias Joseph Scheeben (1835-88), when he wrote: 'the good by which the lower nature is made like to the higher nature [is] not *secundum modum suum* but *secundum modum eius*, that is, not according to the measure of the lower nature's power, but according to the measure of power which the higher nature wills ...' See Scheeben, *Nature and Grace* (Saint Louis, 1954), 37.   108 *IL*, 86.   109 Ibid., 229. We must note that 'deity' here does not mean that man becomes God by nature, but by grace.

nate Lord. He is claiming that the Eternal Word expresses his mode of being in and through a completely human organism[110] or, to put it in more familiar theological language, that the pre-existent Logos has become man.[111] To understand this point it is necessary that we recall the axiom discussed above: transformation from one level to the next does not destroy or eliminate the *law of being* which characterises the lower level.[112] Yet the highest *law of being* determines the status of an organism, and is the expression of that transcending *principle of unity* which flows down from the eternal order. Thornton finds in this description of reality a vocabulary adequate to the task of depicting the structure of the Incarnate Lord. The humanity of the Incarnate Lord is not to be considered a static metaphysical entity but a *spiritual organism*. All the principles of unity which exist in any other human organism exist also in him. The difference is, however, that, while in created human beings the highest law of being is the transcending *principle of unity* which is proper to a human organism on the level of spirit and which flows down from the creative activity of the eternal order, this is not the *highest law of being* in the Incarnate Lord. The *highest law of being* in his case is the law of being proper to deity. There is no abrogation of other *laws of being*. In his organism are all the *laws of being* which exist in every human person. But even the highest of these, that which constitutes him 'the man Christ Jesus', is not the *highest law of His Being*. It is not, therefore, that *principle of unity* which determines his status. Here Thornton introduces the following parallel: 'The human body is not less physical because it is taken up into a *spiritual organism* and has become an organ of spirit. Neither is the human organism less human because it is taken up into union with the eternal Logos and has become an organ of His deity.'[113]

To draw the threads of this particular discussion together, it will suffice to say that Thornton has articulated a theory of the incarnation which seems to safeguard the doctrine of the pre-existence of Christ. Despite the emphasis throughout the first half of *The Incarnate Lord* on the developing incorporation of the eternal order into the successions of events in space-time through an ascending cosmic series,[114] there is no claim in the christology of the second part, that the Incarnate Lord is a product of the creative organic series. Rather Thornton assures us that 'the principle of unity which determines the status of the Incarnate Lord is not a partial manifestation of creative activity, but the Eternal Word Himself, who is the source of all creative activity. Consequently the principle of

---

110 Ibid. 111 Thornton sees his organic interpretation of the incarnation as being 'in line with the fully developed thought of Christian Platonism concerning the Logos-Creator, who embraces in Himself the whole order of Platonic Ideas'. See *IL*, 228. On this point he cites: Thomas Aquinas, *Summa Theologiae*, i. qq. xv., xxxiv. a. 3., xliv. a. 3.; W.R. Inge, *The Philosophy of Plotinus*, vol. 2 (New York & Toronto, 1918), 37 ff., 74. 112 *IL*, 36-40, 230. 113 Ibid., 242. 114 Ibid., 98.

individuality in the Incarnate Lord is not a created manifestation of the principle of individuality, not a further development of that principle in its organic form.'[115] Reductionist views are firmly rebuffed by Thornton: 'if we regard Him as a human individual within the organic series in whom there is a unique manifestation of the eternal order, then we have no ground for supposing that Christianity has the final character which Christians have found in it'.[116]

Evolutionary ideas are also given an unequivocal cold-shoulder, when Thornton insists that the Christ-event constitutes an irruption of something totally new, the Logos-Creator (or the absolute eternal order) into the cosmic series. Christ is characterised as being *super-organic*. The incarnation is interpreted, therefore, as a coming into history, as the entry of something wholly other and not as a product of the historical process.[117] Thus Thornton declares, in what can be seen as a clear

---

115 Ibid., 282.   116 Ibid., 259.   117 This demonstrates that Thornton is not to be considered a process thinker; and he has been severely criticised on this point by process theologians. Norman Pittenger epitomises the general tendency of these criticisms when he draws attention to 'the oddness of Thornton's position' and goes on to say: 'While he [Thornton] is prepared, in the early portions of *The Incarnate Lord*, to accept and to use (to great effect) the philosophy of process developed by Professor Alfred North Whitehead, he draws back as soon as he comes to the consideration of the sense in which Jesus may be styled final and the way in which it may be said of Jesus that he transcends other revelatory activity of God. At this point, but not before or elsewhere, he feels obliged to insist that the whole *Logos*, as we might describe it, is intruded into the world in the incarnation of the Word in Jesus Christ; thus he succeeds, quite contrary to what must have been his intention at the beginning, in making that event partake of an entirely different order from all the rest of the divine revelatory activity in the creation. This comes about because Thornton feels that a specific understanding of finality, must at all costs be maintained firmly ... [In] translating the Patristic view into the idiom of a world-view utterly different from theirs, he is making the Lord a meaningless monstrosity in a world which neither needs him nor (for that matter) can accommodate him. He wants to state that there is some sort of discontinuity within a greater continuity; but what he manages to assert is a contradiction of the very intention of the Fathers themselves, with all they had to say about the eternal Logos in his various modes of operation including that mode which was appropriate to the incarnation in Jesus himself.' See Pittenger, *Christology Reconsidered* (London, 1970), 19-20. Later on Pittenger comments: 'at that moment he deserts the philosophy he has followed and introduces into the picture an intrusion or descent of God the Word into the creative process, an entrance of a sort which flatly contradicts all that he said up to that time. On his own terms this simply will not do'. Ibid., 101. A similarly critical assessment of Thornton comes from J.S. Bezzant: he claims that Thornton has failed 'to show that such a conception of the Incarnation is consistent with, or in any real relation to, "the organic conception of the universe"'. See Bezzant's review, *IL*, *Modern Churchman*, 19 (1929) 222. Yet another critical appraisal is that of Charles Raven who states: 'Thornton's own doctrine was rendered inconsistent by his insistence that although the creative process disclosed a series of emergents, life, mind, spirit, and thereby foreshadowed the culmination of the series in the coming of Christ, yet that event differed radically from all its predecessors and signalized not the consummation of the process but the intrusion into it of a Being wholly distinct and independent'. See Raven, *Natural Religion and Christian Theology*,

defence of the doctrine of the pre-existence of Christ: 'The argument of this book [*The Incarnate Lord*] can find no place for the mediator of an absolute revelation, except His metaphysical status be altogether beyond the organic series and on the level of the eternal order'.[118]

To conclude here, we note that in this section we have seen Thornton articulate an orthodox christology which is heavily indebted to the terminology favoured by a particular school of philosophy and which he considers useful to the Christian apologetics of his day. But there is much more to it than that, significant as it may be. Thornton believes that this organic understanding provides a key which enables us to understand the actual course of the development of christological thought from the Pauline epistles to the declarations of the Council of Nicea.[119] He argues that this development in the knowledge of the person of Christ was the result of a 'slow organic growth'.[120] It was only through an unfolding experience of redeeming love and its transforming fellowship that the historical concept of Jesus of Nazareth was transformed into the metaphysical sonship found in John's Gospel and afterwards in the Fathers and Councils. This process is characterised by Thornton as a 'living development'.[121] Through this 'living development' as recorded in scriptural, patristic and conciliar experiences, there was a growing realisation that the person who became man as did Jesus did not originate with the beginning of Christ's human nature (body and soul) but was always in existence beforehand.[122] Or to put it, once again, in Thornton's organic terms, that the Incarnate Lord had a *super-organic principle of individuality*. In the following section, we shall see how Thornton substantiates this claim by donning his cap as an accomplished biblical theologian and engaging in scriptural exegesis, particularly of Paul and John.[123] This section will draw heavily on Thornton's later book, *The Common Life in the Body of Christ*, in which he spurns the philosophical emphasis that characterised *The Incarnate Lord* and devotes his attentions to a study of the New Testament doctrine of the Church.

Organic development and the Bible
Just as the organic series manifested its moving forward through the advancing incorporation of the eternal order, so too, Thornton argues, the religious revelation as embodied in the historical experience recorded in the literature of the

---

vol. 2 (Cambridge, 1953), 102. See also D.M. Emmet, *Whitehead's Philosophy of Organism* (London, 1932), 254, n. 2 and D.M Baillie, *God was in Christ*, 3rd ed. (London, 1961), 91–3. 118 *IL*, 260. Thornton is reminiscent here of Francis J. Hall's insistence that 'supernatural revelation pertains to the Logos'. See Hall, *The Incarnation* (London, 1915), 272.   119 *IL.*, 286–7.   120 Ibid., xxiii.   121 Ibid., 15.   122 This is the interpretation proffered in K. Rahner & H. Vorgrimler, *A Dictionary of Theology*, 2nd ed. (New York, 1981), 408.   123 The scriptural index of the *IL* has the following number of entries: the Synoptics (41 times); the Pauline corpus (167 times); John's Gospel (154 times).

Hebrew people (the Old Testament) manifested an analogous advance. Thus he comments that in the Old Testament 'there is an advancing revelation with its developing system of mediation, rising to a level where the infinity of God's being and character is apprehended by the prophetic agents of revelation through incorporation of the eternal order in its ultimate and absolute quality into the form of religious experience'.[124] What Thornton is saying here in other words is that in the Old Testament there was a deepening and sharpening sense of Israel's vocation in relation to God as evidenced in concepts such as covenant, law and cult.[125] There is no need to delay on the detail of this argument. It is enough to note that for all 'the advancing revelation of God's character,'[126] the tension of contrasts between the majesty of God and the sinful estrangement of men remained (what Thornton normally refers to as 'the ethical problem of non-attainment').[127] 'This failure to attain harmonisation', of course, following the general law of the cosmic series, was a necessary condition of passage to further transformation.[128] Hence, the New Testament!

When we turn to the New Testament we find that it too records a religious experience in the process of development. The New Testament is at once 'a record of the impression which Christ made upon His first disciples and also in various degrees an interpretation of what that impression signified within the sphere of early Christian experience'.[129] It is clear that in this new dispensation of the Kingdom of God[130] the revelation contained in the prophetic expectations of the Old Testament has been both fulfilled and transcended. It is evident, Thornton goes on, that from the earliest documentary strata of the synoptic tradition we are encountering a revelation which has an absolute and final character in itself.[131] This kingdom, Thornton adds,

> lies beyond the world order; yet its content of heavenly treasure is interior and native to man's heart and need ... [It] is a revelation of a new order of reality, in which the ethical aspects of the eternal order are finally incorporated into a religious form. But the Kingdom is also incorporated into history. It is not simply proclaimed in expectation and promise. It is present in fulfilment; for it is a present reality to the mind of Jesus. The secrets of the Kingdom are His. He knows its treasure and possesses it. Its reality is beyond time and change, beyond historical

---

124 *IL*, 159.   125 Ibid., 161. Examples of this given here include the preaching of the prophets, the stories of the Maccabean martyrs, the rabbinic and apocalyptic forms of Judaism. Ibid., 161-3.   126 Ibid., 161.   127 Ibid., 162.   128 Ibid., 163.   129 As Thornton puts it: 'The New Testament is the literature of a religious experience. It is this which gives it unity ...' Ibid., 165.   130 'The kingdom of God is incorporated into history in the Messiah and His life story'. Ibid., xxii.   131 Mentioned here are 'Q' and Mark as well as such Lucan and Matthean passages as Lk 15 (the three parables of God's mercy: the lost sheep, the lost drachma and the prodigal son) and Mt 11:28-30 (the gentle mastery of Christ). Ibid., 167.

succession. Yet it is embodied in Him who knows it thus. The Kingdom is His Kingdom; for He is able to promise it with assurance to His little flock.[132]

The disciples of the synoptic accounts, Thornton's argument proceeds, recognised that Jesus was the adequate mediator of this absolute revelation. And this experience proved to be the starting point of their interpretations of his person. Thus these Gospels portray him as 'the Messianic head of the Kingdom, in whom Israel's expectations had reached their climax and fulfilment'.[133]

But that was not all. Thornton is aware that the apostolic thinking about Christ has its roots in the experiences of the reality of the Easter Jesus: i.e. of his death, resurrection and bestowal of the Holy Spirit. Thus Thornton asserts that the New Testament as literature 'is the product of these experiences and of the interpretation which they determined'. He draws attention to the Pauline observation that 'the old things are passed away: behold they are become new', and goes on:

> The outlook of the first Christians was determined by their experience of the New. Their minds were fixed upon the new fact which was Jesus the Christ, the new outpouring of [sic] Holy Spirit which was bestowed by Him, the new community in which the Spirit's gifts were manifested, the new power which the Spirit gave, the new way of life which opened out before the disciples of Jesus, the new wisdom by which they might understand the eternal purpose of God and co-operate in its fulfilment, the new covenant in which they shared through the baptism of the Spirit and the common meal of the Eucharist, above all the new κοινωνία or fellowship with God and with one another in which they now participate.[134]

These new experiences meant that the New Testament was characterised by an outlook which, as Thornton remarks, 'developed a new world-view which was eventually formulated in St Paul in his doctrine of the *new creation*. This doctrine became distinctive of New Testament Christianity. For in the fellowship of the Spirit there was experienced a new creative activity of God'.[135]

Thornton identifies the 'deep-rooted experience of salvation from sin' as the fundamental feature of this new life in the Spirit as represented in the New Testament.[136] This new experience is referred constantly to the saving activity of the historical Jesus and particularly to the mysterious efficacy of his death.[137]

---

132 Ibid., 167-8.   133 Ibid., 168.   134 Ibid., 169.   135 Ibid., 170.   136 Ibid., 173. He notes that St Paul seems to find 'a grim satisfaction in piling up descriptions of man's sinful state apart from the gospel', e.g. Rom 1:18 ff., and that in St John's Gospel 'the whole revelation given in Christ is regarded as setting in motion a drama of judgment upon human sin' e.g. Jn 16:8. Ibid., 176.   137 Reference is made in this discussion to the following texts: 2 Cor 5:14-21, Rom 5:4-21.

Increasingly there is an identification of the life of the Christian with the life of Christ as typified, for example, in Paul's exultant cry: 'I am crucified with Christ; but it is no longer I that live; but Christ liveth in me' (Gal 2:20). The Spirit is regarded as the creative source of this new life and Christ as 'not only [the] content of the new life, but also *object* of experience'.[138] Relying particularly on Romans and Galatians, Thornton stresses the importance of Christ's death, burial and resurrection for the identity of the Christian community. One's identification with it is regarded as having been effected through baptism.[139] Through baptism the reality of the kingdom embodied in the messianic life-story and the crowning events of that life are reproduced in the life-story of the baptised (i.e. those whom he also terms the new community).[140] Thornton, developing this theme of incorporation into Christ, notes the Pauline emphasis, especially in Ephesians, on the identity of the new community with its exalted Head.[141]

Thornton firmly underlines the radically Christocentric character of the new community's experience as unfolded in the New Testament. As the inner content of life in the Spirit unfolds itself in the New Testament, so is there a corresponding 'advancing interpretation of Christ's activity as adequate mediator of reconciliation between God and man'.[142] One consequence of this process, as Thornton states, is a developing doctrine of Christ's person in the New Testament.

At this stage it is appropriate that we return briefly to Thornton's understanding of the structure of the eternal order. Bearing in mind the detail of that theory, Thornton feels justified in asserting that 'Christian experience [as unfolded in the New Testament] is an organic whole which finds its principle of unity in Christ'.[143] As we have seen he argues that, while the eternal order does have an immanent aspect, it is ultimately transcendent. Thus it follows that 'what lies at the roots of our spiritual life is recognised in its very penetration to those roots to lie utterly beyond us in an immutable order which commands our allegiance'.[144]

---

138 *IL*, 178–9.   139 Ibid., 179.   140 Ibid. Thornton notes that the New Testament treatment of the conditions for entry into the kingdom passed through several stages of development in Paul, the Synoptics and John. Paul emphasised identification with the Messiah and entry into the new messianic community. They are both effected in baptism. Thornton refers to Rom 6 in particular on this point. The Synoptics stress change of heart and conversion for entry into the kingdom (becoming as little children; e.g. the little child of Mt 18). In this way one identifies with the Messiah and enters into the new messianic community. Finally, John combines and transforms the Pauline and synoptic interpretations with his emphasis in the discourse with Nicodemus upon entry into the kingdom by new birth (the child of Jn 3:4) and through the baptism of the Spirit into the new community. Thornton comments: 'there is a unity of experience underlying all variation and development'. Ibid., 180.   141 Ibid., 182.   142 Ibid., 183.   143 Ibid., xxii. 144 Ibid., 182.

The scriptural and patristic witness

Thornton believes that the New Testament not only vindicates his organic exposition of the reality of the Christ-event, but that it also clearly upholds the doctrine of Christ's pre-existence. We shall acquaint ourselves with Thornton's analysis of how Paul and John in particular treat this question. We shall begin with Paul.

Paul's witness   As a means of introduction to Thornton's interpretation of Paul's witness, we should note his judgement that Paul 'was not, for the most part, consciously elaborating Christological dogmas. He was trying to express the significance of Christ in terms which do justice to the actual facts of his experience.'[145] Thornton feels that Paul's interpretation was based on two lines of thought concerning the identity of Christ. The first line arose from the experience of the risen and ascended Jesus, the Son of Man of St Stephen's vision, the glorified figure of Paul's conversion-vision. Thus Thornton remarks that 'this transcendent glorified Christ dominates Pauline thought and stands both above and within that Christocentric experience'.[146] This experience demanded that Christ be recognised as an adequate mediator between God and humankind, the redeemer who forgives sin and restores us to communion with God, and brings us into a new life in the fellowship of the Spirit (1 Cor 15, Rom 5, Phil 2). Thus Paul formulated an understanding of Christ as the beginning and fountain-head of the new creation.[147] The emergence of this new understanding of Christ, Thornton emphasises, was occasioned by the facts of Paul's religious experience.[148] In the resurrection Jesus was declared to be God's Son.[149] In parenthesis here, we can note that although Thornton's incarnation-centred christology[150] pays the subject of Christ's resurrection rather scant attention, he has a highly orthodox reading of this doctrine too: it reveals, as we have just reported, the personal existence and identity of Christ as God's Son. Thornton also states that the risen Lord in his appearances revealed 'the essential identity which exists under transformed conditions as between the body of the risen life and the body which hung upon the Cross'.[151]

Thornton acknowledges that there was a second line of thought in Paul concerning the identity of Christ. It referred back to Christ's messianic sonship, regarding it as a special relationship to God.[152] This messianic sonship, as

---

145 Ibid., 293.   **146** Ibid., 294.   **147** Ibid.   **148** Thornton also notes that there are possible affiliations with the picture of the Son of Man in Daniel, Enoch and 4 Esdras or with non-Jewish eastern influences. But he goes on to say that if the argument of the *IL* is valid then 'St Paul cannot have derived the religious content of his germinal Christology from such sources'. It could only arise from religious experience. Ibid.   **149** *CLBC*, 290.   **150** Peter F. Carnley has noted that it has been fashionable, particularly in Anglican theology since the mid-nineteenth century, to view the incarnation as the central affirmation of Christian belief, in the light of which other elements within the edifice of Christian doctrine, like the resurrection, may be understood. Thornton is no exception in this regard. See Carnley, *The Structure of Resurrection Belief* (Oxford, 1987), 7.   **151** *CLBC*, 303.   **152** Thornton sees no contradiction in these two

Thornton observes, had its roots in Old Testament expectation of a Davidic sonship and a more general sonship of Israel as God's first-born (Hos 11:1 and Deut 8).[153] Thornton argues that Christ was keenly aware of himself as (messianic) Son in relation to the Father.[154]

Whatever the detail and merits of these arguments concerning this two-fold sonship, Thornton argues that one conclusion is irrefutable: 'St Paul firmly believed in our Lord's pre-existence'[155] and consistently upheld it in his teaching.[156] One passage which Thornton regards as clearly supporting this interpretation of Paul and which he has commented upon in considerable detail is Colossians 1:15-20. In beginning his exegesis of the text in question, he notes that the Epistle to the Colossians was written 'to combat a dangerous heresy ... that Christ was only one of many heavenly beings. The "heavenly bodies" (the planets, etc.) were supposed to embody angelic powers through whom the universe was ruled.'[157] Paul replied to this essentially polytheistic doctrine, Thornton goes on, by declaring that if there be such heavenly powers they were all created by Christ, who was begotten before every creature (1:15). They do not share with him the 'fulness of deity'. For in him the whole 'fulness' was pleased to dwell permanently (1:19, 2:9). Christ is twice described as 'the firstborn'; he is prior to and above every creature, because 'in him' the whole universe was created. He is the agent and goal of creation. He is before all things and all things are held together 'in him' (1:15-17). In assigning cosmic functions to the Messiah, Thornton argues that Paul is identifying him with the pre-existent Wisdom as described in Proverbs 8 and elsewhere in the Jewish wisdom literature.[158] In verse 18, however, Thornton proceeds, a transition is made to the second creation. Here Christ is considered as 'the head of the church'. In that connection he is a second time called 'firstborn', because 'he is the beginning, the firstborn from the dead'.[159] Thus Thornton can deduce that Paul held that Christ 'pre-existed as God's Son, and that he was also declared to be Son in the messianic sense at his resurrection'.[160]

notions of sonship, while acknowledging that at his baptism 'he was named the Beloved Son' (and from then began his mission which issued in his death); it was as the risen Lord, anointed by the Spirit that he exercised 'the fulness of the messianic functions'. Ibid., 272.   153 Ibid., 294.   154 He adds that this attitude to the Father is 'far more important than His attitude to current messianic titles'. This judgment is indicative of Thornton's high Christology. See ibid., 294, n. 3.   155 *CLBC*, 268.   156 Ibid., 290. Among the places where Thornton sees Paul clearly upholding the pre-existence of Christ are the following: 1 Cor 8:6, 2 Cor 8:9, Gal 4:4, Rom 1:3, 8:3, Phil 2:5 ff., Col 1:15 ff. See *IL*, 293, n. 1. and *CLBC*, 268, n. 1.   157 *CLBC*, 289. 158 Ibid., 291. He notes that this identification had already been made in 1 Cor. See also ibid., 296.   159 Thus he is 'the beginning', ἀρχή, i.e. the 'head of the new creation' and so second Adam. In this way Thornton says that Col 1:15-20 builds not only upon Galatians and Romans, but also upon 1 Cor 15. Thus he continues: 'The pattern of St Paul's Christology is one, although its articulation was subject to development'. Ibid., 291 and n. 1.   160 *IL*, 289-90. Thornton also notes that this explains the twofold use of the title Son in Rom. 1:3-4 and that Rom 8:29 introduces the title 'firstborn' in reference to the messianic sonship which was

When we pass on from the Epistle to the Colossians to that to the Ephesians, we find that Paul's thought has developed.[161] Christ is the consummator in history of the plan of God for creation. Thus Thornton comments: 'The Christ of Ephesians bestrides history. He *is* the purpose of God in the time process. Yet He is this as the historical Messiah of Jewish expectation and as the Redeemer in whom Jew and Gentile alike are recreated.'[162] In the Epistle to the Hebrews the eternal glory of the Son's divine life is the fundamental presupposition. Its critical question is, as Thornton observes: 'why was it necessary for One who enjoyed eternal fellowship with God to endure suffering and humiliation?'[163]

At this stage the logic of Thornton's argument is becoming increasingly clear. The new community, in the power of the Spirit, grows in its knowledge of the person of Christ and it is clear that if the language of organism is used to describe this experience of Christ's person, the concept of a *super-organic principle of individuality* in Christ is required.[164] This notion allows us to explain the existence of both immanent and transcendent dimensions in the community's experience. This process continues in John's Gospel and it is to that which we now turn.

John's witness   This evangelist, Thornton affirms, repeatedly asserts the pre-existence of Christ.[165] In John the interpretation of Christ is now developed a good deal further, Thornton goes on, because the prologue to the Gospel

> puts the coping-stone upon the conceptions unfolded in Colossians, Ephesians and Hebrews by expressly introducing a technical word which has philosophical associations for both the Greek and Jew. The language throughout indicates that the writer thought of the Logos as 'personal' both before and after He became flesh (note especially the reiteration of the word αὐτός) ... For John ... the Logos is a Divine Person who became flesh in the historical figure Jesus Christ.[166]

In John's Gospel, Thornton notes that the divine sonship, with its synoptic background, has become deeply metaphysical in character.[167] The prologue,

proclaimed at the resurrection (Rom 1:4). See also *CLBC*, 270-3.   **161** Thornton confesses himself unsure of the authorship of Ephesians. See *IL*, 296, n. 1.   **162** Ibid., 296-7.   **163** *CLBC*, 404.   **164** *IL*, 298.   **165** Ibid. See 6:62, 8:58, 17:5. Sayings like 16:28 are to be interpreted in light of these explicit statements.   **166** Ibid., 297. Thornton notes that the Logos doctrine was 'launched on its theological career by the combined influence of Philo and St John' and that it was destined to provide 'a most important mediating concept for the fusion of Greek, Jewish and Christian thought in the group of problems which concerned the connexion between God and creation; and it brought some of the leading ideas of New Testament Christology to bear upon that stream of speculation. But it could not in itself, as history shows, bear the whole weight of New Testament interpretation concerning Christ'. Ibid., 297-8.   **167** Ibid., 298.

Thornton asserts, 'offers a conception of the Incarnation corresponding to the formative kind of creative activity. Here the Logos, or Word of God, pre-existent and transcendent over creation, becomes incarnate in a human life-story as its transcendent principle of unity.'[168]

Thornton notes that controversy caused in the Synoptics by claims that Jesus was the Messiah have been replaced in John by disputes about his claims to equality with God. Thus the Jews are represented as seeking to kill him when he makes such claims.[169] But the main theme, Thornton states, is the relationship in which the Son stands to mankind as the representative of the Father. Thus, for example, the allegory of the vine in chapter 15 embraces all that is included in the phrase ἐν χριστῷ in Paul's teaching.[170] The discourses are revelations of Christ's redeeming activity, which require for their background a corresponding revelation concerning the Son's relation to the Godhead. Thus, as Thornton remarks, 'Christ is not part of the vine. He is the whole Vine of which we are branches. He is not one of the sheep, but the Shepherd of the whole flock. He is the Bread which feeds all His people and which is offered to all men. He not only raises the dead to life (ch. 5): He is the Resurrection and the Life (ch. 11) ...'[171] In this way Thornton drives home the same point he made in relation to Paul; the *principle of individuality* in Christ is super-organic.[172] Thus Thornton declares that 'the fourth gospel does not differ in principle from the other Christological writings of the New Testament. The evangelist differs only in carrying the argument further back and rendering the conclusions more explicit.'[173]

The main example of this process is the transition from the sonship as conceived in the synoptic narratives of the baptism and temptation to the fully articulate Johannine conception of an absolute sonship belonging to an eternal order. The interaction of apostolic experience and primitive Christian thought-forms meant that the historical concept of the messianic sonship was transformed into the Johannine concept of a metaphysical sonship.[174] Experience demanded a high christology, and consequently Thornton argues that John was right in placing Christ's relationship with the Father within a transcendent order, on the level of deity.[175] But this was not the final word. The Johannine differentiation of persons on the level of deity could not remain stationary. It required a more precise

---

168 Ibid., 327-8.   169 See 5:18; 8:56-59; 10:29-39.   170 *IL*, 300.   171 Ibid., 301-2.   172 Ibid., 302.   173 Ibid., 301.   174 Ibid., 306. Thornton states: 'If we ask how the new creation is constituted in Christ as a man the New Testament has two different answers. i) According to the authors of the nativity stories the human life of Christ derives from a special creative activity of the Holy Spirit. ii) According to the Prologue of St John the pre-existent Word is incarnate in that life'. Thornton points out that the answer to this problem of the double derivation could only be solved on the metaphysical level; and that 'such a level is indeed touched by certain parts of the New Testament; but its full arrival was postponed to a later [post-biblical] age'. Ibid., 321-2.   175 Ibid., 306.

metaphysical statement; something beyond the capacity of Jewish categories of thought.[176] Thus the New Testament gives way to the deliberations of the Fathers as we shall now see. Thornton mentions the contributions to the theology of sonship of such figures as Origen, Tertullian, Clement of Alexandria, Irenaeus, Athanasius, the Cappadocians and Augustine. As Origen is the object of particular attention, we shall briefly dwell upon his significance in the eyes of Thornton and then say a word about Tertullian and Irenaeus.

The Fathers　Thornton's hero in terms of theology is Origen. He brought the Platonic understanding of the order of reality to bear on the New Testament experience of Christ. Thus he was able to view the theology of sonship in terms of the eternal order which is utterly beyond time and sense.[177] The Johannine prologue, while introducing the Logos, did not clearly move outside the category of time. John was content to say that the Logos was 'in the beginning' with God.[178] The result of Origen's construction of Christian Platonism was the advance beyond cosmological speculation in John and Paul to meditation on the Redeemer's place in the life of God. As we have seen, the experience of redemption required that the head of the new creation be the super-organic head of the first creation. Armed with the Platonic ideas, the content of that experience, the κοινωνία, the fellowship of the Spirit whose law is ἀγάπη, is transferred to its transcendent background in the eternal κοινωνία in the life of God.[179] In this way, Thornton goes on, theology has arrived at the ultimate background of redemption, the eternal fellowship of Persons in God.[180] The substance of Origen's doctrine is that a revelation of the eternal order has been given by a mediator who himself belongs to an eternal order.[181] Now a word about Tertullian and Irenaeus.

While acknowledging Origen's contribution to the construction of Christian Platonism, Thornton also recognises the importance of Tertullian's emphasis on the soteriological principle to the community's developing understanding of Christ.[182] And finally according to Thornton, Irenaeus was 'a lesser man' than

---

176 In saying this Thornton acknowledges the considerable infiltration of Platonic ideas into the Jewish world through the wisdom literature, Philo and similar influences. Ibid., 307.　177 Ibid., 309. Thornton notes that Origen's *De Principiis*, book one and book four chapter 28, to which must be added statements scattered throughout his other works, especially the *contra Celsum* and the *Commentary on St John's Gospel*, are of special importance here. Ibid., 307. See also Thornton's additional note on Origen and the doctrine of the Trinity. Ibid., 473-6.　178 Ibid., 304.　179 Ibid., 312.　180 This line of thought will bring Thornton to a consideration of the Trinity. In speaking of the Trinity, Thornton avoids mention of the personality of God, since the term personality as he understands it involves the interpretation that it implies an independent centre of personal reference. As applied to God this would imply either unitarianism or tritheism. He prefers to speak of three persons in One Absolute Individuality. In God the social and individual aspects of personality are perfectly harmonised. Thornton treats the Trinity at length: see ibid., 355-425.　181 Ibid., 314-5.　182 Ibid., 309.

Origen, but he reproduced in some important respects, the full Pauline conception of redemption.[183]

We conclude our examination of Thornton by noting that he holds firmly to the pre-existence of Christ and has been able to postulate a philosophical framework that not only provides metaphysical concepts by which the pre-existence of Christ can be presented but also explains why the Incarnate Lord should be spoken of in such metaphysical terms. The experience of the Christian community demanded that such language be found as could adequately express its experience, through the power of the Spirit, of the risen Lord. Thornton's exegesis of the scriptures and discussion of various Fathers serves to validate his philosophical constructions.

---

183 Ibid., 308. Towards the end of his life Thornton penned an article which heavily criticised liberal theology and modern biblical exegesis. He upheld Irenaeus as an outstanding example of a superior approach to these issues. Irenaeus, he argued, was preoccupied with the unity and wholeness of religious revelation unlike so many contemporary scholars who were intent on separating 'the given whole from the various wholes in which it was given'. See 'St. Irenaeus and Contemporary Theology' in K. Aland & F.L. Cross (eds), *Studia Patristica*, vol. II, Papers Presented to the Second International Conference on Patristic Studies held at Christ Church, Oxford, 1955, Part II (Berlin), 317-27.

3

Eric L. Mascall's interpretation of Christ's pre-existence

INTRODUCTION

Eric Lionel Mascall was born in 1905; the product of 'no grand background'. [1] He was brought up as an only child in south London where he attended Latymer Upper School. There he displayed academic flair and developed a particular love of mathematics. In 1924 he won an open scholarship to Pembroke College, Cambridge, where he took a First in the Mathematical Tripos. He intended to take a PhD[2] with a view to seeking a college fellowship, but when no such offer was forthcoming he went instead to teach mathematics at Bablake School, Coventry. He spent three years teaching there (1928–31) and, as his memoirs attest, they were thoroughly miserable ones.

The young Mascall imbibed little by way of active religious conviction or pattern of practice from his all but lapsed Evangelical-Anglican parents. They rarely went to Church, 'Though they were ready to indulge in it occasionally for a special reason, and they thought that the British social fabric was so thoroughly permeated with religious and moral principles that, provided that you preserved its official and external profession, there was nothing more that you needed to do about it.'[3] Nevertheless, the young Eric's religious awakening as a boy saw him become firstly a keen Evangelical-Anglican; his penultimate year at Latymer Upper School, however, saw him become an ardent Anglo-Catholic,[4] and he would remain so for the rest of his long life. Mascall explained that his conversion to Anglo-Catholicism was occasioned by a bout of illness: the sickness meant that

1 Anon., 'Dr E.L. Mascall [Obituary]', *The Times* (February 17, 1993), 17.   2 In Relativity, Quantum Theory or Unified Field Theory. See his *Saraband: The Memoirs of E.L. Mascall* (Leominster, 1992), 73.   3 *Saraband*, 31. In later years they were to 'become devout Catholic churchpeople'. Ibid.   4 Anglo-Catholics owe their origin to the High Church movement in the Church of England. They 'hold a high doctrine of Church and Sacraments; they attach great importance to the "apostolic succession", that is, to an episcopal order derived from the apostles; to the historical continuity of the existing Church of England with the Church of the earliest centuries; and to the Church's ultimate independence of the State'. See F.L. Cross & E.A. Livingstone (eds), *The Oxford Dictionary of the Christian Church*, 3rd ed. (Oxford, 1997), 69; hereafter *ODCC*.

he spent several months in Brighton where he was introduced, in the parish of St Bartholomew's, to 'the ecclesial riches .... of Anglo-Catholicism'.[5] He commented that he returned for his last year to Latymer 'fully restored to health and fully convinced that the Church of England was Catholic and not Protestant ....'[6] In due course, Mascall, who had for sometime been developing an interest in theology, went to Ely Theological College in 1931 to study for the ministry.

Ordained only a year later in 1932, and without any real formal theological training, Mascall served as curate in two Anglo-Catholic parishes: St Andrew's, Stockwell and St Matthew's, Westminster. In 1937 he became sub-warden of Lincoln Theological College;[7] his career had taken the academic path which it was to follow until his retirement. While in Lincoln he wrote the book, *He Who Is*, (1943) which established his reputation as a major philosopher and theologian. In 1945, he went to Oxford, becoming a lecturer in the philosophy of religion at Christ Church College; and from there he moved, in 1962, to fill the newly created chair of Historical Theology at King's College, London, a post which he held until his retirement in 1973. While teaching in London he lived in the clergy house of St Mary's, Bourne Street, and served in the parish as an unofficial but distinguished curate.[8] He was awarded a DD by Oxford in 1948 and by Cambridge in 1958.

Mascall published theological and philosophical books, essays and reviews for more than fifty years and, as John Macquarrie commented, these writings were designed to expound Anglican Theology in its Catholic form.[9] In later life Mascall's publications became more polemical as he became increasingly disenchanted with the growing influence of liberal theological ideas within the Church of England.

He was wholeheartedly committed to the ecumenical movement and had many personal contacts in Europe and North America with the Orthodox Church and the Catholic Church. He spent a semester teaching, as a visiting professor, at the Gregorian University, Rome, in 1976, describing it as 'an exhilarating and rewarding experience'.[10]

As to the man, those who knew this serious-minded scholar marvelled at his impish sense of humour and apparently unlimited fund of anecdotes, sometimes expressed in verse. He published a short selection of them in his popular *Pi in the High* (1959) and in his memoirs, *Saraband* (1992). His attachment to theological orthodoxy (especially in the wake of the secularising pressures that accompanied

5 *Saraband*, 51.   6 Ibid., 52.   7 Mascall notes in his memoirs: 'as I had never had any academic training in theology at all, all my equipment as a theologian really consists of what I was able to acquire for myself during my eight years at Lincoln'. Ibid., 120.   8 Mascall lived in this clergy-house, as he puts it, 'chiefly because of my conviction of the importance for academic theologians of keeping in close relation with the pastoral and evangelistic ministry of the Church and of the serious harm that has been done to theology and to the Church when they have failed to do this ...'. Ibid., 281.   9 J. Macquarrie, 'Obituaries: Canon E.L. Mascall', *The Independent* (February 17, 1993), 25.   10 *Saraband*, 368.

the 1960s and since) did not win him many friends in the higher circles of the Church of England. Harry Smythe,[11] in his tribute to Mascall at the time of the latter's death, commented that 'the Church of England did not seem to want him and had nothing in particular for him to do'. The only ecclesiastical recognition that he ever received from the Anglican Church was being made the canon theologian of the diocese of Truro in 1974. Smythe comments that 'Mascall himself had remained untroubled by official neglect, or at worst antipathy, because he had no ambition other than the attainment of excellence in the fields of intellect and personal faithfulness and integrity ...'[12]

Mascall bore it all with admirable serenity: 'Anglican to his fingertips, he had an abiding loyalty to the Church in which he was brought up'.[13] Macquarrie commented after his death: 'As a cleric who combined learning and orthodoxy with rationality, and honest regard for truth with courtesy toward those who differed, and tempered it all with a sense of humour, Mascall may have been the last of a type which the Church of England can ill-afford to lose.'[14]

Mascall's main publications

Mascall's first published book, a slight volume entitled *Death or Dogma* (1937), dealt with the social implications of Christian theology. *Man, His Origin and Destiny* (1940) showed Mascall's concern for Christian sociology and carried a criticism of capitalist economics. *Christ, the Christian and the Church* (1946) and *Corpus Christi* (1956) were contributions to dogmatic theology on the mutually related topics of the incarnation, the church and the eucharist. *He Who Is* (1943), *Existence and Analogy* (1949) and *Words and Images* (1957) were written as replies to the linguistic positivism which dominated Oxford philosophy at the time. The ecumenical questions involved in the formation of the Church of South India were the issues discussed in *Priesthood and South India* (1944) and in its follow-up, *The Convocations of South India* (1955). *Via Media* (1956) maintained that on the cardinal points of Christian doctrine, orthodoxy consists in holding together two notions which appear to be, but are not, incompatible. *The Recovery of Unity* (1958) argued that doctrinal impasses between the different Christian denominations were due much more to uncriticised assumptions held in common than to consciously recognised disagreements. He delivered the Bampton Lectures of 1956 and they were subsequently published under the title *Christian Theology and Natural Science* (1956); they explored the relationship between modern science and the Christian faith. His American Bampton Lectures, delivered in Columbia University, New York City in 1958, were published under the title *The Importance of Being Human* (1958) and were concerned with theological anthropology.

11 The former director of studies at Pusey House, Oxford and the sometime director of the Anglican Centre, Rome. 12 H. Smythe, 'Obituary: Eric Mascall' *The Tablet* (20 February, 1993), 256-7. 13 Anon., 'Dr. E.L. Mascall [Obituary]', *The Times* (see n. 1 above). 14 Macquarrie, 'Obituaries: Canon E.L. Mascall', *The Independent* (see n. 9 above).

The 1960s ushered in great political, social and theological changes in Western society. Mascall was alarmed at the consequences of these developments for the Church of England, where liberal theological ideas soon gained a firm foothold. For the rest of his career, the bulk of his books were written as critiques of the heterodox ideas which were increasingly gaining currency: *Up and Down in Adria* (1963), *The Secularisation of Christianity* (1965), *The Christian Universe* (1965), *Theology and the Future* (1968), *Theology and the Gospel of Christ* (1977), *Whatever Happened to the Human Mind?* (1980), and the slim volume, *Jesus: He Who Is And How We Know Him* (1985). These publications were generally dedicated to the twin tasks of unmasking the unacceptable presuppositions of liberal theology and displaying the overriding superiority of theological orthodoxy.

Mascall also turned his attention to the task of restating a more viable natural theology in both *The Openness of Being* (1971) which was based on his Gifford Lectures of 1970-1 and *Nature and Supernature* (1973) which was based on lectures he delivered at Gonzaga University, Spokane, in 1973. The first of these two books involved him in a detailed critique of transcendental Thomism and process theology. Mascall's last principal work, *The Overarching Question: Divine Revelation or Human Invention?*, a critique of modern theories of revelation and an analysis of the challenges facing contemporary Anglican ecclesiology, remains unpublished: it is to be found with the rest of his papers in the archives of Pusey House, Oxford.

The early Mascall (1929-62) – confident orthodoxy

Mascall's career was characterised by two distinct phases: the early one lasting until his departure from Oxford in 1962, and the later one coinciding with his change to King's College, London and lasting until the time of his death. In the former phase, he found himself a member of the promising Anglo-Catholic movement in Anglican theology and Church life. The tone of his writings at this time was consistently positive as he rejoiced in the decline of the old Victorian certainties of scientific atheism and in the intellectual revival of religion.[15] In the latter stage, however, in the wake of the 1960s' turn to liberalism (in social, cultural, political as well as theological terms), Mascall, as we have already noted, would find himself increasingly disillusioned with the prevailing mood of theological thought in England, and much of his academic energy was spent on refuting the central tenets of this liberal agenda. To assist us in our attempts to get to terms with Mascall, we shall begin by hearing something of his youthful optimism concerning the task of theology in England in the years between the two world wars. But before doing this we should recall that, while the tone of his theological discourse differed between the two phases, as he struggled to respond to the challenges

---

15 *Christian Theology and Natural Science* (London, 1956); hereafter *CTNS*, is dedicated to an in-depth analysis of the new possibilities emerging in the relationship between science and religion.

presented by different intellectual climates, the substance of his christological argument remained consistent, though, as we shall see below, it was enriched by the
insights provided by certain scholars admired by Mascall.

The theological climate

The increasing sympathy in the 1930s for orthodox Christianity both within the
Church of England and in the universities[16] meant that the young Mascall, like
many of his Anglo-Catholic colleagues, entertained high hopes for a growing
recovery of orthodox theological thought after the ravages of the liberal dominance in this field during the previous century.[17] This confidence is clearly
reflected in his own writings, even if those of a specifically theological character
were not so numerous during this stage. His earliest articles in the periodical
Theology, his *Christ, the Christian and the Church* (1946) and *Via Media* (1956)
show a man confident that Anglican theology was about to opt decisively for a
'Catholic orthodoxy' in matters pertaining to doctrine. Thus in one of his very
earliest publications, Mascall the school master in Bablake commented that

> it is therefore gratifying, in view of the many problems that science has
> raised for religion in the past to find that the philosophical position to
> which, on purely physical grounds, scientists have been recently led, pro-
> vides, if not a solution of the problem (for this we cannot expect), at any
> rate an indication as to where the solution lies. Relativity and the Quantum
> theory have made it more than ever clear that time and space are modes
> rather than objects of our experience ....[18]

In charting the new theological future in the wake of a changed intellectual
climate, Mascall was adamant that the future was as bleak for the Anglican Liberal
Catholic Modernists as it was for the unorthodox liberal theologians. Mascall
acknowledged that Liberal Catholicism had

16 Mascall comments in his memoirs: 'In these days [following the rise of theological liberalism
in the 1960s], when for so many theologians the fundamental theological categories seem to be
drabness and obscurity, it is comforting to remember the life and work ... of highly intelligent
laymen and women – T.S. Eliot, Dorothy L. Sayers and C.S. Lewis spring at once to mind –
whom the Anglican Church possessed in those days, who wrote grippingly, lucidly and
enlighteningly because they were convinced of the truth of orthodox Christianity and its
relevance to the problems of mankind. The strength of their conviction gave their writing more,
not less, apologetic force.' *Saraband*, 200.   17 Similar sentiments had already been expressed
by Francis J. Hall when he wrote: 'There are signs ... that modern scholarship is ere long to
justify itself as a chosen means of the Holy Spirit for the guidance of the Church into a riper
understanding of her primitive faith.' See his *The Incarnation* (London, 1915), x.   18 'The
Incarnation and Space-Time', *Theology*, 19 (1929) 315. Mascall would later dwell more
extensively on the issues involved here in *CTNS*.

never set out to be unorthodox .... [but its] distinguishing feature was that it was a break from the past. Instead of discussing its problems in the light of theological principles and attempting to continue the development of traditional theology, it tried to build up theology entirely *de novo* upon the basis of contemporary science and philosophy. Its primary concern - and it was a laudable one - was to retain within the Church those who had grown up in a Christian atmosphere and were temperamentally disposed to be Christians, but whose faith had been undermined by modern scientific research. In many cases its success was remarkable.[19]

As to its defects, Mascall, writing in 1960, asserted that it was too willing, in general, to accept the contemporary presuppositions of the secular sciences as reliable and ultimate; this resulted from its natural tendency to show how little humanity needed to believe in order to be justified in practising the Christian religion. It also tended to a dogmatically attenuated type of religion which was somewhat lacking in appeal to those who were not professional or amateur intellectuals, and was singularly impotent in bringing a Christian critique to bear upon the modern mind's prejudices and assumptions in both the intellectual and social realm.[20]

If this liberalism could be said to belong to the past, 'the younger movement in theology', Mascall went on to say, 'might be described as a return to dogma'.[21] It was concerned not so much with trying to prove by the methods of contemporary thought that the Christian religion can make a compelling case for itself as with 'taking the Faith as something revealed by God in Christ and examining how it can be applied to the problems of the present-day world, though this must not be taken to mean that it is uninterested in apologetics ...'[22]

Adrian Hastings has characterised this epoch as 'the high summer of Anglo-Catholic orthodoxy' and identified Mascall as one of its principal luminaries.[23] That the movement could look to the future with great confidence, Mascall would seem to have had little doubt. There can hardly be another explanation of the

19 'The Future of Anglican Theology', *Theology*, 39 (1939) 407. 20 'Anglican Dogmatic Theology, 1939-1960', *Theology*, 63 (1960) 2. 21 'The Future of Anglican Theology', *Theology*, 39 (1939) 408. Mascall notes that for many of the 'younger men', this return to dogma was not to be in terms of neo-Calvinism or neo-Lutheranism and that 'it would be a complete misunderstanding to see in them only a group of Papalists or medievalists. Whether they should be described as "scholastics" or not is largely a matter of words. There is certainly little to be said for the common use of the terms "scholastic", "Thomist" and "medievalist" as synonymous pejoratives ...' Mascall goes on to say that these 'younger men' would lay stress on St Thomas and the great Anglican divines, such as Hooker, Andrewes, Taylor and Hall. Ibid., 409-10. 22 Ibid., 408. 23 A. Hastings, *A History of English Christianity 1920 -1985* (London, 1986), 298. Prominent also in Anglo-Catholic circles were the rather older scholars, Lionel Thornton, A.T. Herbert of Kelham, Michael Ramsey, Dom Gregory Dix of Nashdom Abbey, Kenneth Kirk (Bishop of Oxford) and Mascall's contemporary and personal friend, Austin Farrer.

extravagant confidence of his claim that 'liberalism would seem to have been a *temporary* [italics mine] divergence from the main stream of Anglicanism, largely due to pressure of circumstances and by no means wholly valueless, but incomplete, lacking continuity with the past and without solid foundation'. As to what the shape of this new theological future would be, Mascall felt confident enough to predict that in the work of 'a quite large and vigorous group of younger men' (by whom he meant Anglo-Catholic scholars) it would be characterised by an appreciation of the fact that the 'great system of dogmatic theology which the Church of England inherited from the Middle Ages, which was unbroken until the arrival of Hanoverian latitudinarianism, and which reappeared in a rather attenuated and one-sided form in the Tractarians is the proper sphere of thought in which Anglicans should move'.[24]

Mascall also expressed the aspiration that if the work of Anglican biblical revival and the permanent gains of the (Anglo-Catholic) liberal period (which he fails to list)[25] could be brought into the traditional structure of dogmatic theology, then 'Anglicanism may do for the twentieth century what the Dominicans did for the thirteenth'.[26]

Thus as we shall soon see, Mascall's early theological publications saw him confident that a retrieval of orthodoxy pointed the way forward for theology, especially in the field of christology. We shall now see how the early Mascall attempts to come to terms with the mystery 'that in Jesus of Nazareth human nature is permanently and inseparably united to the Person of the Eternal Word'.[27] We shall confine our attentions to the salient elements of Mascall's christological thought with particular reference to those points which seem important to a discussion of his understanding of the pre-existence of Christ.[28] Firstly, we shall touch upon his theological method.

A modern Thomist

The bulk of the early Mascall's christological writings are to be found in his *Christ, the Christian and the Church* (1946), *Via Media* (1956) and in a number of articles published over a period of some thirty years since 1929. While Mascall rarely tackled biblical exegesis, a glance at the index of the earlier of these two

24 'The Future of Anglican Theology', *Theology*, 39 (1939) 410. 25 Save for the comment that 'Anglican liberalism at its best has never quite forgotten its roots in historical Catholicism; that is why Anglican biblical criticism has been at once so much saner than that of the German school and so exasperating a phenomenon to those, who not being in the Catholic tradition, could see in it nothing more than an attempt to run with the critical hare and follow with the Catholic hounds'. Ibid., 411. 26 Ibid., 410-1. 27 *Christ, the Christian and the Church: A Study of the Incarnation and its Consequences* (London, 1946), v; hereafter *CCCH*. 28 Although Mascall has been the subject of very little scholarly research in his native England, he has been the topic of four doctoral dissertations at the Gregorian University; one of which is devoted to his christology: E.L. Piotrowski, *The Christology of E.L. Mascall* (Rome, 1987).

books shows that he drew heavily from that other great font of Anglican theology, the Church Fathers. It comes as no surprise to note his familiarity with the Anglican divines and the other major figures of subsequent English theology.[29] Where Mascall departed from the Anglican norm, however, was in his intimate knowledge of medieval thought, especially that of St Thomas, and in his acquaintance with more recent Continental, neo-Thomist Catholic theology, principally that current in France. (These would be two consistent characteristics of his writings throughout his long theological career.) While the wide range of his theological interest was clearly demonstrated by the sheer breadth of the sources to which he appealed in his various writings, it is quite evident that Mascall was pre-dominantly a Thomist in his philosophy and theology. He relied heavily on the writings of the Angelic Doctor and authors from the Thomist tradition such as Maritain, Gilson and others.[30] The Thomism he expounded in his important early work, *He Who Is* (1943) had a decidedly dynamic character and, in the judgement of John Macquarrie, anticipated what came to be called 'transcendental thomism'.[31] In the preface of his *Existence and Analogy*, (1949) Mascall described the general outlook of the book as one of 'modern Thomism' and went on to say:

29 Thus, for example, in *CCCH*, Mascall appealed to the following authors: the Anglican divine, Hooker (13 times), recent Anglican theologians like Gore (13 times), Thornton (10 times), Relton (14 times) and, interestingly, such Continental authors as Maritain (15 times), Mersch (16 times), and de Lubac (14 times). St Thomas Aquinas is the one to whom recourse is most frequently made (45 times). It comes as some surprise to observe that there is no mention of such prominent Anglican divines of the seventeenth century as L. Andrewes, W. Laud, H. Thorndike, J. Taylor, J. Cosin and T. Ken.   30 It is unclear as to who, or what, first stimulated Mascall's interest in Thomism. His memoirs attest that he was a member of the Socratic Club (as was C.S. Lewis) and that 'it provided a valuable battle-ground for religious apologetics'. Mascall also notes that 'more private and inconspicuous but in its way perhaps of not less value was the small group of philosophers and theologians which Michael Foster and I got together ... and of which I was secretary until I left Oxford.' It was known as 'The Metaphysicals' and numbered among its members were such people as Austin Farrer and Basil Mitchell. *Saraband*, 253-4. One clue as to why he found Thomism so intellectually rewarding comes from his own mathematics background at Cambridge and his attachment to clear and exact thought. He comments in his memoirs: 'several years [spent] grappling with the concepts and methods of mathematics, pure and applied, is in itself of inestimable value in forming habits of clear and exact thought, whether one is going to be a professional mathematician or not; nor in my experience has it a narrowing tendency. There are, of course, notorious exceptions, but my observation is that mathematicians tend if anything rather more than other specialists to have interests outside their own subjects. Having myself moved later into another field of research, I have often found myself wishing that some of the theologians whose work I have had to read had been subject to the same rigorous training. Conscious as I am of my weakness in never having had an academic theological training, I have never regretted as a theologian the training I had as a mathematician.' Ibid., 60.   31 J. Macquarrie, *Twentieth-Century Religious Thought*, 4th ed. (London, 1988), 386.

I can only plead that if, on the broad issue and in a number of details, I have had the temerity to agree with the Angelic Doctor, it is not because of nostalgia for the thirteenth century, or because Dominicans are picturesque, or even in order to scandalize some of my elders, but simply because, having given a good deal of thought to these questions, I have come to the conclusion that what St Thomas said about them was on the whole correct.[32]

While there is not the space here to dwell on the characteristics of Thomism, it is clear that he identifies himself as a Thomist in 'the widest sense', that is, 'anybody who, basing his cosmology upon the principle *Nihil in intellectu quod non prius in sensu*, maintains in addition that the existence of the finite world apodictically indicates the self-sufficient transcendence cause to which Christian theology applies the name "God"'.[33]

Having noted Mascall's orthodox, Thomist theological predispositions, we shall now turn to an examination of his christology.

MASCALL'S CHRISTOLOGY AND INTERPRETATION OF CHRIST'S PRE-EXISTENCE (1929-62)

The shape of his early christology
The Oxford Dictionary of the Christian Church defines christology as 'the study of the Person of Christ, and in particular of the union in Him of the divine and human natures'.[34] While many christologies, both ancient and modern, fight shy of, or even deny, the assertion that Christ is both human and divine, Mascall's is not numbered among them. He is uncompromisingly orthodox in his teaching about Christ, accepting without qualification the doctrine of the incarnation laid down in the great Catholic confessions of faith and especially by the Council of Chalcedon (451).[35] Mascall does not adopt this view as a conclusion of argument

---

32 *Existence and Analogy* (London, 1966), xvi. Mascall, in his memoirs, notes that Anglican ecclesiastical authorities have never looked approvingly upon Thomism and commented that 'it did me no good, ... in higher ecclesiastical circles, ... the suspicion of Thomism was as much of a disqualification in official eyes as was that of Communism or homosexuality'. *Saraband*, 125. Although Mascall does not refer to it in his memoirs, Owen Chadwick reports that he, along with Stephen Neill and Michael Ramsey, was a candidate for the vacant post of Regius Professor of Divinity at Cambridge in 1950. Mascall, Chadwick relates, lost the post to Ramsey, in part, because of the feeling of the selection board that neo-Thomism 'was a retrograde movement in divinity'. See O. Chadwick, *Michael Ramsey: A Life* (Oxford, 1990), 68-9.   33 'Theism and Thomism: Some Answers to Professor Emmet', *Theology*, 53 (1950) 129. A. Nichols has spoken of Mascall as 'the distinguished Anglican Thomist'. See his *A Grammar of Consent* (Edinburgh, 1991), 82.   34 *ODCC*, 336.   35 The definition of this Council reaffirmed the earlier conciliar teachings of Nicea (325) and Constantinople I (381), asserting them to be

or of reasoning based on premises the truth of which is evident to us. Like Thomas Aquinas, he begins with it.[36] Everything he has to say about Christ is an attempt to explore the sense and significance of the creedal and conciliar teaching (which, of course, are in accordance with the scriptural testimony) concerning him.[37] It is hardly surprising, therefore, that Mascall has been characterised as an outstanding Anglican example of 'Catholic orthodoxy'.[38] We shall now familiarise ourselves with the more important detail of his reading of certain creedal formulations and of the definition of the Council of Chalcedon.

The importance of the creeds

On the first page of *Christ, the Christian and the Church*, Mascall begins his christological endeavour by referring to 'the two great Catholic confessions which the early Christian centuries bequeathed to the Church' and which proclaim 'with incandescent clarity' that Jesus Christ is truly God and truly man. He reproduces that part of the Niceno-Constantinopolitan Creed which asserts the Church's belief 'in one Lord Jesus Christ, the only-begotten Son of God, begotten of the Father before all ages, Light from Light, Very God from Very God, begotten not made, consubstantial with the Father, through whom all things were made'. He then goes on to recall that this same Lord, 'for us men and for our salvation came down from heaven, and was made flesh of the Holy Ghost and Mary the Virgin, and was made man.'[39]

sufficient accounts of the orthodox faith about the person of Christ, but declares that the new errors of Nestorius and Eutyches must be formally repudiated. Chalcedon upheld the title *Theotokos* for the Virgin Mary and the non-confusion of the two natures, divine and human, in Christ. See *ODCC*, 315.　**36** For an introduction to St Thomas' christology, see B. Davies, *The Thought of Thomas Aquinas* (Oxford, 1992), 297-319.　**37** Mascall, on a number of occasions, draws attention to his inadequacy as a biblical scholar and it is true to say that his christology is not characterised by any great emphasis on questions of biblical exegesis (though in later life he would write disparagingly of the historical scepticism so typical of scriptural studies during the second half of the twentieth century). See his *Theology and the Gospel of Christ* (London, 1977), 65-120; hereafter *TGC*. Nonetheless, on a few occasions he underlines his argument by reference to biblical texts. Thus, for example, when combating the kenoticists, Mascall argues that 'the New Testament writers never seem to find the human nature of Christ an embarrassment to the exercise of his divine prerogatives' and draws attention, in support of this contention, to the following passages where Christ is described as: 'the image of the invisible God' (Col 1:15); 'the impress of his substance' (Heb 1: 3); and man as made in God's image (Gen 1:26-27). See *CCCH*, 49. Another example is found when Mascall disputes Gore's (among others) interpretation of Phil 2:5-7, arguing that 'emptied' (ἐκένωσεν) does not imply that the Word stripped himself of some element or elements proper to his divinity. It is thus not intended in the metaphysical sense, but rather as a strong and graphic expression of the completeness of his self-renunciation. *CCCH*, 25.　**38** So wrote John A.T Robinson in his *The Human Face of God* (London, 1973), 106.　**39** *CCCH*, 1.

If we are to pass beyond 'the mere recognition of historical fact' that is recorded in this and other creedal formulations, 'and ask how this miracle [of the Incarnation] is possible', then, Mascall asserts, 'we are led to those more subtle and philosophical statements which we find in the Chalcedonian definition and the *Quicunque Vult*'.[40] Thus, as we shall now see, Mascall views christology as basically an ontological concern. L.B. Smedes has remarked that Mascall's entire work in christology may be considered a commentary on one sentence in the *Quicunque Vult:*[41] 'And although He be God and Man, nevertheless He is not two, but is one Christ: one, however, not by conversion of the Godhead into flesh, but by taking up of manhood into God.' A brief glance at some of the more conspicuous points of Mascall's general christology may be helpful before turning our attention to the main focus of this study, the pre-existence of Christ.

His 'no' to kenoticism

A strong theme in Mascall's writing is his rejection of the kenotic theories[42] which had enjoyed considerable influence in English theology following the publication of *Lux Mundi.*[43] Thus he asserts that whatever 'the Incarnation means, it cannot imply that any change takes place in the divine Word. With St Thomas we must affirm our belief in 'the Word of God, proceeding forth yet leaving not the Father's side'.[44] Appealing to the words of the *Quicunque Vult,* he declares that the incarnation is not a 'conversion of the Godhead into flesh'. Mascall is resisting here any suggestion that God is anything other than immutable and impassible: 'it must be said quite plainly that neither the Incarnation nor anything else can involve a change in God himself'.[45] It was thus a matter of regret for Mascall that 'many modern English discussions of Christology adopt precisely the [opposite] standpoint' and 'take as their starting-point human nature as it is known to us, and then in effect inquire what must happen to the divine Word if he is to be compressed within its limits'. The consequence of this approach, says Mascall, is that 'their

---

40 Ibid., 42-3. *The Quicunque vult*, a profession of faith widely used in Western Christendom, is also known as the Athanasian Creed, even though the attribution of its authorship to St Athanasius has been generally abandoned. See *ODCC*, 119. It is found in *The Book of Common Prayer*, intended to be recited at certain Feasts.   41 L.B. Smedes, *The Incarnation: Trends in Modern Anglican Thought* (Amsterdam, 1953), 31. This assessment of Mascall's christology remains valid for the entirety of his career.   42 For a very useful contemporary discussion of kenotic christology, see L. Richard, *Christ the Self-Emptying of God* (New York, 1997). See also S.W. Sykes, 'The Strange Persistence of Kenotic Christology', in A. Kee & E.T. Long (eds), *Being and Truth: Essays in honour of John Macquarrie* (London, 1986), 349-75.   43 *Lux Mundi* is a 'Series of Studies in the Religion of the Incarnation' published in 1889 by a group of Anglican teachers under the editorship of Charles Gore. Its purpose was 'to put the Catholic faith into its right relation to modern intellectual and moral problems. By accepting in principle the new critical views in Old Testament scholarship, it represented a break with the older school of High Churchmen'. See *ODCC*, 1011.   44 *CCCH*, 15. These are the first two lines of a hymn (*English Hymnal*, 330) which translates Aquinas' *Verbum supernum prodiens*.   45 Ibid., 14.

Christology thus becomes a degradation of the divine Person rather than an exaltation of human nature'.[46] In becoming incarnate, the Son of God undergoes no diminution in his divine functions and attributes. Rather, 'he adds to these all the functions of a complete human life which go to make up the complex which is human nature'.[47] Any change of relations which seems to occur in the incarnation is real only for the creature. For God, the change is only logical.[48] We now come to Mascall's understanding of the relationship between the human and divine natures and their union in the one divine Person of Christ.

The Person of Christ

At the centre of Chalcedonian doctrine, as Mascall recalls, is the conviction that in Jesus Christ there are 'two natures, a divine and a human, [which] are inseparably and unconfusedly united in one divine Person'.[49] Thus 'Christ had a complete human nature, but no human person'.[50] All the acts of the incarnate life are to be considered as *theandric* acts.[51] In the philosophical categories employed by the Council, it was said, or at least clearly implied, that Christ had no human *prosopon* (human person) in him, but only a divine *prosopon* (divine Person). Mascall stoutly rebuffs any suggestion that Christ has no human energy or operation (monergism) or that he lacks a human will (monothelitism), and goes on to state that 'nothing human in Christ is missing except a human person or *hypostasis*; and the absence of a human person does not mutilate the nature, for "person" is not the name of a constituent of human nature, it is a purely metaphysical term'.[52]

46 Ibid., 15. Mascall argues that the enthusiasm of kenotic christology to transpose christology into the realm of the more fashionable science of psychology represents what he feels can best be described 'as a failure of theological nerve'. See *CCCH*, 42.   47 Ibid., 15–6. See also *He Who Is* (London, 1943), 112, n. 4.   48 *CCCH*, 17. Mascall refers to St Thomas in a footnote here: *Summa Theologiae*, 3, 2, 7c: 'Every relation which we consider between God and the creature is really in the creature, by whose change the relation is brought into being; whereas it is not really in God. And hence we must say the union of which we are speaking [i.e. the Incarnation] is not really in God, except only in our way of thinking (*non est in Deo realiter, sed secundum rationem tantum*); but in the human nature, which is a creature, it is really.' Ibid., 17–8, n. 1.   49 *CCCH*, 20.   50 *Via Media* (London, 1956), 101; hereafter *VM*.   51 That is to say, the acts of a divine Person in a human nature. Ibid. 98.   52 Ibid., 101–2. Mascall uses the term the 'impersonal manhood' to characterise the absence of a human person in Jesus Christ. See ibid., 103; *CCCH*, 3 and *Up and Down in Adria* (London, 1963), 66. He explains that Christ's manhood is impersonal 'not in the sense that Christ is not a person, but in the sense that the function in relation to his nature which would ordinarily be performed by a created human person is performed by an uncreated and pre-existent Person of the divine Word', *CCCH*, 3. Mascall is striving here to avoid any suggestion of Nestorianism and to underline the fact that Jesus is fully personal because his nature is possessed by the Second Person of the Trinity. As to how useful the expression 'the impersonal humanity' is, there is some doubt. W.N. Pittenger, for one, has roundly condemned the term, accusing Mascall of a tendency to treat Jesus' human nature in such a manner as to suggest that Jesus has 'no genuine humanity at all'. See his *The Word*

Mascall's reasoning is open to the charge of ambiguity on this point: surely nature is also a metaphysical term? In general it must be said that Mascall's treatment of the concept of *person* is somewhat lacking even if he does show that he is aware of the problems it presents, when at the beginning of his *Christ, the Christian and the Church* he comments that

> the assertion that in Christ there is a divine but no human *persona* does not in itself explain anything. For, we naturally want to know, what does *persona* mean? What is this factor in a human being which is not a constituent of the human nature but is nevertheless the subject of all the human experiences and activities?[53]

With such concerns prominent in his mind, Mascall acknowledges that he is aware of the difficulties presented by Boethius' famous definition of *person* (*Persona est rationalis naturae individua substantia*)[54] for the christological formula that two natures or substances cohere in one *Person* and for the trinitarian formula that three *Persons* cohere in one substance.[55] (Boethius argued that a person *is* a substance of a particular kind.) Having said this, however, the younger Mascall is too reticent to tackle the problems that Boethius' formula presents since it 'has generally been accepted by Christian theologians and defended by St Thomas himself'. Instead he settles for the (unconvincing) thesis that Boethius' definition presents problems for theology only 'at first sight' and that upon further reflection these difficulties disappear.[56] That said, Mascall goes on to assert that 'the person is the concrete individual and all that finds realization in him: he who is, and what he is, in their concrete union'. He acknowledges that 'in ordinary life we hardly ever need to distinguish, except in thought, between the *who* and the *what*; the person and the nature go together' and that 'the question therefore does not press itself as to whether the nature is to be understood as what the person *has* or as what the person *is;* the nature is the person in its concrete activity and individuality'.[57] Thus Mascall, writing in 1966, defined *person* as 'what each of us has for himself; it is the seat of his incommunicable self-identity', and nature as that which 'the human being shares with the whole human race'.[58]

Incarnate (London, 1959), 89. And G.C. Stead asserts that 'Mascall has fallen into the trap ... [since] he never himself refers to Jesus as "a man". God became man, he assumed human nature, but he was not a man'. See his review of *VM, Journal of Theological Studies*, 8 (1957) 384.   **53** *CCCH*, 4.   **54** Translation: 'a person is an individual substance of a rational nature'.   **55** *CCCH*, 7.   **56** Ibid. Mascall argues, in support of this contention, that the solution to the problem 'is to be found in the adjective *individua*. It is "individual substance" that is in question, that is, *substantia prima* in its most concrete application: not the specific essence which the person shares with other individuals of its kind, nor even that essence taken in conjunction with the individual characteristics shared by no one else, but the individual himself in whom that essence is realized with those characteristics, the *suppositum* in the strictest sense.'   **57** Ibid., 7-8.   **58** *The Christian Universe* (London, 1968), 104.

When Mascall turns his attention to the incarnate Word, he argues that 'the *who* and the *what* must of necessity be distinguished, for while the latter is created, the former is God himself'.[59] Thus Mascall claims that while in Jesus Christ 'two natures, a divine and a human, are inseparably and unconfusedly united in one divine Person .... [they] are not both related to the Person in precisely the same way'.[60] While Jesus' human nature and divine Person are not to be considered absolutely identical (although their union is the most intimate and substantial), his divine nature and Person are in fact really identical and only logically distinct.[61]

While the detail of Mascall's understanding of *person* cannot delay us here,[62] it is appropriate that we note the principal difficulty it poses: the divine Person has arguably been reduced to the level of being only a quality of the nature. This position is clearly in conflict with Chalcedon's insistence upon the distinction between nature(s) and person in Christ.

In drawing this discussion to a close, it must be observed that the early Mascall's uncritical acceptance of Boethius' definition of *person* meant that he failed to develop a viable understanding of the concept of *person*. As we shall report below, however, Mascall's understanding of the notion of *person* did develop in the later stage of his career when he availed of the insights provided by J. Galot on the concept of *person* as pure relational being.

This examination of Mascall's earlier understanding of the concept of *person* should not conclude without mention of his attraction to the terminology adopted in the theology of the sixth-century theologian Leontius of Byzantium on this issue.[63] Leontius, Mascall recounts, stated that 'the human nature of Christ is neither unattached to a *hypostasis* nor does it inhere in the human *hypostasis* of the Second Person of the Holy Trinity. It is neither itself a *hypostasis* nor is it *anhypostatic*, but it is *enhypostatic* in the divine Word'.[64] Mascall can thus assert that 'the fundamental wonder and mystery of the Incarnation is that it is possible for a created nature, without being destroyed or absorbed, to inhere in an uncreated Person'.[65] As *enhypostatic*[66] in the person of the Word, Christ's human

---

59 *CCCH.*, 8.   60 Ibid., 20.   61 Ibid.   62 It receives extensive treatment in Piotrowski, *The Christology of E.L. Mascall*, 240–63.   63 Mascall draws attention to the importance attached to Leontius' work by such scholars as H.M. Relton in his *Study in Christology* (London, 1917) and R.V. Sellers, in his *The Council of Chalcedon* (London, 1953). See *VM*, 103.   64 Although Leontius himself was strongly influenced by the Aristotelian revival, his essential contribution to christology arose from his assertions (against the Monophysites) that a nature cannot exist without a *hypostasis* and (against the Nestorians) that Christ, having a human nature, must have a human *hypostasis* in addition to his divine *hypostasis*. See *VM*, 103–4. Mascall seems to have grown in his appreciation of Leontius because, in a work ten years earlier, he stated that Leontius' doctrine of the *enhypostasia* 'provides a convenient way of expressing this fact [i.e. the doctrine that the humanity of Christ is constituted in the person of the divine word], though I am not sure that it gives us anything much more'. *CCCH*, 8.   65 *VM*, 104.   66 Mascall regards this doctrine of the enhypostasia as in essence nothing else than that doctrine of St

nature is as real and concrete, says Mascall, as that of any man or woman who ever lived.[67] In the face of this 'profound mystery', where 'the Creator should become the subject of a created nature', we can conclude our discussion of this point by acknowledging Mascall's recourse to the *Summa contra Gentiles* where St Thomas states: 'We must now speak of the mystery of the Incarnation, which of all the works of God most greatly surpasses our reason; for nothing more wonderful could be thought of that God could do than that very God, the Son of God, should become very man (IV, xxvii).'[68]

We shall now turn our attention to a discussion of Mascall's interpretation of the significance of 'the assumption of humanity into God' in the incarnation.

The deification of Christ's humanity

A persistent theme in Mascall's writings is the insistence that human nature, as created, possesses a passive fitness (*potentia obedientialis*)[69] for *hypostatic union*[70] with God. Be that as it may, however, Mascall goes on to argue that the hypostatic union of Christ's divine and human natures raises the latter (as the result of the *communicatio idiomatum*)[71] to a still higher metaphysical level: 'to the level of God-head and on that level [it] is caught up into the eternal filial offering of the Son'.[72] Smedes regards this point on 'the deification of Christ's humanity .... [as] the most important point in Mascall's thought'.[73] For Mascall then, in the incarnation, God became man, but in becoming man, took manhood up into Himself. Thus, whereas the human nature of Christ, considered in itself, is created and finite, when considered in its union with God it is taken up into the life of God and placed on a higher metaphysical plane than is man apart from Christ.[74] Thus Mascall can comment that 'the Incarnation is not to be thought of as the com-pression of the divine Word within the limits of human nature but as the

---

Athanasius and St Cyril 'that in the Incarnation the Logos did not simply come and dwell in a man who already existed but himself became man'. Ibid., 104.   **67** *He Who Is*, 112, n. 4.   **68** *VM*, 118-9.   **69** Human nature, insofar as it is open to divine grace.   **70** By this is meant the union between full divinity and humanity in the one (divine) Person of Jesus Christ, which occurred when 'the Word became flesh' (Jn 1:14); see *DS* 252-63.   **71** This is the exchange of attributes which results from the union of divinity and humanity in the one person of the incarnate Son of God. This means that the attributes of one of his natures may be predicated of him even when he is named with reference to the other nature; see *DS* 251.   **72** *CCCH*, 92.   **73** Smedes, *The Incarnation*, 34. Smedes also asserts that R.I. Wilberforce is 'the one Anglican theologian who anticipates Mascall to any great extent. In him, too, we find an extreme elevation of Christ's human nature as a result of the union with the Word ...' Ibid., 38.   **74** Thus Mascall can say: 'There is thus in Christ a new creation of manhood out of the material of the fallen human race ... In Christ human nature has been recreated by the very God who was its first Creator; and the new creation is effected, not like the first creation by the mere decree of the omnipotent will ... but by the Creator himself becoming man and moulding nature to the lineaments of his own Person.' *CCCH*, 3.

exaltation of human nature to the level of Godhead by its union with the Person of the divine Word'.[75] Smedes asserts that in Mascall 'there is no suggestion that humanity can change into the *who* of God, ... It remains created, derived existence, but in that mode, the mode of derived being, it shares in all the *whatness* of God.'[76] We can conclude this discussion by noting that for Mascall, human nature, as a result of its union with God, is elevated to the level where it is capable of sharing in the essence of God (though, of course, without involving a change from humanity to Godhead).[77] The elevation effected in the incarnation constitutes the supreme honour conferred upon human nature. Mascall, writing towards the end of his time at Oxford in 1958, put the point succinctly when he commented: 'if God has himself become man in the Incarnation, he has sealed human nature with a certificate of value whose validity cannot be disputed'.[78]

The early Mascall and Christ's pre-existence

In this section we shall focus in detail upon Mascall's understanding of *who* the subject of this divine Person of the eternal Word is, and in so doing examine his interpretation of the doctrine of Christ's pre-existence. It is important at the outset to appreciate that the question of pre-existence is not one that he, during this stage of his career, expressly set out to explore. His whole approach to christology, however, clearly assumed its validity.

As has been stated, Mascall's commitment to the Church's doctrine of the incarnation is absolute. In his first serious theological publication, an article of eight pages in *Theology*, published in 1929, he examined the bearing of the contemporary mathematico-physical philosophy of science[79] upon the doctrine of the incarnation and came to the conclusion that they were not in the least incompatible. Thus as a man of science he had no hesitation in asserting that 'Christ is true God and true man'.[80] The subject of the divine Person is 'the Divine Logos [who] continued His life in the Holy Trinity during the time when He was incarnate on earth'.[81] The incarnation is 'the assumption by the Logos of a complete set of human relationships, which he added to the Divine relationships'. Mascall argues that there are no grounds for denying *a priori* that the Person of the divine Logos could, without his individuality being impaired, be the subject of

75 Ibid., 48.   76 Smedes, *The Incarnation*, 39. In making these points, Smedes is drawing on the language used by Mascall in a discussion of the results of incorporation into Christ when the latter comments: 'Even if, in a strictly guarded sense, we can say, with some of the mystics, that Christ and God are what we become, we can never say that they are *who* we become'. *CCCH*, 97.   77 Since, as we have seen, the basic and decisive difference between them must remain: i.e., that which exists between derived and underived being.   78 *The Importance of Being Human* (Oxford, 1959), 22.   79 'The Incarnation in Space-Time', *Theology*, 19 (1929) 315. These themes would be dealt with more fully in his *CTNS*.   80 Ibid., 312.   81 Ibid., 316. By the way, there is no attempt here to explore the background or significance of the concept of 'the Divine Logos'.

two natures.[82] God is the creator of the universe; he is antecedent, not just temporally but also, causally, to the temporal and spatial experience which has arisen as a consequence of his act of creation.[83] There is no suggestion, says Mascall, that the incarnation involved for the divine Logos 'an addition to the mode of existence of God which is incompatible with His eternal changelessness through which He shares in the eternal life of the Holy Trinity'.[84] At the time of the incarnation, Mascall adds, the divine Logos

> adds to His timeless and spaceless existence in the bosom of the eternal Father a complete and perfect human life under the conditions of space and time, but this appears to us as an addition to His functions solely because we view it from within the space-time order. From the standpoint of His divinity, from 'outside' space-time, He is the Subject in His divine nature of all the spaceless and timeless relations involved in His Godhead as the Second Person of the Holy Trinity, and is also the subject in His human nature of the whole fabric of spatio-temporal relations involved in His manhood as the Son of Mary.[85]

Mascall returns to this theme *en passant* in his *Christ, the Christian and the Church* (1946)[86] when he comments that 'the act of Incarnation in relation to the Person of the Word is not in time, for, as God the divine Word is not in time; but in relation to Christ's human nature and to us it is in time, for Christ's human life is lived in time and so is ours'.[87]

To sum up here, it is clear that Mascall's understanding of the nature of creation and the relationship between space and time present no obstacle to his embracing the doctrine of the eternal pre-existence of Christ. We must note, however, the absence of any sustained reflection by Mascall on the doctrine in terms of the eternity/time relationship. While this is not the place to develop this point (it will be dealt with in a later chapter), it is enough for our purposes here to state that

---

82 Ibid., 314. 83 Ibid., 315. 84 Ibid., 314. 85 Ibid., 316. 86 He argues: '*In relation to God,* we may say, creation is not in time, for God who creates is not in time. But *in relation to creatures* it is in time, because creatures are in time, and time is the mode of existence with which they are created. Creation is thus a relation spanning the gulf between time and eternity; it is in the scholastic phrase, real in the creature but only logical or "rational" in God. That is to say that it involves a change in them – indeed that total and radical change which draws them out of non-existence into existence – but it involves no change in him'. *CCCH*, 17. 87 Ibid. Mascall states: 'The divine nature belongs to the Word from all eternity, in virtue of the very fact that he is the Word – 'before all ages, πρὸ πάντων τῶν αἰώνων in the words of the Nicene Creed – while his human nature was taken by him at a particular moment in the world's history. Ibid., 20. Elsewhere Mascall acknowledges: 'the Father communicates his divine nature to the only-begotten Word from all eternity'. See his 'The Dogmatic Theology of the Mother of God', in E.L. Mascall (ed.), *The Mother of God* (London, 1949), 39.

this constitutes a significant oversight by one so apparently well versed in philosophical concerns in theology. (After all, a clear interest in the issue was detectable as early as the sixth-century Boethius, was apparent in Thomas Aquinas and was the cause of much controversy in the new mathematically inspired metaphysics of the seventeenth century.)[88] While Mascall did not deal at length with the specific issue of pre-existence at this stage, clearly presupposing its unquestionable validity, he did make a few fleeting references to it. Thus (to mention but two) he could comment in one place that the doctrine of the incarnation is 'the re-creation of human nature by elevation into union with the pre-existent Son and Word of God, who is the Second Person of the Ever-blessed Trinity'.[89] In another place, he could say that 'the Person of this [Christ's] human nature was not created, as is the case with all other human beings; it was the pre-existent Word or Logos'.[90]

MASCALL'S CHRISTOLOGY AND INTERPRETATION OF CHRIST'S PRE-EXISTENCE, 1962-1993

The beginning of the second stage of Mascall's academic career coincided with his appointment, in 1962, to the newly created post of Professor of Historical Theology at King's College, London. In this new phase his commitment to theological orthodoxy was to continue undaunted,[91] but there was to be a shift in the tone of his writings. In the wake of the emergence in the 1960s, within the Church of England, and beyond, of an influential radical theology deeply critical of theological orthodoxy and mirroring the changes in society in general, Mascall would find himself obliged to defend the traditional doctrines of the Church against the attacks of such leading liberal theologians as J. Knox, G. Lampe, H. Montefiore, D.E. Nineham, J.A.T. Robinson, P. van Buren, and M.F. Wiles.[92] His writings of

88 P. Manchester, 'Eternity' in M. Eliade (ed. in chief), *The Encyclopedia of Religion*, vol. 5 (New York, 1987), 170.   89 *CCCH*, 68.   90 Ibid., 2. This point is also made in *VM*, 103.   91 At his inaugural lecture at King's College, London, in 1962, he set out clearly his understanding of the theologian's role as that 'of theologising within the great historical Christian tradition; *theologizandum est in fide*. Even when he feels constrained to criticise adversely the contemporary expression of the tradition, he will be conscious that he is bringing out from the depths of the tradition its latent and hitherto unrecognised contents; he is acting as its organ and its exponent. He will also offer his own contribution for it to digest and assimilate if it can. Like the good householder he will bring out of his treasure things new and old. But he will have no other gospel than that which he has received,' *Theology and History* (London, 1962), 17. A trenchant criticism of those Anglican theologians who have neglected to do this is Mascall's 'Whither Anglican Theology?', in A. Kilmister (ed.), *When Will Ye Be Wise?* (London, 1983), 30-49. He asks: 'Is the Christian religion something revealed by God to man in Christ having an unconditional claim on our obedience, or is it something to be constructed by us for ourselves in response to our own desires and the pressures and assumptions of contemporary culture?' Ibid., 40.   92 Interestingly,

this period are generally characterised by a critique of his opponents' theological presuppositions and an indication of the riches latent in theological orthodoxy.[93] Mascall noted in his memoirs: 'Ever since leaving Oxford I had become more and more concerned with dogmatic theology and less with philosophy, not least because of the growing number of urgent problems in the former field and the lamentably small number of Anglicans prepared to interest themselves in it.'[94]

One of the principal targets of this liberal theology was the doctrine of the personal pre-existence of Christ, and Mascall was to find himself compelled to defend it. In this section we shall see him in the thick of dispute with a few of its assailants,[95] but before doing so, it is useful to comment, if only in the briefest of terms, on the general shape of his christology during this later stage of his career.

It continued to be characterised by an abiding attachment to the creedal and conciliar teaching of the Church, and supremely to that of Chalcedon.[96] As before,

Mascall states in his memoirs: 'Possibly through an unconscious motive of defence I have always enjoyed reviewing other people's books as well as writing my own, and I wrote an inordinate number of reviews for a large number of periodicals ...' *Saraband*, 296-7.   93 Thus, for example, in his *The Secularisation of Christianity* (London, 1965), Mascall selects J.A.T. Robinson, *Honest to God* (1963) and P. van Buren, *The Secular Meaning of the Gospel* (1963) as two 'outstanding expressions of a radical and destructive attitude to traditional Christianity which has obtained a foothold in many academic circles in the United States and the United Kingdom, though until the publication of *Honest to God* it was little known to the general public and to the majority of the parochial clergy'. Ibid., x. Consequently, the two main chapters of Mascall's volume are a critique of both books. The rest of the book is concerned with an examination of the intellectual setting which gives rise to the ideas of Robinson and van Buren. 94 Ibid., 296. Adrian Hastings claims that Mascall is to be compared with Hans Urs von Balthasar and Cardinal Ratzinger because of his critique of contemporary theological fashion. See his *A History of English Christianity 1920-1985*, 652.;   95 Thus a former doctoral student of Mascall, Robin Gill, has written that 'there was a polemicism about Mascall which belied his self-perception as a neo-Thomist. In some respects he was more like Augustine than Aquinas. A gentle, pious, considerate and ascetic person in private, he was a fierce and sometimes belligerent defender of the faith in print'. See Gill, 'Michael Ramsey: A Theological Speculation' in R. Gill & L. Kendall (eds), *Michael Ramsey as Theologian* (London, 1995), 185. Lest the impression be given that Mascall was alone in his disenchantment with the age we can note the following judgement by an Anglo-Catholic historian: 'the new liberal theology which started to be expressed at this time in a particularly strident manner, and in a "popular" form, did have a corrosive effect in the ranks of High Churchmen. It both undermined and unsettled many Anglican Catholics, and also found a home in some quarters. It was a disturbing phenomenon for churchmen who in any case were struggling with their own problems of identity and purpose, and were beginning to have a collective sense of insecurity and uncertainty about their distinctive beliefs and their special role and function within the Church of England.' See K. Hylson-Smith, *High Churchmanship in the Church of England* (Edinburgh, 1993), 329.   96 He has spoken of the definition of Chalcedon as 'the classical and authoritative expression of the Church's belief about her Lord' in his 'On from Chalcedon' in S. Cipriani (ed.), *Parola e Spirito. Studi in onore di Settimio Cipriani*, vol. 2 (Brescia, 1982), 1043.

Mascall rarely had direct recourse to scriptural texts nor does he dally with the great figures of post-Enlightenment christology. What is particularly striking about Mascall's christology at this stage, as it battled with certain liberal 'new christologies',[97] is that in addition to its recourse to the fonts that he had appealed to during the earlier part of his career (Councils, Fathers and Thomas Aquinas), and almost uniquely among his fellow Anglican theologians of the day, he kept himself acquainted with the theological writings of contemporary, Catholic, Continental writers[98] (whose theological interests, it needs to be said, extended beyond the boundaries of Thomism). He was particulary indebted to the writings of L. Bouyer and J. Galot, and integrated many of their insights into his christology. This is clearly evidenced in the profound change that Galot's notion of *person* as *subsistent relation* (or as Galot prefers to say, *relational being*) wrought in Mascall's understanding of the concept of *person*.[99] This concept allows Mascall to overcome the difficulties that had arisen in his earlier christology due to his adherence to Boethius' definition of *person*.[100] Gone is his earlier suggestion that there is only a

---

97 John McIntyre has said of one of Mascall's books from this period, *Whatever Happened to the Human Mind?* (London, 1980), hereafter *WHHM*, that it 'is one of the ablest answers to the problems raised by ... those who felt that their criticisms of classical Chalcedonian christology spelt the death of that type of doctrine'. See McIntyre's review of *WHHM*, *Expository Times*, 92 (1981) 153. 98 This point has been acknowledged by the English theologian, Brian Hebblethwaite, when he commented that 'Mascall, is for the most part, an untypical figure [in the Church of England], in that his christological writings are based on the very interesting contributions of French Roman Catholic writers'. See his *The Incarnation* (Cambridge, 1987), 61. To underline this point, we can note an observation of Bernard Leeming: 'it is singularly sad to consider the extent to which English theology was cut off from Catholic [Continental] writing', in 'Reflections on English Christology', in A. Grillmeier & H. Bacht (eds), *Das Konzik von Chalkedon*, vol. 3 (Würzburg, 1954), 716. 99 Another aspect of Mascall's thought which was to undergo profound change owing to the insights of Galot and also Bouyer, as well as those of W. Pannenberg and K. Rahner, is in relation to the human consciousness of Jesus. In this later stage he comes to reject the position that he outlined in 1946 when he maintained that Jesus from the moment of his conception possessed a beatific vision and that there was a direct infusion of knowledge into his human mind from his divine Person. See *CCCH*, 56. Now, Mascall argues that the fact that Jesus Christ lived in his complete human nature a real human life, implies that his human consciousness and knowledge were limited and growing in conformity with the development of his human organism. As Mascall indicates: 'since human nature, in any individual, is not given from its beginning in a fully developed state but develops from the unrealized potentialities of the original fertilized ovum through birth, infancy, childhood and adolescence to its climax in adult manhood, we must surely hold that the mentality of Jesus, like that of any other human being, developed *pari passu* with the development of his bodily organism. To say this is not to imply that it was in any way defective in the early stages; on the contrary, at each stage it was precisely what at that stage it is proper for the human nature to be ...' See *WHHM*, 44. 100 It is tempting to enquire here as to why Mascall did not make more of Thomas Aquinas' treatment of the divine Persons as subsistent relations. See *Summa Theologiae*, 1, 29, 2.

logical distinction between Christ's person and divine nature. Employing Galot's insights, he insists, on the contrary, that 'a human person cannot, anymore than a divine person, be a quality of the nature, or a mode, or existence itself, or the act of existing; it must be a subsistent relation'.[101]

In parenthesis here we can note that Mascall, in opposing liberal challenges, holds firmly to the reality of Christ's bodily resurrection,[102] rejecting as inadequate 'any interpretation of the resurrection in either naturalistic, existential or mythological terms'.[103] He had insisted early on in his career that 'The human organism which the Son of God took from his Virgin Mother and in which he died and rose from the dead was not destroyed by his resurrection and ascension; it was transformed and glorified and made accessible to men.'[104] Mascall is thus clear on the personal existence and identity of the risen One and is aware, in the words he quotes directly from C.F.D. Moule, that 'it is not just that, owing (somehow) to Jesus, they [the first Christians] found new life; it is that they discovered in Jesus himself, alive and present, a divine dimension such that he must always and eternally have existed in it'.[105]

The later Mascall and Christ's pre-existence
Whereas, in the section above devoted to the early Mascall's treatment of Christ's pre-existence, we found that he paid little direct attention to the issue, we shall find here that he has much to say on the matter. In what will follow here, we shall set out the broad outline of the interpretations of Christ's pre-existence advanced by J. Knox, J.A.T. Robinson and G.W.H. Lampe. We shall begin with the views of the American Anglican, J. Knox.

John Knox (1900-92)   The *sine qua non* of Knox's christology is his determination to defend the completeness of Christ's human nature and, consequently, to avoid falling into the pitfalls of Apollinarianism, monophysitism or monothelitism, according to which if Jesus was literally divine he could not be genuinely human. Knox holds that pressures to succumb to this temptation were already evident in

---

101 *Theology and the Gospel of Christ* (London, 1977), 153; hereafter *TGC*. It must be said here, *pace* Mascall, that while the divine Persons of the Trinity may be defined as subsistent relations, it is not at all clear that human persons can be spoken of as such. See W. Kasper, *The God of Jesus* (London, 1982), 154, 281.   102 *Jesus: Who He Is And How We Know Him* (London, 1985), 11-2; hereafter *Jesus*. Mascall comments: 'It is this conviction of being personally united with the risen Jesus, the same yesterday, today and forever, and not just sharing in an "Easter experience" or (to use another popular modern term) being edified by an impersonal "Christ-event", that drew from Bishop Polycarp [a figure of particular devotion for Mascall] in the stadium at Smyrna the declaration: "I have been his servant for eighty-six years and he has never done me any wrong. How can I blaspheme my king who saved me?"' Ibid., 11.   103 Ibid. 104 *CTNS*, 314. See also 'The Nature of the Resurrection', *Theology*, 21 (1931) 203-13.   105 C.F.D. Moule, *The Origin of Christology* (Cambridge, 1977); quoted by Mascall in his Jesus, 8.

New Testament times. He discerns three stages in the unfolding of christology up to the end of the first century, and he designates them as: adoptionism (the belief that Jesus was a man who by his resurrection was made Lord and Christ by God); kenoticism (the belief that Jesus had pre-existed as a divine or heavenly being who by a voluntary emptying (*kenosis*) had become a man and lived on earth); docetism (a belief rejected by the Church but held among dissident groups that Jesus was wholly an other-worldly figure who appeared on earth but only seemed to be a man).[106]

Knox contends that the earliest christology was adoptionist 'almost by necessity',[107] and that 'in its basic structure it was, and might conceivably have continued to be, an entirely adequate christology'.[108] But that was not to be: 'the whole environment of early Christianity',[109] with its reflection on the resurrection and Jesus' present Lordship, led immediately to the affirmation first of his foreordination to that office and soon afterwards of his pre-existence.[110] Thus the idea of pre-existence entered into christology to make it abundantly plain that God had not just found a man who happened to be suitable for elevation to christhood, but that this man had been sent by God. Once the notion of pre-existence had been introduced, however, the dangers inherent within it became actualised, and a threat to belief in the true humanity of Christ arose. This began very early, as early in fact as the Pauline epistles and the epistle to the Hebrews.[111] It reached its apogee in John's Gospel, which, Knox argues, trembles on the very edge of docetism. The Church was subsequently unable, Knox's argument proceeds, either to reject the *story* outright or to recognise it as simply a story. Thus it changed it into something else in the hope of making it more credible; it turned it into a mixture of kenoticism and docetism. 'The result is a christology, half story and half dogma, a compound of mythology and philosophy, of poetry and logic, as difficult to define as to defend.'[112]

---

106 J. Knox, *The Humanity and Divinity of Christ* (Cambridge, 1967), 17. This scheme is later modified by Knox when he asserts that between kenoticism and docetism there was another stage which he calls 'incarnationism' (the belief that a pre-existent divine hypostasis took in Jesus a genuinely human life), but this fourth possibility is not so clearly defined as the others. It does not emphasise self-emptying, but at the same time it avoids lapsing into docetism. Ibid., 38. 107 This was because it corresponded so closely to the actual experience of the Church as to be hardly more than a simple account of it. See ibid., 95. Knox cites Acts 2:36 ('God has made this Jesus, whom you crucified, both Lord and Messiah') as 'the clearest example' of an adoptionist christology. He then proceeds to ask 'how can this passage be interpreted to mean anything else than that this man Jesus crucified simply as such, was at the resurrection exalted to his present messianic status?' Ibid., 7-8.   108 Ibid., 56.   109 Ibid., 97.   110 Ibid., 39.   111 Knox, unlike Robinson and Macquarrie, who will be studied below, holds that Paul's belief in the pre-existence of Jesus is beyond doubt. See Macquarrie's criticism of Knox's position in his *Jesus Christ in Modern Thought* (London, 1990), 144-5.   112 Knox, *The Humanity and Divinity of Christ*, 99; quoted in *TGC*, 126.

To conclude here, it will suffice to say that Knox has submitted the doctrine of pre-existence to a barrage. As far as he is concerned, 'we can have the humanity [of Jesus] without the pre-existence or the pre-existence without the humanity. There is absolutely no way of having both'.[113] He then proceeds to redefine the divinity of Jesus as simply 'a transformed, a redeemed and redemptive *humanity* [Knox's italics]'.[114] As we shall see below, Mascall is outraged by Knox's analysis and rises to champion the doctrine in the face of such onslaught. But, we must first examine the reflections of other liberal Anglican critics, J.A.T. Robinson and G.W.H. Lampe, on this question.

John A.T. Robinson (1919–83)   As Robinson's stand on the doctrine of the pre-existence of Christ will be the subject of a later chapter, the discussion here will confine itself to the task of outlining the principal features of his thought on this theme. We shall begin by noting that Robinson first came to prominence in 1963 with the publication of his *Honest to God*. This popular paperback offers a criticism of the image of God held among Church people – an image in which God's transcendence of the world is exaggerated to the virtual exclusion of any sense of his immanence, so that he is a God 'up there' or 'out there', not a God 'in the midst'. Robinson's reflections have consequences also for christology. At the heart of Robinson's christology[115] is the intention to reawaken, as far as possible, what he regards as the long lost sense of the humanity of Christ and of his full sharing of our human condition. As we shall see in greater depth later, Robinson argues that the doctrine of the incarnation does not necessarily entail the pre-existence of a supernatural being who, at a certain point in time, assumes flesh. Rather, he argues, pre-existence should be interpreted not as an alleged fact but as 'a way of speaking that ... can no longer be taken literally or descriptively and is so misleading as to be unsuitable today'.[116] He suggests that it is perfectly satisfactory to interpret pre-existence as referring to 'pre-existence in the mind of the Father' (a pre-existence which is common to us all), and not a personal pre-existence of the eternal Son.[117]

Be that as it may, Robinson still expresses the most unqualified devotion to Jesus of Nazareth, so that, in his own words, 'it could be said, and has to be said, of that man, "He was God's man", or "God was in Christ", or even that he *was* "God for us".'[118] He finds the greatest difficulty, however, in saying that Jesus was begotten of the Father before all ages, and that 'for us men and for our salvation he came down from heaven and was incarnate by the Holy Spirit of the Virgin Mary and became man'.

---

113 Ibid., 106; quoted in *WHHM*, 36.   114 Ibid., 113; quoted in *TGC*, 121.   115 It received its most comprehensive articulation in his *The Human Face of God* (London, 1973),   116 Ibid., 144.   117 Ibid.; quoted in *TGC* 128.   118 Ibid., 179 (italics in the original).

For Robinson, then, it is the humanity of Jesus that matters. Whether he is personally divine is at best of secondary importance, even if, in virtue of his complete self-dedication to the Father, God was active in him as in no other human being. We shall now turn our focus to the reflections of the third and final liberal theologian whose understanding of pre-existence provoked Mascall to write a vigorous criticism, G.W.H. Lampe.

Geoffrey W.H. Lampe (1912-80)   Of the three liberal critics of the doctrine of pre-existence singled out for special attention by Mascall, Lampe presents the most radical case. Sometime Regius Professor of Divinity at Cambridge, he was the final editor of the prestigious *Patristic Greek Lexicon*. Mascall has acknowledged that 'his knowledge of the New Testament and especially of the Fathers is exhaustive'.[119] Yet in the course of his academic career Lampe came to reject two dogmas.[120] The first to be jettisoned is the belief that God is not one person but three, and that the Spirit, consequently, is a distinct divine Person. Lampe views the Spirit as simply the unipersonal God seen in his activity towards and in the world; hence the title of Lampe's *magnum opus* in systematic theology, *God as Spirit*.[121] The second dogma to be discarded, and the one that is of precise interest to this study, is that which teaches that Jesus is the eternal Son and Word, the Second Person of the Trinity, incarnate in human nature. For Lampe, Jesus is simply a man in whom God as Spirit is uniquely and incomparably active. Mascall has no reservations in arguing that Lampe's views designate him as an unitarian and adoptionist.[122] With his repudiation of the doctrine of the incarnation there goes the disavowal of 'salvation as a decisive act of God performed at a definite point in history'.[123] To the question 'What has God in Jesus done for man that man himself could not do?', Lampe offers the answer that He has 'brought the process of creation to the point where perfect man appears for the first time'.[124] There would seem to be no reason why another person should not be as perfect as Jesus *and in the same sense*.[125]

It can come as no surprise that Lampe rejects the notions of the pre-existence and post-existence of Jesus. He asserts that 'we do not need the model of a descent of a pre-existent divine person into the world. Nor do we need the concept of

---

119 Review of G.W.H. Lampe, *God as Spirit* (Oxford, 1977), *Journal of Theological Studies*, 29 (1978) 618.   120 See C. Basevi, 'La Cristologia de G.W.H. Lampe o una cristologia en disolución', *Scripta Theologica*, 12 (1980) 483-96.   121 This book was the published form of his Bampton Lectures of 1976 (Oxford, 1977).   122 *WHHM*, 99.   123 Lampe, *God as Spirit*, 15. 124 Ibid., 17.   125 The idea of redemption (though the use of the very word would be rejected by Lampe) is purely exemplarist: 'Jesus became both the pattern of sonship and also the inspiration and power which can create in us a response, analogous to his own, to the Spirit of God that was in him and is in us. The interpretation of divine Spirit with human spirit presents itself to us, and takes effect within us, in terms of the character, actions, and words of Jesus.' Ibid., 24-5.

a "post-existent" continuing personal presence of Jesus, himself alive today, in order to interpret our own continuing experience of God's saving and creative work'.[126] Lampe argues that the emergence of the doctrine of pre-existence derived from one colossal error:

> Paul's failure to complete the identification of the Spirit with the present Christ is to assign a 'third place' to the Spirit .... This reduction of the Spirit to a second, and very ill-defined, place in God's out-reach towards the world could have been avoided if the term 'Spirit' had been allowed to express the totality of God in his creativity: in the whole process of his creative work which has its focus in Jesus Christ and continues now in believers. Paul and John, however, and the other New Testament writers, were unable to do this because they wished to affirm the personal pre-existence of Jesus Christ as Son of God, the continual personal 'post-existence' of Jesus Christ, resurrected and ascended and also experienced by present believers, and the future return of the ascended Christ in glory.[127]

Lampe damningly assesses the subsequent unfolding of classical christology (hardly a surprise in view of his thoughts on the scriptural testimony, as outlined above). Thus he can contend that 'according to this Christology, the eternal Son assumes a timeless human nature, or makes it timeless by making it his own; it is a human nature which owes nothing essential to geographical circumstances; it corresponds to nothing in the actual concrete world; Jesus Christ has not, after all, really "come in the flesh"'.[128]

When, as we have seen above in looking at the arguments of Knox, Robinson and Lampe, a large and influential body of Anglican theological life opted for a heterodox mode, Mascall was to emerge as a strident critic. A clear admission of his astonishment at this turn of events is evident in the following statement made in 1977: 'One of the most surprising recent theological phenomena has been the recrudescence at a high professional academic level, especially in the more ancient English universities [Oxford and Cambridge], of the views commonly known as unitarianism and adoptionism.'[129] That being so, Mascall was anxious to demonstrate that such ideas in relation to Christ are without foundation.[130] In what will follow in this section we shall see Mascall sifting through the arguments concern-

---

126 Ibid., 33; quoted in *WHHM*, 106.   127 Ibid., 118-9; quoted in *WHHM*, 112.   128 Ibid., 144; quoted *WHHM*, 113.   129 Review of Lampe, *God as Spirit*, 617-8.   130 He had a feeling of *dèja vu* about the influence once again of liberal ideas, as in the 1920s: 'there is the same assumption that the theologian must fall into line with the intellectual climate of the day, though rather less confidence that the climate will be permanent', and he confesses that in these new ideas he could hear once again, as during his student days at Cambridge (when he was a religiously interested lay man studying mathematics), 'the voice of Bethune-Baker', the liberal champion of his day. *TGC*, 42.

ing Christ's pre-existence proposed by Knox, Robinson and Lampe, and arguing
that christological orthodoxy, based on the scriptural testimony (although he
attends only in the most fleeting of ways to the details of exegesis),[131] Chalcedon
and the classical tradition, is far more successful in terms of 'fertility and flexi-
bility' than the various formulations emanating from the 'New Theologies'.[132]

Mascall acknowledges the integrity and high-mindedness that inspired the
liberal thinkers to criticise the doctrine of pre-existence. Their goal was to uphold
uncompromisingly the full humanity of Christ and Mascall recognises this when
he attests that 'the insistence of these writers upon the reality and completeness of
Christ's human nature is the one really strong point in their position, and it is
wholly admirable'.[133] Mascall elsewhere explains that the *sine qua non* of the liberal
project in theology is

> the assumption that the primary need is to emphasize the reality and the
> normality of the *humanity* of Jesus, that traditional Christology has con-
> sistently and mysteriously failed to do this, that no special problems arise in
> doing it, and that when this has been done the *divinity* of Jesus can be left
> to look after itself, since in the last resort it can either be denied or ignored
> or else redefined in terms of the humanity.[134]

And again, in criticising the various christological approaches of Knox,
Robinson and another Anglican author, W.N. Pittenger, Mascall comments that
for them

> it is the humanity of Jesus that matters, whether he is personally divine is at
> best of secondary importance, though they hold that, in virtue of his com-
> plete self-dedication to the Father, God was active in him as in no other
> human being. They express great admiration for the Antiochene christol-
> ogists of the fifth century and a corresponding suspicion of, and indeed
> antipathy for, the Alexandrians.[135]

131 Among the few exceptions to this is his brief response to the question: 'What is the New
Testament picture of Jesus?' He responds by drawing attention to the following passages: Phil
2:6ff., Col 1:15ff, Heb 1:3, 1 Cor 15:14, Lk 24:42-43, Jn 20:27 and Acts 10:41. *Jesus*, 47.   132
WHHM, 52. In speaking of the various 'New Theologies', Mascall intends not only those
constructed by Knox, Robinson and Lampe, but also those fashioned by other Anglo-American
theologians such as J. Hick and M.F. Wiles and such Continental theologians as R. Bultmann
and P. Schoonenberg.   133 *TGC*, 130-1.   134 Ibid., 121. Mascall singles out Knox as a clear
exponent of these ideas, especially in his comment already noted above: 'We can have the
humanity without the pre-existence and we can have the pre-existence without the humanity.
There is absolutely no way of having both'. See Knox, *The Humanity and the Divinity of Christ*,
106 and 113.   135 'But, strangely enough', Mascall adds, 'they have little sympathy for the
point in which the Antiochenes took pride and which constituted their chief objections to the
Alexandrians, namely their unqualified and persistent stress upon the impassibility of God;

Mascall flatly rejects these claims. Was the primitive Church, he asks, as ambivalent about the divinity and pre-existence of Christ as our radical authors would have us believe? Is the doctrine of pre-existence to be taken only metaphorically? Has the true humanity of Christ been short-changed throughout the Christian centuries? Mascall, of course, denys these assertions and argues that the rejection of the supernatural element in Jesus rests in the last resort not upon biblical scholarship, but upon a preconceived and consistently applied dogma about the impossibility of the supernatural.[136] Moreover, he holds that authentic scriptural exegesis supports the doctrine of pre-existence, and not just in a figurative sense. We shall turn now to his argument concerning an anti-supernatural presupposition and then say something about his reading of the testimony of the scriptures.

The critical element in allowing radical theologians[137] to reject the classical understanding of the doctrine of pre-existence, Mascall argues, is the extent to which their argument is controlled by unrecognised theological and, in the wide sense, philosophical presuppositions. He accuses them of what he terms a 'methodological anti-supernaturalism or nonsupernaturalism'.[138] As to the precise shape of this presupposition, Mascall gives the following account:

> whether or not there is a God and whether or not, if there is one, he has made a unique intervention into the world in the person of Jesus of Nazareth, the production, development, contents and significance of the records about him can be, and can only be, adequately and honestly studied if the ostensibly supernatural elements are treated as having a purely natural explanation. The supernatural is allowed in, if at all, only at the end of the investigation, as a possible or provisional explanation of any residue that is

Pittenger in particular is a fervent proponent of process-theology ...' Ibid., 130.   **136** Ibid., 67-8.   **137** In his *WHHM* and *Jesus* Mascall is also concerned with refuting the unorthodox christological ideas which emerged at the symposium entitled 'The Myth of God Incarnate' in 1976 and were published as *The Myth of God Incarnate* (London, 1977). Prominent among its contributors were: J. Hick, M.F. Wiles, D.E. Nineham and D. Cupitt.   **138** *Jesus*, 14-5. It must be said that the English philosophical tradition has readily disposed the English towards such anti-supernaturalism. C.S. Pierce succinctly describes English philosophy as follows: 'From very early times, it has been the chief intellectual characteristic of the English to wish to effect everything by the plainest and directest means, without unnecessary contrivance ... In philosophy this national tendency appears as a strong preference for the simplest theories, and a resistance to any complication of the theory as long as there is the least possibility that the facts can be explained in the simpler way. And, accordingly, British philosophers have always desired to weed out of philosophy all conceptions which could not be made perfectly definite and easily intelligible, and have shown strong nominalistic tendencies since the time of Edward I, or even earlier.' Quoted in A. Quinton, 'British Philosophy', in P. Edwards (ed. in chief), *The Encyclopedia of Philosophy* (London, 1967), vol. 1, 369-96. The twentieth century has been no exception to this as can be seen, for example, in the prominence of Logical Positivism.

unaccounted for. Grace, if it exists at all, is assumed not to perfect but to ignore, or at most to supplement nature.[139]

Having described the characteristics of the 'anti-supernatural' presupposition held by so many theologians, Mascall takes great joy in outlining how unacceptable such an assumption would be to many within the world of contemporary science. They would see this type of reasoning as belonging to an out-moded and thoroughly discredited post-Newtonian cosmology.[140] Well versed in the sciences[141] (and conscious of the prominent part that the advance of the scientific mentality played in the undermining of religious belief in England during the previous century or so), Mascall is aware that under the twin influences of relativity and quantum theory 'scientists have altogether abandoned the view of the world as an aggregate of indestructible particles inhabiting three-dimensional Euclidean space and interacting according to deterministic laws for which all interactions are either physical impacts or, in the most literal sense, "action at a distance"...'[142]

Tantalisingly brief and incomplete on this issue, Mascall comments: 'how fruitfully the new physics can partner a thoroughly traditional Christology has been shown by Dr T.F. Torrance'[143] (especially in his *Space, Time and Resurrection*).[144] Torrance proposes building a new scientific theology on the foundation provided by the insights of the new cosmology. Mascall emphasises the significance of such a new scientific theology, when he says that it reveals those ' "liberal" or "radical" theologians who reject the traditional views of the birth and the resurrection of Jesus .... as uncritical adherents of an out-moded world-view. It is the view of a world in which Jesus in first-century Palestine and I in twentieth-century London are separable from each other by two distinct gulfs of space and time in mutual metaphysical isolation'.[145] Mascall points out that in the wake of this 'new physics' the world is viewed in very different terms:

---

139 *Jesus*, 15. Mascall concedes that the advantages of this approach are two-fold: firstly, academic theologians can win academic respectability (even among their unbelieving colleagues) and, secondly, that as a purely intellectual enterprise – to discover how far a purely natural explanation of the phenomena can go – can have a certain limited usefulness. 'But when it becomes the overarching and all-embracing methodological principle, it deprives theology of its distinctive character and makes it simply a selection of material from other disciplines – ancient history, anthropology, palaeography, psychology and so forth – on which it becomes parasitic.' Ibid., 16. 140 Ibid., 42-3.   141 Mascall notes in his memoirs that his early training in applied maths at Cambridge had the offshoot of encouraging in him a lifelong interest in the philosophy of science, and this led in turn to a concern with natural theology. *Saraband*, 137.   142 *Jesus*, 43. Mascall also cautions that 'no doubt our relativity-and-quantum universe will appear to scientists of a future age as outmoded as Newton's does to those of ours. But in the meantime theologians may, with prudence, legitimately profit from the lessons of both'. Ibid., 45.   143 Ibid., 45.   144 Edinburgh, 1976.   145 *Jesus*, 44-5.

we can say that the world now appears as a spatio-temporal manifold of centres of energy, whose causal activity is constitutive of their very being; in such a world the notion of gulfs needing to be bridged is wholly inapplicable. The notion of space and time as receptacles, pre-existing with their respective characteristics of vacancy and flux antecedently to their occupancy by really existing beings is gone for good, but St Augustine's famous assertion that God has created the world not *in time* but *with time* can be welcomed back in the amplified form that God has created the world not in but with space-time.[146]

Mascall, then, is in a position to dispute the claims that have emerged from the radical quarters under the guise of what he ironically terms 'the assured results' of modern critical work in the New Testament.[147] Thus he comments that

behind the whole of the modern neo-adoptionism, of which Knox, Pittenger, and Robinson are in various ways exponents, there lies a deep rooted assumption, which as we have seen, is fully explicit in Knox, that humanity and divinity are not only diverse in their metaphysical basis but are also radically incompatible, in such a way that if Jesus was fully and completely man he could not also be literally and personally God. It is this assumption that I wish to deny.[148]

He adds that this presupposition

although it is highly debatable, it is rarely debated. It is the axiom that, whatever the Church and its greatest thinkers may have thought throughout the ages, it is impossible for the Son of God to be on the one hand divine and pre-existent and on the other to have really become man. Now it is not surprising that in the New Testament itself we can see a development of Christology; as Knox himself says, the Christian not only sings and prays, but also thinks. But that the primitive Church was led to accept pure nonsense I find it difficult to suppose; especially when on closer examination its thought turns out not to be nonsense at all.[149]

---

146 Ibid., 45.   147 Mascall offers an extended critique of the prevailing historical scepticism of current biblical criticism (discussed at length under the chapter title, 'History and the Gospels'). He is particularly effective in drawing our attention to the work of Morna Hooker, especially her article in *Theology* (1972) 'On Using the Wrong Tool'. There Hooker shows that the current criteria for judging what biblical material can be reliably attributed to the historical Jesus cannot be applied without contradiction. See *TGC*, 65-120.   148 Ibid., 130.   149 Ibid., 126. Mascall refers in passing here to the ultra-extreme theory held by Martin Werner that 'the Church invented the deity of Jesus to console itself for the delay in his second coming, but only slightly so'. Ibid., 126-7.

Mascall asserts that he is not alone in this conviction. He lists the following authors as being among those who share his outlook: the English scholars Canon A.E. Harvey and C.F.D. Moule, and Continental ones such as M. Hengel, L. Bouyer and J. Galot.[150] Mascall is particularly indebted to the writings of Moule, Bouyer and Galot since they are unencumbered by this 'methodological anti-supernatural presupposition', and he devotes much space in his publications to disseminating their views.[151] These authors adhere uncompromisingly to the appropriateness of the doctrine of the pre-existence of Christ and, very importantly in light of the criticisms proffered by the radical Anglican theologians above, uphold the doctrine's scriptural foundations. We shall now examine Mascall's reading and presentation of the main detail of their arguments concerning the pre-existence of Christ.

C.F.D. Moule (b. 1908)   Mascall holds Moule, a fellow Anglican priest and one time Lady Margaret Professor of Divinity at Cambridge (1951-76) in high regard, describing him as 'one of the most learned and judicious of contemporary New Testament scholars – and also one of the most readable'.[152] He states that Moule's *The Origin of Christology*[153] 'is an extremely important book and a timely one'.[154] It deals 'with the astonishing fact' that the primitive Church, although it was deeply rooted in Jewish monotheism, came without any sense of strain to accept Jesus as sharing in the attributes of God.[155] Moule, Mascall comments, finds no use for the expedient by which some 'reductionist' scholars (e.g. Robinson) have interpreted Jesus' pre-existence as merely his existence in the mind of God. To let Moule speak for himself, we can note that he argues (against the *religions geschichtliche Schule* of New Testament studies)[156] that the christology of the New Testament did not 'evolve' through assimilation to Jewish and pagan conceptions, but 'developed' through reflection upon an experience of Jesus which was there from the beginning and which has left irreducible traces in the records.[157] Prominent among such 'developments' was the realisation of Christ's pre-existence. Evidence of this development, Moule goes on, is seen in the distinctive Johannine use of the christological title, 'the Son of Man', in 3:13 and 6:62 where, Moule asserts, 'the dimension of pre-existence' is clearly apparent. This happens

150 His treatment of these authors is divided between *WHHM* and *Jesus*.   151 It should be noted here that the predominant writing style of Mascall on christological matters, during the later stage, was to quote (directly and at length) from those authors whose work he admired. This had the advantage of allowing him to acquaint an English readership with ideas which might otherwise have been denied them, especially French Catholic ones. However, it has the disadvantage that it means that Mascall's treatment of christological matters in general, and of the pre-existence in particular, has to be gleaned from many incomplete quotations and statements scattered throughout his various writings.   152 *WHHM*, 55.   153 Cambridge, 1977.   154 *WHHM*, 59.   155 *Jesus*, 7. We shall see below that Macquarrie makes a very similar claim.   156 Moule, *The Origin of Christology*, 139.   157 Ibid., 1-10.

as 'a legitimate development' on the Synoptics (where no such claims about the pre-existence of the Son of Man are made) and not as an evolutionary borrowing from outside the Christian data.[158] Moule also posits the opinion that Christ's pre-existence is implied in John 17 and Colossians 1,[159] and he stresses the close link that there is in the New Testament between the personal pre-existence of Jesus and his resurrection.

To return to Mascall now, we can observe that he is happy when Moule's work demonstrates that 'far from it being the case that the pre-existent divine Jesus was invented as a subject of a variety of myths about salvation, it would be far truer to say that the myths (if that is what we are to call them) were constructed as analogies in the attempt to describe the salvation that his followers had found in Jesus'.[160] The implications of Moule's reflections, Mascall adds, is that his 'is a Christology of the assumption of human nature by the pre-existent word of God, and not a Christology of the gradual apotheosis of a revered teacher by his followers, that is not only true to the New Testament evidence itself, but also makes Christianity relevant to human life and culture in general and to the insights and problems of our own time in particular'.[161]

Louis Bouyer (b. 1913) Mascall esteems greatly the writings of this French Catholic theologian and in particular his *Le Fils éternel*,[162] which he describes as 'an outstanding work'.[163] Mascall admires the author's determination to build a christology upon a firmly biblical foundation[164] and welcomes his criticism of Bultmann's postulate of a discontinuity between Jesus and the Church and any relegation of the Gospels to the category of myth and folklore.[165] Mascall finds one passage from Bouyer particularly agreeable:

> In spite of certain inevitable hesitations of thought and still more of expression, adoptionist christologies, far from being primitive christologies, are only late products which can be labelled reactionary. The most immediate

---

158 Ibid., 18. 159 Ibid., 139. 160 *WHHM*, 101. 161 Ibid., 59. 162 Paris, 1974. 163 *TGC*, 151. 164 Mascall is also attracted by Bouyer's 'conviction of the need to rescue Christology from a growing and excessive individualism which he sees as having characterised it in the West from the Middle Ages onwards, and also from a psychologism whose roots he discerns in St Thomas Aquinas and which he judges to have reached later on the dimensions of an invasion and to have resulted in a virtual expulsion of metaphysics from Christology. For a Biblical Christology as he sees it, is essentially ecclesial; Jesus cannot be detached from the Church which is his Bride and his Body, the People of God, the New Israel.' Ibid., 144. 165 Mascall notes approvingly Bouyer's assertion about 'how few of the multitude of books dealing professedly with the Resurrection are devoted to a really critical study of the documents and to an effort to get to the essential facts and how many are absorbed in the development of *a priori* philosophical positions for which the philological and historical critique is often a pretext or simply a façade'. See *Le Fils éternel*, 239; quoted and translated in *TGC*, 145.

and sure effect of what we can call the experience of the resurrection, as the experience of the Christian faith in its first outburst, is quite different. It is a recognition (what St Paul denotes by the term *epignosis*) of what had been there in Jesus all the time and is now taken account of. He himself had suggested, and more than suggested it by his words, and perhaps still more by his actions. But God, by raising him from the dead, has in one stroke both confirmed and manifested it for those who believe in him.[166]

Mascall comments that the French author 'shows convincingly how unforced is the development of an explicit Christology in the New Testament'. Unfortunately, however, Mascall expects us to take his word for this, since he does not furnish the reader with the details of Bouyer's scriptural analysis. But he does comment at this point: 'there is no trace with [Bouyer] of Dr Knox's extraordinary contention that it is impossible to have both the pre-existence and the humanity'.[167] Nor is there any need for Robinson's interpretation of the pre-existence as 'merely a way of speaking', and still less for Lampe's reduction of the doctrine to the level where it is seen as originating in myths about salvation.

Mascall's appraisal of Bouyer is not without its criticism: he is uneasy with Bouyer's idea of a certain pre-existence not only of Christ's divinity, but also of his humanity in the life of the Trinity.[168] (Bouyer's argument here is inconsistent with Chalcedon.)[169] The crux of the controversial point is Bouyer's assertion that 'the Father begets his Son eternally, not only as going to be incarnate but as the Word made Flesh'.[170] Mascall agrees that 'from God's standpoint his relations to all created beings, even to the human nature of Christ are non-temporal and *in that sense* eternal'. But Mascall feels that there is a 'danger of confusing, in view of their common non-temporality, the necessary begetting of the divine Word by the Father with the contingent willing of his created humanity'. While acknowledging that it is 'peculiarly appropriate' that the Son become incarnate in human nature, Mascall insists, *pace* Bouyer, that 'it does not mean that the Word is concretely incarnate in the eternal life of the Trinity; nor do we need to assume this'.[171]

Jean Galot (b. 1919)   Mascall is deeply impressed by the work of the Belgian Jesuit, Jean Galot, and notes that, while it is independent of Bouyer's, it shows a remarkable affinity of outlook. Mascall, writing in 1977, described Galot as 'the most constructively creative, and also one of the most judicious, of living Christologists'.[172] Galot takes Chalcedon as the starting-point of his christology and is

---

166 Ibid., 254; quoted and translated in *TGC*, 145.   167 *TGC*, 145.   168 Ibid., 148.   169 This Council taught that Christ is one in being (*homoousios*) with us as to the humanity (*DS* 301). Thus to imply that Christ's humanity pre-existed; something that cannot be said of ours, is to posit a radical difference between Christ's humanity and our humanity, and consequently, to be at odds with Chalcedon.   170 Bouyer, *Le Fils èternel*, 486; quoted and translated in *TGC*, 119.   171 *TGC*, 149.   172 Ibid., 151.

totally committed, in Mascall's words, to showing 'the unexhausted fruitfulness' of its doctrine.[173] For Galot there are no dotted lines between the New Testament experience and the teaching of Chalcedon, and he emphasises that 'what was imposed at Chalcedon was neither philosophical concepts nor a particular system of thought, but rather the best way of expressing what is found concretely in Christ; it was a matter of translating the gospel datum, for it is always to this fundamental datum that the Fathers refer'.[174]

Mascall notes that Galot, like Bouyer and Moule, sees the New Testament as containing a clear doctrine of pre-existence. He directly quotes Galot's comment: 'the Incarnation is characterized by the involvement (*engagement*) of a pre-existent divine person. These three elements: involvement, divine person, pre-existent person, give the mystery its true bearing'.[175] Mascall quotes Galot directly, and at some length, on the question of the pre-existence, and in the following order:

> A divine person is necessarily pre-existent, but I wish to stress that this pre-existence gives a very special value to the involvement ... Eternity is thus introduced into human existence.
>
> Pre-existence is not a luxury of theological speculation, which we could set aside in the interest of simplification. It concerns us because it effects the relation of Christ to mankind ... He who possesses eternity in its fulness in common with the Father has the power to make man share it by communicating eternal life to them.
>
> Furthermore, it is in the pre-existence that there is situated the decision of the redeeming Incarnation, the act of love which has brought about the Son among men. The mystery is governed by a divine attitude; it is the expression of a divine dynamism which dominates all the earthly life of Jesus by being anterior to him.[176]

Mascall thoroughly approves of Galot's argument and notes that 'it provides the answer to those who, like Robinson, are content to reduce the pre-existence of the Son to a merely psychological existence and idea in the mind of God'.[177] Mascall notes that Galot 'is every bit as emphatic as any of the proponents of the "New Approach" upon the totality and reality of the human experience of Jesus'. But he is equally emphatic that the subject of this human experience is the divine Word himself.[178]

---

173 Ibid., 169.   174 J. Galot, *La Personne du Christ* (Gembloux & Paris, 1969), 7; quoted and translated in *TGC*, 151.   175 J. Galot, *Vers une nouvelle christologie* (Gembloux & Paris, 1971), 62; quoted and translated in *TGC*, 174.   176 Ibid. 62ff.; quoted and translated in *TGC*, 174-5.   177 *TGC*, 175.   178 Ibid., 183. Mascall goes on to quote Galot's own words on this point: 'To bring this human experience into full light it is not helpful to withdraw into the shade the divine person of the pre-existent Son of God or to question its reality as the "New Approach" does. The denial of the divinity of the person not only fails to make Christ more human, it prevents

Mascall raises a criticism of Galot: he confesses himself 'not altogether happy with the way in which Galot describes the divine *démarche*'.[179] Mascall asserts that he finds himself

> uneasy with the suggestion .... that the decision to become incarnate was made by the divine Word at some moment or moments in time; this seems to envisage God as himself within the time-process and to be almost reminiscent of the 'tournament of Love' of Dodat de Balsyé .... For what is spoken of here is not a decision taking place within the human mind of the incarnate Lord, but of a decision alleged to be made by the divine Word in his pre-incarnate state .... I must record my impression that Galot has for once succumbed to a sense of the dramatic and also that, as on an earlier occasion on which I commented, he has surprisingly shown a rather inadequate understanding of the relation between time and eternity.[180]

As we have seen, then, in this section, Mascall has recourse to the findings of other orthodox scholars, Moule, Bouyer and Galot, so as to underline his conviction that the New Testament clearly teaches the pre-existence of Christ. In doing this, he concurs with Helen Oppenheimer's assertion that 'to take one's stand .... upon Christ's pre-existence is not just an obsolete mythological speculation, but the necessary condition of the first Christian thinkers being right about his significance'.[181]

As to the subsequent unfolding of the doctrine, and of classical christology in general, Mascall argues vigorously that it posed no threat to the completeness of Christ's humanity and he holds firm to the Chalcedonian teaching that the subject of Christ's two natures, human and divine, is none other than the eternal and pre-existent Son.[182] Nothing needs to be absent from Jesus' human nature in order for the divine Word, who is absolutely impassible in his Godhead, to be really and literally passible in his manhood. There is no place for even the most attenuated form of docetism. Thus we can end here with Mascall's insistence that

one from recognizing the value of the human experience which the Incarnation constitutes. That value resides in the fact that a person who is God has willed to undergo and experience the existence which is proper to man...' See *Vers une nouvelle christologie*, 95; quoted and translated in *TGC*, 183. **179** Galot's description of the divine *démarche* to which Mascall takes exception reads as follows: 'The Incarnation ... presents the sole case in which a human existence was first of all expressly wished by him who was going to live it. Christ is the only man who has lived his human life in virtue of an antecedent personal commitment ... This experience deserves more than another the name of "adventure", in view of the distance that exists between the divine person of the Word and the new existence on which he entered ... The Incarnation is the great divine adventure, that of a human existence deliberately faced and totally lived'. See Galot, *Vers une nouvelle christologie*, 95; quoted and translated in *TGC*, 184. **180** *TGC*, 184. **181** H. Oppenheimer, *Incarnation and Immanence* (London, 1973), 214; quoted in *TGC*, 130 and *Jesus*, 8, n. 8. **182** *WHHM*, 64.

traditional Christology, with its roots in Chalcedon, is committed no less strongly to defending, in its concrete fullness, [Christ's] humanity .... [N]othing could be clearer than Chalcedon's affirmation that Jesus is "truly man, the same of rational soul and body", with its deliberate exclusion of the Apollinarian view that in Jesus the person of the divine Word took the place of a rational soul; and further emphasis was added by the Council of 680 (Constantinople III) with its insistence that the rational soul included a human will. Nothing, it was implied, needed to be absent from Christ's human nature to make room for the divine Word, for the Word was not *part* of the human nature but its metaphysical *subject*; *person* and *nature* are not on the same level of being.[183]

The concluding chapter will assess the strengths and weaknesses of Mascall's approach to the doctrine of Christ's pre-existence. For now, we acknowledge that his is clearly a classical approach. One of the most pressing issues to be addressed later will be to establish whether Mascall, as one well versed in philosophy (and Thomism in particular), has dealt adequately with the philosophical considerations that are unavoidably involved in any satisfactory presentation of the doctrine of Christ's pre-existence. It must be said in his defence at this point that he never set out to outline systematically his position on the doctrine. On the contrary, his observations on the issue, were either made very much in passing, as during the early years of his career, when the doctrine was not under fire, or, as during the later years, they were framed in response to the reductionist interpretations emerging from certain pens. In consequence, they are fragmentary and incomplete. We shall finish here, nevertheless, by observing that it is a matter of regret that, Mascall, as one so well versed in classical theology and philosophy, did not attempt to explore the significance of the relationship between time and eternity for the doctrine of Christ's pre-existence. (It must be said, however, that alone of the four Anglican authors under review in this study, he did show that he was aware of the issue, even if he failed to develop the point sufficiently.)[184] The need to reflect on time and eternity has very deep roots in the Christian tradition, not least in Boethius and Thomas Aquinas, but was to fall into disfavour in the wake of the Enlightenment. It has, however, been recognised in recent times that those who argue that the doctrine of the incarnation of the eternal Son of God is not

---

183 Ibid., 33.   184 In the course of an examination of Galot's christology, Mascall criticises the former's tendency 'to speak as if the divine Logos, not only in his human but also in his divine nature, exists in time and makes decisions in time. Thus he [Galot] never seems to be quite explicit that what we rightly describe in our temporal language as *pre*-existence is in fact timeless existence, just as what we describe as divine *fore*-knowledge is in fact timeless knowledge. (This, of course, [Mascall goes on] does not reduce the pre-existence of the Logos to a merely ideal or conceptual existence in the mind of God; quite the contrary).' *WHHM*, 94.

inherently impossible or self-contradictory should also reflect on eternal and temporal existence. It will be our task to investigate below the possibilities such reflection offers towards a more coherent and accessible articulation of the doctrine of Christ's pre-existence and incarnation.

4

John A.T. Robinson's interpretation of Christ's pre-existence

INTRODUCTION

John A.T. Robinson was born in 1919 and grew up under the shadow of Canterbury Cathedral. Both his grandfathers were canons there and as Robinson himself once commented: 'if you are an Anglican you can't get much nearer than that to the heart of the establishment'.[1] His father, Arthur William Robinson, held a DD from Cambridge University and in 1907 was a candidate for the Lady Margaret Professorship of Divinity. He was the author of a dozen books. Six of John's uncles were ordained priests.

Robinson was educated at Marlborough College, where his career was not noteworthy. Yet he was awarded a Rustat Exhibition to Jesus College, Cambridge, and went on to win the Burney Prize, and the Burney Scholarship for 1942-43 which took him to Trinity College. His unpublished thesis in the philosophy of religion, *Thou Who Art*, which gained him his PhD in 1946, was judged by Professor John Baillie, his external examiner, 'the best ever to have come my way'.[2] Robinson decided not to opt for an academic career immediately and, consequently, did not pursue the possibility of becoming an assistant professor in the philosophy of religion at Swarthmore College, Pennsylvania, USA.

He was ordained a deacon in 1945 and took up a curacy in the city parish of St Matthew Moorfield's, Bristol, with Mervyn Stockwood as his vicar. A year later he was ordained to the priesthood.[3] In 1947 he married Ruth Grace and they were to have three children. From 1948 to 1951, he was chaplain at Wells Theological College, and it was here that he wrote and published his first book, *In the End God* (1950). Emerging as 'a promising scholar in the New Testament',[4] he became dean (at a young age) of Clare College, Cambridge, in 1951.

---

1 *The Roots of a Radical* (London, 1980), 10; hereafter *RR*.   2 E. James, *A Life of Bishop John A.T. Robinson* (London, 1987), 16.   3 Adrian Hastings has commented that Robinson had so many clergy in his ancestry that 'he might hardly have been able to imagine not becoming a priest'. See Hastings, *Robert Runcie* (London, 1991), 8.   4 An observation proffered by O. Chadwick in his *Michael Ramsey: A Life* (Oxford, 1990), 370.

In 1958, Mervyn Stockwood was nominated Bishop of Southwark and invited his erstwhile curate to become his suffragan as Bishop of Woolwich. Despite contrary advice from fellow academics at Cambridge and the Archbishop of Canterbury, Geoffrey Fisher, Robinson accepted, and was consecrated as a bishop in Canterbury Cathedral in 1959. Robinson threw himself with great zeal into his duties as a bishop. In 1960 he came to national prominence in England when he gave evidence for the defence against those who sought to prove that D.H. Lawrence's novel, *Lady Chatterley's Lover*, was pornographic. The Archbishop of Canterbury publicly censured him, but Robinson had no regrets.

He caught the public eye again, in 1963, with the publication of *Honest to God*. He wrote the book while recuperating in hospital from back trouble. John Macquarrie has described it as 'the most important book on English christology ... [in] a quarter of a century'.[5] The message of the book summed up crudely in a headline in *The Observer* newspaper: 'Our Image of God Must Go'. The argument of the book inflamed strong passions, for and against. It sold over a million copies and was translated into seventeen languages. Robinson received over four thousand letters about it.

After ten busy years as Bishop of Woolwich (during which time he still found time to write), Robinson decided to return to full-time academic life at Cambridge. Thus in 1969, he became fellow, dean of chapel, and lecturer in theology at Trinity College. Within eight months he delivered the Hulsean Lectures at Cambridge in the autumn of 1970. Adding to them material from lectures given to Lancaster and Aberystwyth Universities in 1971, he published *The Human Face of God* (1973). He was thus what Maurice Wiles has termed, 'one of the small band of scholar-bishops of our time'.[6] He made an unsuccessful application for the post of Lady Margaret chair of Divinity at Cambridge in 1974. This was a cause of some disappointment to him.

Robinson's appointment to Trinity afforded him the opportunity to travel extensively (even if the College was unhappy that it did not see more of him). He made at least six lecturing visits to the United States of America, as well as going to South and Central America, South Africa, Israel, India, Sri Lanka, Hong Kong, Japan, New Zealand and Australia. In 1980 he was made an honorary DCL of the University of Southern California. In 1982 he spent some time as visiting professor at McMaster University, Hamilton, Ontario, Canada, where he was able to pursue his deep interest in the issue of nuclear disarmament.

In June 1983 it was diagnosed that Robinson had terminal cancer. In the short time that remained to him he laboured hard to prepare the Bampton Lectures which he was due to give in Oxford the following year. As things turned out, death intervened all too quickly; but the lectures were ready save

5 J. Macquarrie, *Jesus Christ in Modern Thought* (London, 1990), 333.   6 M. Wiles, 'John Robinson', *Theology*, 87 (1984) 85.

for some editing. Robinson's friend of many years, C.F.D. Moule, delivered the lectures, and they were subsequently published as *The Priority of John* (1985).

As to the man, Alistair Kee has described him as 'awkwardly shy, incapable of malice, of profound faith and of childlike integrity'.[7]

Robinson's main publications
Robinson wrote on an extensive number of different topics. Shortly before he died he listed these books and divided them into three categories. These classifications are as follows: i) the way of theological exploration; ii) the way of biblical interrogation; and iii) the way of social responsibility. It may be useful to arrange the various books according to their appointed classification.

'The way of theological exploration': Robinson considers this first group (writing in an abbreviated fashion) as 'constantly pushing out; questioning accepted doctrine; stripping away; cutting to the heart; revisioning, re-interpreting; being stretched; never resting content; pressing out from edges'.[8] In this group he places his doctoral dissertation *Thou Who Art* (1946), a study of the philosophy of Martin Buber. *In the End God* (1950) was an investigation of eschatology. *Honest to God* (1963) was his most important book; we have indicated its contents in the previous section. *The Honest to God Debate* (1963), co-edited with D.L. Edwards, was a collection of various responses to the controversy that arose following the publication of *Honest to God*. His next book *But That I Can't Believe* (1967) was a further exploration on these lines. *Exploration into God* (1967) was an attempt to exhibit more fully and positively the foundations of the Christian conception of God than had been possible in *Honest to God*. *The Human Face of God* (1972) articulated a christology that took seriously the humanity of Christ. *Truth Is Two-Eyed* (1979) reflected on the insights and challenges that Eastern religions bring to Christianity.

The books listed in the second category, 'The way of biblical interrogation', are described as 'digging to roots; probing; compelling the Scriptures to give up their message for us now; going behind the interpretations; refusing to accept stock answers; return to source; centre; rooted to be radical'.[9] We find listed here *The Body* (1952) and *Wrestling with Romans* (1978): they were devoted to the study of certain Pauline themes. *Jesus and His Coming* (1957) was a study of biblical eschatology. *Twelve New Testament Studies* (1961) and *Twelve More New Testament Studies* (1983) were collections of essays on various biblical themes. *Redating the New Testament* (1975) was one of Robinson's most significant books: C.F.D. Moule considered it 'a brilliant tour de force',[10] The radical and controversial thesis of the book was that all the books of the New Testament were written before AD 70. Its arguments were presented in a

7 A. Kee, *The Roots of Christian Freedom* (London, 1988), xv.   8 James, *A Life of Bishop John A. T. Robinson*, 299.   9 Ibid.   10 Ibid., 236.

more popular style in *Can We Trust the New Testament?* (1976). *The Priority of John* (1985) was his *magnum opus* in New Testament studies. In it he argued that John's Gospel has much more historical validity than contemporary scholarship (post-Bultmann) tends to recognise.

The books in the third and final category, 'The way of social responsibility', are defined as 'responding to what God is saying to us through his world of people; the call of the kingdom and the claims of love; reading the signs of the times; forcing us out into the world'.[11] Since the works in this grouping are not of immediate concern to us in this study, and since the titles are generally self-explanatory, it will suffice (with one exception) to list the titles of the different works without offering comments on the contents. *On Being the Church in the Modern World* (1960); *Liturgy Coming to Life* (1960); *Christian Morals Today* (1964); *The New Reformation?* (1965); *Christian Freedom in a Permissive Society* (1970); *The Difference in Being a Christian Today* (1971); and *The Roots of a Radical* (1980). This last title was a collection of nine articles, one of which was devoted to christology. It was entitled 'Honest to Christ Today' and it was an attempt to comment on some of the issues raised by 'The Myth of God Incarnate' Symposium.

A radical thinker

Before identifying the forces, intellectual and social, which shaped Robinson's thought, it is appropriate to note that his starting-point was very different from that of Thornton and Mascall. Both of them were highly convinced Anglo–Catholics who, in their different ways, were, as we have seen, committed to theological orthodoxy. Robinson's theological outlook within the Church of England differed markedly from theirs. His family background was clearly more influenced by the currents of reformed theology present therein and he was drawn towards the writings of such Continental, radical Protestant theologians as Dietrich Bonhoeffer, Paul Tillich, and Rudolf Bultmann, as well as towards those of the French Jesuit, Pierre Teilhard de Chardin.[12] He seems to have seen himself in terms of the 'complete Church of England man ... a both-and man rather than an either-or, Catholic *and* Reformed ...'[13] Unlike the two Anglo–Catholic writers, he was so unencumbered by much of what the theological tradition held as sacrosanct that Adrian Hastings has described him as being 'apparently willing to de-mythologise almost anything of which modernity might conceivably be suspicious'.[14]

In addition to this, Robinson's academic competence lay predominantly in the field of New Testament studies,[15] whereas both (the early) Thornton and Mascall

---

11 Ibid., 299.   12 It must be recalled here that Thornton's (unnamed) obituarist has claimed that the elderly Thornton also found Teilhard's ideas stimulating: but this interest came too late to be reflected in his published works. See *Church Times*, 148 (1960) 11.   13 *RR*, 21.   14 A. Hastings, *A History of English Christianity, 1920-1985* (London, 1986), 537.   15 Yet, as we have seen, his PhD was in the philosophy of religion.

were more at home, for the most part, as we have seen, in theological and philosophical discourse. This would not prevent Robinson, however, from frequently crossing-over and commenting (often controversially) on many of the central themes of systematic theology: not least in relation to the God question and christology.[16]

The primary motivating force behind Robinson's theological endeavour (as opposed to his New Testament writings where a more conventionally academic purpose was normally apparent) was the pastoral alarm that he experienced, as a scholar and a bishop, at the accelerating decline of Christian faith in England in the decades after the Second World War. It is against this background that he published *Honest to God*. This popular paperback was a criticism of the image of God commonly held among Church people: an image in which God's transcendence of the world is exaggerated to the virtual exclusion of any sense of his immanence, so that he is a God 'up there' or 'out there', not a God 'in the midst'.[17] It followed that the Church's traditional presentation of Christ was also flawed. John Macquarrie has summarised Robinson's position when he says: 'Already in *Honest to God*, Robinson found himself also criticising the popular incarnational christology of the Church of England. It had led, he believed, into a widespread docetism ... Jesus was also a figure "out there", he had come from a heaven in which he pre-existed, sojourned for a brief while on earth, and then returned to the realm from which he had come.'[18]

What Robinson was arguing (here and elsewhere), in other words, was that the Church herself bore her own burden of responsibility, for the growing secularism of society, because she had failed to present an image of God and of Christ which could dialogue with the age. In order to understand what is at stake in Robinson's criticism of the received theological tradition, it is necessary that we familiarise ourselves with the detail of his argument concerning the changed religious consciousness of modern (Western) humanity. Having done that we shall be in a position to tackle the constructive aspect of his christological endeavour (i.e. his response to these changes) and, more specifically, his interpretation of the doctrine of Christ's pre-existence. We begin then by attending to the detail of Robinson's argument concerning the anato-

---

16 John Knox, aware of the sheer breadth of issues upon which Robinson commented, has asked: 'was he [Robinson] the theologian, the ecclesiastical administrator, the New Testament scholar, the liturgist, the pastor?' Knox is of the opinion 'that all who have closely followed his career or read his books will agree that he is to be thought of principally as a New Testament scholar'. See his 'J.A.T. Robinson and the Meaning of New Testament Scholarship' in *Theology*, 92 (1989) 251-2. 17 Robinson relied heavily in this book on the ideas of several German theologians: Tillich, Bultmann and Bonhoeffer. Karl Barth, like many others, was not much impressed with the result. Thus he went so far as to say, in Macquarrie's paraphrase that 'Robinson had mixed together three good German beers, and produced a lot of froth'. See J. Macquarrie, *Twentieth-Century Religious Thought*, 4th ed. (London, 1988), 426. 18 Macquarrie, *Jesus Christ in Modern Thought*, 333.

my of these changes. He discusses them in detail in his christology book *The Human Face of God*,[19] under the heading 'Four fundamental shifts'[20], and it is to an analysis of them that we shall now turn our attention.

Robinson argues that the traditional language of theology in general and of christology, in particular, 'has been shaken if not shattered'[21] by the impact of four fundamental shifts in popular religious consciousness. These changes (which have come *post* Darwin, Marx, Freud and the cracking of the genetic code)[22] have served to undermine four of the great pillars that had hitherto supported the edifice of orthodox theology. These pillars are as follows: i) the concept of myth, ii) metaphysics, iii) the language of the absolute, and iv) confidence in the absolute historicity of Christian preaching concerning the incarnation. Before looking briefly at these four pillars, it is well to note Robinson's practice of pursuing issues that interest him through the secondary literature – an approach to scholarship that C.F.D. Moule found rather *ad hoc*.[23] In what is about to follow, we find Robinson making strong criticisms of the classical orthodox tradition. It will be clear to us that Robinson does not always deal adequately with the theological and philosophical intricacies involved in his claims.

The concept of myth   Myth has to do with what is deepest in human experience, with something more primal and archetypal and potent than intellect. Until quite recently myth was interpreted quite realistically (which is not to say literally). Thus Adam's fall explained why giving birth was painful for women and work oppressive for men. As Robinson reminds us, to be a Christian had necessarily involved believing in a series of events of salvation history, all stated as if they were objectively true in the same kind of way (e.g. the assertions of the Apostles' Creed concerning God's only Son, our Lord, Jesus Christ). No need was felt to distinguish between what was to be taken as history, what as myth, and what as a mixture of both.[24] Following Bultmann, Robinson asserts that today, in our modern, scientific age, 'myth cannot be taken as a description of how things did, do or will happen. For us it is an expression of significance, not an explanation for anything'.[25] It is to be considered as 'a way of speaking'.[26]

Metaphysics   Robinson comments that 'what myth is to the imagination, metaphysics is to the intellect',[27] and that the latter, in common with the former, has come today to be associated with unreality.[28] He declares that modern humanity

---

19 London, 1973; hereafter *HFG*.   20 *HFG*, 19.   21 Ibid.   22 Ibid., 39.   23 Moule is quoted in James, *A Life of Bishop John A.T. Robinson*, 233.   24 *HFG.*, 20-1.   25 Ibid., 21. Robinson refers here in n. 60 to G.D. Kaufman, *Systematic Theology: A Historical Perspective* (New York, 1968), 203. For a fuller appreciation of Robinson's reading of Bultmann see his 'Rudolf Bultmann: A View from England', in B. Jaspert (ed.), *Rudolf Bultmanns Werk und Wirkung* (Darmstadt, 1984), 149-54.   26 *HFG.*, 32.   27 Ibid.   28 The criticism of metaphysics had been a consistent theme in Robinson's writings. Although he is to be considered first

no longer has confidence in the type of supernaturalistic ontology to which Christian theology in its classical presentation has been attached. According to this, what is 'really real' (*to on*) is located in another realm, above, beyond or behind phenomena (the latter belonging to the world of appearance rather than reality).[29] Robinson asserts, however, that while 'we cannot ... dispense with metaphysics ... the *logos* is lacking with which to give it anchorage in what for our generation lies "beyond the physical"'.[30] This would seem in practice, in spite of Robinson's protestations to the contrary, to involve the disavowal of metaphysics, on the grounds that we have no agreed metaphysics today.[31]

Demise of the language of the absolute Closely related with metaphysics is the concept of the absolute. Influential in classical thought, it speaks of ultimate reality in terms of 'uniqueness, of finality, of once-and-for-allness, of timeless perfection, of difference not merely of degree but of kind'. Through the lens of this language of the absolute, 'truth has been seen as unitary, rising like a Gothic Arch and meeting in the One who is the answer to all possible questions'.[32] Robinson goes on to argue, that as with the categories of myth and metaphysics, 'this monistic model has lost its power over our thinking, whether about space or time. Ours is a relativistic, pluralistic world in which we are compelled to be more modest about our claims'.[33] As will emerge below, this development has profound

and foremost a New Testament scholar, we must not lose sight of the fact that he wrote his PhD in the field of the philosophy of religion under the supervision of Professor H.H. Farmer. The thesis, as we noted above, was entitled *Thou Who Art* (1946) and was a study of the contemporary 'I – Thou' philosophy of Martin Buber. It was written as a conscious counter to E.L. Mascall's Thomist work, *He Who Is: A Study in Traditional Theism* (London, 1943). While there is not the space here for an adequate treatment of the argument of the dissertation, we can put it thus: the classical theological tradition, with its heavy reliance on Greek thought (as epitomised in Thomas Aquinas' *Summa Theologiae*), uses categories that 'are not such as can do justice to the "living God" of the Biblical revelation'. To achieve this goal, Robinson turned from the classical tradition, with its heavy reliance on Aristotle, as reflected in Boethius' influential classical definition of person, to the philosophy of Martin Buber. For a further discussion of this point, see A. Kee, *The Roots of Christian Freedom*, 67. 29 HFG, 22. 30 Ibid., 23. 31 This is the judgement of B.C. Butler who goes on to comment that 'metaphysics, explicit or implicit, cannot be exorcised from our thinking. If you try to do without it, it crops up unknown to you to make non-sense of your affirmations or to show the emptiness of your difficulties'. See his 'Notes and Comments: Bishop Robinson's Christ', *Heythrop Journal*, 14 (1973) 427. 32 HFG, 24. 33 He notes Paul van Buren's observation that we live in a world characterised by 'the dissolution of the absolute' and his comment that 'the question may fairly be asked whether theology and faith can survive this shift of focus: whether Christianity, for example, which for so long proclaimed a monistic view of the universe, a single and unique point of reference as the only valid one, with a single and unique revelation of this truth, can learn to live in a world from which the Absolute has been dissolved'. Ibid. See P. van Buren, *Theological Explorations* (London, 1968), 29-42.

consequences for christology because 'as a changeless Absolute, the Christ cannot come as good news'.[34] Robinson finds in the thought of Teilhard de Chardin an altogether more stimulating and fruitful approach.

Demise of confidence in the absolute historicity of the incarnation   At the heart of this issue is the question: 'can we know *anything* of what the Jesus of history was really like, and *does it matter anyhow* [italics Robinson's]?'[35] Robinson argues that the existence of this question has as much to do with popular impression (and is none the less potent for that), as with the consequences of any established results of scholarly inquiry.[36] Thus he explains that he wants to question what he regards as 'the tyranny of the unexamined presuppositions in much of the current post-Bultmannian critical orthodoxy'.[37] He claims to be 'increasingly convinced that there is a lot of very good history in the gospels – not least in the Fourth Gospel'.[38] Thus he has no intention of acquiescing in 'a sort of treason of the clerks at this point',[39] and giving way to the undue and almost impossible scepticism of certain scholars. B.C. Butler may have got to the heart of the matter when he comments that Robinson's polemic against the exaggerated lengths of much modern biblical scholarship 'suits his purpose, because in large measure he wants to substitute a historical for a "metaphysical" Christ'.[40]

ROBINSON'S CHRISTOLOGY

Having acquainted ourselves with the detail of Robinson's rather *ad hoc* sketch of the changed contours of modern religious consciousness, we are now ready to examine his attempts to construct a new christology sensitive to these new realities. It is to be a christology which responds to that question posed by Dietrich Bonhoeffer from his prison cell when he wrote: 'what is bothering me incessantly

---

34 *HFG*, 25.   35 Ibid., 28.   36 Ibid., 29. Robinson goes on to dismiss certain works which argue that Jesus never lived or that in all essentials he was a mythical construction of the early Church: e.g., G.A. Wells, *The Jesus of the Early Christians* (London, 1971) and the enthusiastic commendation it received from the pen of Hugh Trevor-Roper, sometime Professor of Modern History at Oxford. He is also unimpressed with the findings of J. Wren-Lewis, *What Shall We Tell the Children?* (London, 1971).   37 *RR*, 70.   38 *HFG.*, 31. He also states (in stark contrast to the sentiments of Mascall), that the new methods of biblical study 'so far from reducing the historical content of the gospels to vanishing point as is often supposed, enable one to strip off the layers of church tradition to reveal more of what lies beneath them'. Ibid.   39 *RR*, 69.   40 B.C. Butler, 'Notes and Comments: Bishop Robinson's Christ', 426. An outstanding example of another thinker who wanted to disengage theology, and therefore christology, from its traditional setting and to articulate it afresh in historical terms is Friedrich Gogarten (1887-1967). It must be said, however, that Gogarten takes more trouble than Robinson to analyse the changes that the Enlightenment has brought about: he argues that metaphysics has been superseded by history. See his *Demythologizing and History* (London, 1958), 25-6.

is the question ... who Christ really is for us today'.[41] Before attending to Robinson's response to that question, it may be useful to consider his criticism of the traditional presentation of Jesus Christ, since his own christology arose out of his dissatisfaction over earlier deficiencies. This will prepare the ground for an examination of Robinson's treatment of Christ's pre-existence.

The legacy of classical christology
Robinson's christological endeavour, as we saw in chapter one, was undertaken against a background of a real crisis of faith in England and indeed throughout the Western world. He argues, as we have noted above, that this situation will not change so long as the Church's presentation of Jesus Christ continues to be tied to supernaturalistic categories of thought which only serve 'to invite blank incomprehension in a modern listener,'[42] and which ensure that 'a Christological *tour de force* [is] impossible'.[43] To overcome this stasis, Robinson insists that we should realise that theology need not judge itself to be inextricably wedded to these supernaturalistic categories. Indeed, he asserts that the understanding of Christ which they imply (the divinity compromising the humanity), is inconsistent with the New Testament portrayal of him. The Matthean-Lucan genealogies, the 'historical' portrait of all four Gospels, the epistle to the Hebrews, with its conception of Jesus' growth in *teleiotes*, the pre-christological formulae and Paul's own christology, and lastly the christological presentation of John's Gospel demonstrate that in the New Testament Jesus is presented, Robinson argues, not as a divine visitor from another world in human guise, but as a human being emerging from the nexus of human history (hints of Teilhard), who yet embodies 'the divine initiative and saving presence' so completely as to be the incarnation of God. Thus Robinson comments:

> the New Testament shows quite clearly that the early Christians began with a view of Christ which left this memory uncomplicated and unthreatened. They certainly did not see him to be of *merely* human significance:

---

41 D. Bonhoeffer, in E. Bethge (ed.), *Letters and Papers from Prison. The Enlarged Edition* (London, 1971), 279; quoted in *HFG*, 13, 16 and 237. Macquarrie's preface to *Jesus Christ in Modern Thought* carries a similar appeal to Bonhoeffer. 42 *HFG*, 39. 43 *Honest to God* (London, 1963), 67. Robinson comments, in rather irreverent terms, that 'the traditional supernaturalistic way of describing the Incarnation almost inevitably suggests that Jesus was not a man born and bred - he was God for a limited period taking part in a charade. He looked like a man, he talked like a man, but underneath he was God dressed up – like Father Christmas. However guardedly it may be stated, the traditional view leaves the impression that God took a space-trip and arrived on this planet in the form of a man. Jesus was not really one of us; but through the miracle of the Virgin Birth he contrived to be born so as to appear one of us. Really he came from outside.' Ibid., 66.

he spoke of what God had done in their midst. But that he was *not* in their memory a man in every sense of the word is incredible in the light of Peter's speech on the day of Pentecost [Acts 2:22-24] (which, whenever it was written, clearly represents a very primitive, not to say simplistic, Christology).[44]

But this situation was soon to change: 'the pressure began ... within a decade or two ... [and] the foreordination of God became translated as the pre-existence of Christ. As soon as Jesus Christ was, or could be, represented as a pre-existent being who could come down from heaven, then the genuineness of his humanity while he was on earth was open to question'.[45]

We shall return below to Robinson's argument concerning what the New Testament writers actually intended by pre-existence. What is of significance to us now is to note that Robinson interprets the emerging orthodox theological tradition as a departure from the biblical witness. He goes on to identify four particular post-biblical 'ancient presuppositions,'[46] handed down from the Fathers, whose expressions of what it meant for Christ to be both divine and human are, he feels, hopelessly unsatisfactory for us today, and totally out of step with the scriptural witness. These presuppositions are: i) the notion of the *individuality* of the Second Person of the Trinity; ii) the metaphysical bias or weighting in favour of the divinity over against the humanity of Christ; iii) the doctrine of the *anhypostasia*; iv) the doctrine of the two natures.

The individuality of the Second Person of the Trinity   Robinson notes how the Fathers held that the Logos himself as a member of the Trinity was a being, a person, an 'individual substance', (to use Boethius' later definition 'of a rational nature'). He then points to the problem (which he admits was largely created by the terms of the debate)[47] of how 'the same terms hypostasis and persona were used subsequently in the Christological debate to indicate the selfhood of one who, as man, was a person in the modern sense of the word [i.e. a distinct centre of conscious selfhood]'.[48] Robinson thus states the problem that has arisen for theology in the wake of this in the following striking terms: 'if you start the

44 *HFG*, 36-7. See also his 'The Most Primitive Christology of All', *Journal of Theological Studies*, 7 (1956) 177-89; reprinted in *Twelve New Testament Studies* (London, 1961), 139-53.
45 Robinson appeals to John Knox's comment that as long as the primitive, 'adoptionist' christology prevailed, 'the simple actuality of the humanity was in no sense or degree compromised. Not only could it be whole and intact, but it was also subject to no theological or mythological pressure of any kind'. See Knox's *The Humanity and Divinity of Christ* (Cambridge, 1967), 6f. *En passant*, let us recall the trenchant criticism that Mascall reserved for the ideas contained in this book. Robinson, on the other hand, designates it 'a beautiful little study'. *HFG*, 37.   46 Ibid., 102.   47 Ibid., 104.   48 Ibid., 103.

Christological sum with one substance (divine), it means that you cannot introduce another (human) without finding yourself with the impossible exercise on your hands of trying to put two billiard balls on the same spot'.[49] He holds that the theological tradition has tried to merge the two billiard balls by either arguing that the divine displaces the human (as in the doctrine of the *anhypostasia* to be discussed below), or the human exists, in Cyril's words, 'as another individually beside him (*heteron par' auton idikos*)'.[50]

The metaphysical bias in favour of the divinity   Robinson asserts that even if the theological tradition has argued strenuously that Christ had two equal natures, the raw reality is that 'one was more equal than the other', since 'the person who "had" these natures was firmly on one side of the line: He was divine'.[51] (Where has the tradition stated this? Robinson's argumentation is seriously flawed here: orthodox theology has not in fact thought of Christ's two natures in terms of their being equal.) Robinson acknowledges that 'no classical statement of the person of Christ was more concerned than the *Tome* of Leo to preserve a true balance between the divine and the human', yet he argues that it singularly failed in its task: 'The balance is not in fact preserved. The divinity always has the edge.'[52] This forces Robinson to state that 'it is difficult to escape the conclusion that, however much they insisted otherwise, the Fathers did believe that Christ was God but that he was made like us (in everything but sin)'.[53]

The doctrine of the anhypostasia   The third ancient patristic presupposition under fire from Robinson is the doctrine of the *anhypostasia*.[54] He notes that Bonhoeffer dubbed it 'the last refuge of docetism'.[55] Robinson defines it as the view that 'Christ was not a human person, but a divine Person who assumed human nature without assuming human personality'.[56] In consequence, Jesus is a superhuman figure.[57] Robinson, (in contradistinction to Mascall), condemns the doctrine of the *anhypostasia* as strange and remote both from common sense and from scriptures[58] and says that 'it requires a considerable effort of the imagination to

49 Ibid.   50 Ibid., 103-4.   51 Ibid., 104.   52 Ibid.   53 Ibid., 105.   54 Robinson notes that this doctrine has always been controversial: it was vigorously resisted by the Antiochene, as opposed to the Alexandrian school, and 'in modern times the theory has been rejected by many theologians who would not dream of supposing that they were abandoning the doctrine of the Incarnation but were trying rather to be true to its real meaning'. He mentions as examples of those who subscribe to this approach the following theologians: N. Pittenger, D. Bonhoeffer, P. Schoonenberg, J. Mackey, T.F. Torrance and G. Lampe. See *RR*, 64.   55 D. Bonhoeffer, *Christology* (London, 1971), 81; quoted in *HFG*, 107.   56 *HFG*, 105.   57 Ibid., 108. Robinson singles out the christology of the Anglican theologian, Bishop Frank Weston, as a good example of such a presentation of Christ. See his *The One Christ*, 2nd ed. (London, 1914), 106.   58 He is similarly unconvinced by the later refinement of *enhypostasia* (i.e. the doctrine of Christ's fully human nature, personalised through

understand what can ever have been meant by it, let alone why it has been so generally regarded as essential'.[59] Robinson realises that at the root of this doctrine is the wish to deny Jesus' independent existence as a human being apart from God but is 'persuaded that the truth at stake can be preserved without the theory that Jesus had no human personality'.[60] He notes that his own thoughts on this issue are 'very much in line' with those of Dutch Catholic theologian, Piet Schoonenberg.[61]

The doctrine of the two natures   This constitutes the fourth and final legacy of patristic times to the christological tradition that Robinson sets out to scrutinise. This doctrine of two separate 'natures', each with its own inalienable properties, and yet belonging to the one subject, was regarded as essential if Jesus was to be both Son of God and Son of Man.[62] Robinson is entirely unconvinced of the need to speak of Jesus having a second, divine nature since he interprets it as implying that Jesus possessed 'his own independent divinity'. He acknowledges that 'obviously Christ was a man', but states that 'our questions relate to the functions for which it is alleged that he required a second, divine nature'.[63] He adds:

> if we wish, as assuredly as the New Testament does, to go on to say that Jesus' words and works are not simply those of any man faithful and open to God but the self-expression of God acting in and through him, this is still not because there were some things he could not say or do as a man, and which therefore required of him a second nature, but because what he said and did must also be seen as 'bespeaking' God as well as man.[64]

being assumed by the *hypostasis* or person of the *Logos*). *HFG*, 107.   59 Ibid., 106.   60 Ibid., 201, n. 89. Robinson has an extended quotation from Karl Barth here upholding the necessity of the doctrine to guard against Christ's being one man among many whom God could have taken. See *Church Dogmatics*, vol. IV/2 (Edinburgh, 1958), 48. Robinson then goes on to summarise Barth's argument by quoting van Buren's paraphrase of it: 'Jesus was indeed a man as we are men, but the fact that he existed as a man was totally dependent on the fact that God the Word, the eternal Logos, had called him into being to be the historical bearer of this divine Word'. See van Buren, *The Secular Meaning of the Gospel* (London, 1963), 31. Robinson goes on to assert that 'this does not mean that he could not also be "taken" out of countless millions. For he is elected not for exclusive privilege but for representative service ...'   61 *HFG.*, 109, n. 44. This observation is to be found in a footnote added after Robinson had completed writing *HFG*. He describes Schoonenberg's rejection of the anhypostatic manhood as well as that of the two natures of Christ as 'a real breakthrough in Roman Catholic Christology'. See Schoonenberg, *The Christ* (London, 1972), 54-66 and 80-91.   62 Son of Man is used here as equivalent to Christ's humanity. Admittedly a number of the Fathers used it in this way, but in the New Testament, as well as indicating some human properties and activities of the incarnate Son of God, this designation also refers to some divine prerogatives: for instance, being the final Judge of all nations.   63 *HFG*, 112.   64 Ibid., 113.

Robinson thus concludes with the request that henceforth christology should speak 'not of one superhuman person with two natures, divine and human, but of one human person of whom we must use two languages, man-language and God-language'.[65]

Robinson's proposals for a new christology
Robinson's assertions about the shifts that have occurred in modern religious consciousness and his criticism of some of the principal tenets of classical christology is a *cri de coeur* against any attempt to tie up our talk about Jesus Christ with outmoded views of the universe, be they mythological or onto-logical, which modern humanity, with the best will in the world, cannot adopt. These two ways of expressing reality only serve today to

> make God less real rather than more real. And the same is true in Christo-logy. The Christ becomes evacuated of reality – a remote, unreal, docetic figure, who can be God for us only at the expense of being a genuine human being. The mythology of the pre-existent person and the meta-physic of the two natures has very limited cash-value in our world – though their devotional and "antique" value (as part of the 'poetry' of the old city) are not to be underestimated or despised.[66]

What does Robinson propose 'to put in the place of this currency for those for whom it has lost its purchasing power'?[67] Two salient points emerge. The first is that he is drawn towards 'an earlier way of putting things'; a (third) way of representing reality,[68] which he believes to be basic to both the Old and the New Testaments and which 'is not tied to the supernaturalist projection (though it can be expressed in terms of it, as God from on high lighting upon and raising up a man). And this freedom is surely a strength today when that projection is so counter-productive of reality'.[69] We are speaking of what he terms, the *functional* mode.[70] The second point is that he is drawn towards making evolving creation the primary focus of the incarnation. Thus Gerald O'Collins has commented that in his christology, 'one detects, peeping over Robinson's shoulder the looming figure of Teilhard'.[71] We shall first address his arguments concerning a functional christology.

---

65 Ibid.   66 Ibid., 195-6.   67 Ibid., 196.   68 Ibid., 182.   69 Ibid., 196.   70 Ibid., 32. We must acknowledge Robinson's reliance here on a classification by C. van Peursen, that humanity has moved in the ways in which it has sought to represent reality from a mythological way of thinking to an ontological, and is moving from an ontological to a functional. See van Peursen, 'Man and Reality - The History of Human Thought', *The Student World*, 56 (1963) 13-21; reprinted in J. Bowden & J. Richmond (eds), *A Reader in Contemporary Thought* (London, 1971), 115-26.   71 G. O'Collins, *What Are They Saying*

A functional approach   We have already seen above how classical christology has been greatly indebted to the categories of myth and metaphysics. We shall not rehearse again Robinson's reflections on them, save to remark that today they are 'no longer thought of as representing the real, essential events of which occurrences in the contingent, existential order are the reflection or consequence.'[72] Indeed, Robinson argues that the truth is to be found in the contrary position:

> these mythical or metaphysical 'events' are ways of speaking (and to us fairly strange ways of speaking) about the profoundest realities of *this* historical order. The real world ('where we are down here') is the starting-point: the rest is interpretation, in terms of the imagination or the intellect. This means that we have to start any Christology today from this end – from this world rather than the heavenly, the human rather than the divine. To begin by asking Anselm's question, *Cur deus homo?* – why (or who) did God become man? – is to move from the unknown to the known rather than *vice versa*.[73]

This third way of representing reality which Robinson is proposing, the *functional* approach, will be seen to assert identity not in terms of substances (ontology) or substantives (mythology), but in terms of verbs. As we have observed, Robinson argues that modern humanity experiences very grave, if not insurmountable, difficulty in trying to make its own the language of agencies or essences behind the scene. The language of *function*, however, provides no such stumbling-block. Indeed, Robinson claims that it has the advantage of appealing naturally to an empirical, scientifically trained generation (like the present one). He is conscious that the functional approach seems vulnerable to the charge that it 'looks as if it is saying much less than the other two, having neither the robust rotundity of personification nor the solidity of substance. Yet it is another, equally serious way of asserting identity'.[74] Through its lenses, the Christ

> is the one who does what God does, who represents him. He stands in the place of God, speaking and acting for him. The issue is not where he comes from or what he is made of. He is not a divine or semi-divine being who comes from the other side. He is a human figure raised up from among his brothers to be the instrument of God's decisive work and to stand in a relationship to him to which no other man is called. The issue is whether in seeing him men see the Father, whether in mercy and judgement, he *functions* as God, whether he *is* God to and for them.[75]

About Jesus?, 2nd ed. (New York/Ramsey, 1983), 16.   **72** *HFG*, 32.   **73** Ibid., 33.   **74** Ibid., 183.   **75** Ibid., 183-4.

Robinson is also quick to stress that this functional mode is not to be pre-judged as a newfangled idea. He asserts that it has a deep affinity with the Hebraic prophetic tradition before the latter was influenced by the currents of thought that entered Judaism in the centuries immediately before and after the Christian era.[76] He spells out the difference that the functional approach makes to presenting Christ's divinity or identity with God by introducing a rather trying contrast between the different models of royalty to be found in contemporary Japan and Sweden. The former, he tells us, has much in common with the mytho-logical and ontological stories of the incarnation which use the image of a divine visitant, of the king who becomes a commoner. This has presupposed two orders of being: 'The king is a royal personage, *not* a commoner. He may enter upon his royal estate, he may become in every respect a commoner, but, like the Japanese emperor, nothing can ever stop him *being* different. He remains a being of com-pletely other blood.' Whereas when we examine the latter, the Swedish model, we discover that 'the king is a commoner, who has a royal office. He embodies royalty, he exercises it, discloses it, wears it. He is part of the ordinary human scene. He does not have to come on to the scene or make a visitation: he has grown up within it. You may see him on the streets anyday. There is nothing different to see – yet you have seen the king.'[77] The consequence of all this for christology is that 'we may view the Christ as a man who embodies divinity, or what the gospels call the kingly rule of God, who exercises it, discloses it, wears it – rather than a divine being who takes on humanity. He is a completely ordinary human being, a "com-mon man", born and bred, who is nevertheless the carrier of the divine disclosure – all that Barth magnificently expounds as "the royal man" '.[78]

He firmly rejects the charge that to speak of Jesus in such terms is reductionist and cautions that we recognise that '*any* contemporary Christology is bound to appear reductionist compared with that done in the more "full-blooded" (but actually rather bloodless) categories of classical ontology'.[79] He entreats us not to succumb to the mendacious pre-supposition that 'what is sometimes called a "degree Christology" is somehow lower-class or less respectable than one which asserts that Jesus was different *in kind* from all other men'.[80] To do so is to

---

76 Ibid., 184. Following van Peursen, Robinson argues that the first transition reflected in the specific field of christology was the shift from Jewish categories to Greek. 'The former viewed finality in terms of the eschatological act of God in history, embodied in the sending of the Messiah as saviour and judge of everything in heaven and earth and under the earth. The latter saw ultimate reality not in terms of final act but of timeless being, in the categories of substance rather than will.' Ibid., 33.   77 Ibid., 184-5.   78 Ibid., 185.   79 Ibid., 34.   80 Ibid., 35. Jacques Dupuis is unimpressed by Robinson's (and Macquarrie's; see Chapter 5, n. 45, above) 'degree Christology'. He comments that 'no matter how valid is the upward advance toward the christological mystery, more often than not, Christologies following it fail to reach out adequately to Jesus-the-Son-of-God. Christology thus becomes a "degree Christology", in which Jesus is reduced to an ordinary man in whom God is present to an

threaten, if not to destroy, his total solidarity with all other men.[81] In insisting on the *Christus pro nobis*, the Christ for us, Robinson forewarns that we must be 'prepared for the charges of cultural relativism and psychological subjectivism which this has constantly brought into Christian history. But it is a risk that any genuinely incarnational theology must be ready to run. For the truth with which Christology wrestles is essentially of the absolute *made relative* – "the mystery", as Paul puts it, of "Christ *in you*" [Col 1:27]'.[82]

Evolving creation and the incarnation   As we saw above in our exposition of Robinson's arguments concerning the four shifts in contemporary humanity's understanding of reality, modern consciousness is said to have passed from a static to a dynamic way of looking at the world. While Robinson does not delay much on the intricacies of what is involved in this judgement, it is clear that his christology adopts this new, dynamic *Weltanschauung* with its awareness of creation as something evolving. It differs profoundly from the older vision of a once-for-all creation, of a number of fixed species, and of the world as an unchanging stage upon which successive generations play their essentially representative role. One of the great champions of the new evolutionary way of thinking was Pierre Teilhard de Chardin (1881-1955) and Robinson makes frequent reference to him in his various writings.[83] This French Jesuit theologian and scientist of high distinction set out to combine a dynamic world-view with the central teachings of Christian theology. His starting-point is scientific and naturalistic.[84] B.C. Butler has summarised his project by first noting that Teilhard de Chardin

extraordinary degree. In such cases, Christology from below ends up in a "low Christology".' Dupuis states that Robinson is one 'who expressly professes a "low", "degree" Christology'. See his *Who Do You Say I Am?* (Maryknoll, New York, 1994), 35 and 38, n. 31. Illtyd Trethowan argues that Robinson's 'degree Christology' constitutes 'a loss of contact with the Christian tradition' and laments the fact that Robinson's is an example of 'the current tendency, not only among Protestants but also to some extent among Catholic theologians, to concentrate so exclusively upon safeguarding Christ's humanity from any suggestion of docetism that the need to safeguard God's imprescriptible absoluteness is lost sight of, if not disavowed'. See his review of *HFG, Downside Review*, 91 (1973) 233-4. Carl E. Braaten applies Karl Barth's famous criticism of Wilhelm Hermann's christology to Robinson's: it is 'a case of trying to raise the level of a lake by means of a handpump'. Braaten proceeds to assert that Robinson 'ignores that our interest in Jesus lies not in all the respects in which he is just like us; it lies in the essential respect in which he is other that us and can therefore be and do for us what we cannot for ourselves. The assertion that he is one of us would have no soteriological significance on its own. His identity with us derives its salvific power from the personal unity with God the Father'. See his review of *HFG, Journal of Religion*, 55 (1975) 484-5. 81 Ibid., 210. Thus Robinson comments: 'If one has to choose [between a difference in kind or degree], I should side with those who opt for a "degree Christology" – however enormous the degree.' Ibid., 209-10. 82 Ibid., 35. 83 Thus the index to *HFG* carries eleven entries under Teilhard de Chardin. 84 Macquarrie, *Twentieth-Century Religious Thought*, 4th ed 272.

identifies the world as a place of progressively emergent reality, in which temporality and change are of the essence of things; a world in which we can trace out in retrospect, the upward path from sub-atomic particles, on through atoms, molecules, living cells, mammals, to man and, in the humanity of Christ, to man's own highest peak; from which point we turn to look forward, our vision directed by what we have learnt from the past, to an Omega-point of ultimate fulfilment.[85]

As Macquarrie states, for Teilhard de Chardin God is the final rather than the efficient cause of the universe, drawing all things towards perfection in himself.[86] Like Thornton, Teilhard de Chardin sees Christ as the centre of the evolutionary process. Thus Macquarrie comments that in the Teilhardian scheme of things, 'Christ is, so to speak, the reflection into the heart of the process of the omega-point which stands at its end. Christ assures us of its reality by actualizing it in our midst, and in the Christian society of self-transcending love the end is already being realized'.[87]

Robinson characterises theology as *logos* (talk) about *theos*, and christology as *logos* about *Christos*, the mystery of theos incarnate.[88] And building upon the Teilhardian intuition, Robinson claims that in the mystery of *Christos*, of Immanuel or God with us, we meet 'the primal mystery as it is earthed, expressed, embodied in the process of nature and history, reaching its fullest articulation (so far) in the meaning and destiny of man'.[89]

At this point, we shall turn to examine how Robinson brings the insights gleaned here to bear upon his christological constructions. It goes without saying that he regards every human being as a product of the evolutionary process, and he will argue that, if the genuine humanity of Christ is not to be threatened, then he too, like everyone else, must be 'a genuine product of the evolutionary process'.[90] Robinson is thus demanding that theology take the functional language of the bible seriously, and he recognises in a Teilhardian evolutionary consciousness, a new openness to this.[91] It follows logically, then, that Christ 'will have all the pre-history of man in his genes',[92] since 'to be a member of the species *homo sapiens* includes having genes and chromosomes shaped and transmitted by millions of years of evolution. No one can just *become* a man out of the blue: a genuine man (as opposed to a replica) can only come out of the process, not into it'.[93]

To have it any other way would be to erect, as it were, 'a *cordon sanitaire* between the manhood of Jesus and what the Fathers called "common" humanity'.[94] Robinson acknowledges, however, that from the time of the Fathers to Karl

85 This summary comes at the beginning of the Catholic Bishop Butler's highly critical review of *HFG* in the *Heythrop Journal*, 14 (1973) 425. 86 Macquarrie, *Twentieth-Century Religious Thought*, 4th ed, 273. 87 Ibid. 88 *HFG*, 5-6. 89 Ibid., 6. 90 Ibid., 148. 91 Ibid., 202. 92 Ibid., 42. 93 Ibid., 43. 94 Ibid., 48. He sees the traditional interpretation

Barth, there has been a persistent tendency 'to assume that Jesus could not be both a genuine product of the process and the Word of God to it'. Thus he goes on to assert that there has always been a presupposition (using Whiteheadian terms), that 'the divine initiative must come as an external exception to, rather that the supreme exemplification of, the created order ...'[95] Robinson's difficulties with this line of reasoning are obvious to us after seeing his objections to anything which might undercut the genuineness of Christ's humanity. With the assistance of Teilhard de Chardin, and other writers who stand within the tradition of process philosophy, notably Norman Pittenger,[96] Robinson is confident that he has overcome classical christology's need of recourse to supernaturalistic language in order to speak of the incarnation. This has become possible because the new way of thinking has provided the categories 'to see the natural and the supernatural not as two layers of being that have to be joined together, so much as two sets of languages, man-language and God-language, in which it is possible to speak of the single cosmic process. In other words, what we are talking about is not two storeys, but two stories'.[97]

In this new dispensation, Christ is to be thought of as a product of the process, Robinson goes on, rather than as an invader of it. He appeals to Whitehead's observation that God is the chief cause, not the only cause. There is no overriding or overruling: 'there is eruption rather than inruption. The Incarnation does not mean insertion into the living stream, an intervention by God in the form of a man, but the embodiment, the realization of God in man'.[98] This means therefore, for example, that Jesus Christ is to be seen as 'a slow product of the species *homo sapiens*, whom God raised up though the normal process of heredity and environment... [not] an afterthought or an *ad hoc* creation, the Christ is prepared for and elected from a progeny as countless as the sands of the sea. He is indeed selected, "taken from among men", to be their representative before God.'[99] Thus Christ has been in the process from the beginning, and in this sense Robinson believes that 'we may speak of the eternal generation of the Son'.[100]

It is not our task at this point to offer a critique of Robinson, but two important questions do press for mention, and he alludes to them himself (saying that

of the virgin birth story as an example of such a cordon sanitaire. **95** Ibid., 200. We shall recall that this was in accordance with Thornton's view; something for which he was heavily criticised by such process theologians as Pittenger. **96** The index to *HFG* carries fifteen entries under his name: in one of them, Robinson comments that Pittenger's *The Word Incarnate* (London, 1959), 'seems to me to be one of the great books in this field'. Ibid., 202. **97** Ibid., 116–17. Robinson adds that 'the one is natural, scientific, descriptive. The other is supernatural, mythological and interpretive. The former views the course of events in the categories of an evolutionary cosmology, the latter in terms of "moments" like the Creation, the Fall, the Incarnation, the Parousia'. **98** Ibid., 203. **99** Ibid., 200. Robinson notes that the significance of this last category, Christ as the 'representative of God', the one who dares stand *in loco dei*, 'is brilliantly worked out by Dorothee Sölle' in her book, *Christ the Representative* (London, 1967). Ibid., 191. **100** Ibid., 203.

Moule[101] has already raised them): first, is the Christ-event being interpreted here as simply an 'emerging' as by evolution or as a result of 'human striving'?[102] We can note that Colin Gunton is unhappy with the direction of Robinson's argument. He comments that 'if there is an incarnation, it takes place on the initiative of God. The alternative, and it is what appears to be the teaching of this book [*The Human Face of God*], is to place the initiative somewhere in the created order and idolatrously to divinize either man or the process from which he emerges'.[103]

And second, is being a member of a 'genuine evolutionary process' not a rather impoverished understanding of what it means to be human? Surely there must be some more personal, more interior criterion to bring out the full and the true humanness of Jesus?[104] (It seems fair to suggest that we might have expected more on this point from one who had written his doctoral dissertation on the personalist philosophy of Martin Buber. We shall return to this criticism, and others besides, later).[105]

ROBINSON AND CHRIST'S PRE-EXISTENCE

If one sets out to articulate an adequate account of the doctrine of the incarnation, there must come a point where one faces the question of Christ's pre-existence. In Paul, in Hebrews and in John (and in other parts of the New Testament as well), classical christology has seen Christ presented as a pre-existent divine being who is continuous in personal existence with Jesus of Nazareth. This divine being is thought of not merely as having existed with God from all eternity, certainly from before creation, but also as having appeared on various occasions in Israel's history. The tradition has tended to see Christ, Robinson ventures, as 'an eternal, heavenly being who enters the conditions of our history and humanity to dwell within it from the *outside* [italics mine]'.[106] From what we have already seen

---

101 See C.F.D. Moule, 'The Manhood of Jesus in the New Testament', in S.W. Sykes, & J.P. Clayton (eds), *Christ, Faith and History* (Cambridge, 1972), 107.   102 *HFG*, 205.   103 Gunton then proceeds to assert: 'that this is in fact Dr Robinson's position is suggested by his frequent appeals to the incredible and nonsensical process theology'. See his review of *HFG*, *Theology*, 76 (1973) 487   104 Robert Butterworth has suggested that Robinson would have been better employed in exploring the concept of faith as being definitive of humanness rather than seeing it as arising from one's belonging to the cosmic process. See his 'Bishop Robinson and Christology', *Religious Studies*, 11 (1976) 85.   105 As a hint of Robinson's reaction to such criticism, we note an assertion of Pittenger, approvingly quoted by Robinson: 'emergent humanity is itself the instrument for expressive Deity; the Word is made flesh, in one of our own kind, our Brother, without over-riding or denying the humanity which is ours, but rather crowning and completing all that is implicit in humanity from its very beginning. The divine intention ... is ... "enmanned" among us'. See his *The Word Incarnate*, 131; quoted *HFG*, 206.   106 *HFG*, 143.

of Robinson's thought, it is obvious that this doctrine presents a huge question mark against the approach to the incarnation which he has been proposing.[107] For, if the doctrine can be traced to the New Testament, and the writers there can be shown to uphold a doctrine of a pre-existent divine being who was personally continuous in existence with Jesus of Nazareth, then there are surely good grounds to indicate that they must have held some sort of a doctrine of a God-man, of a Christ who was something *more* than a man. This line of reasoning stands in stark contrast to that displayed in Robinson's christology: a superhuman Christ would not be a *genuine* man at all (not a genuine product of the evolutionary process).

Hardly surprisingly, Robinson flatly rejects such a supernaturalistic understanding of Christ. He is unable to locate any scriptural evidence to substantiate classical christology's claim that the writings of Paul, the Letter to the Hebrews or John uphold a personal pre-existence of a distinct divine being. He does not deny the presence of pre-existence language in the New Testament. Indeed, he states that 'since it is so deeply imbedded in the New Testament presentation of Christ – far more deeply than that of the virgin birth – it is at least worth asking what the New Testament authors had in mind when they used it and whether they saw it as the threat to humanity that we do – and if not, why not ...'[108] He argues that pre-existence language is certainly not to be interpreted in the terms proposed by the classical, supernaturalistic understanding since it inevitably results in the undermining of the authentic humanity of Christ.[109] Thus he comments: 'I have felt that there must be some other explanation, and that our dilemma did not exist for the New Testament writers because, in some way, we are attributing to them presuppositions which they did not share.'[110]

This hunch forces Robinson to go back and examine the roots of the doctrine of pre-existence.[111] He claims, to begin with, that it was not part of the extremely

---

107 Robinson can take comfort from the favourable estimation of his thesis written by the New Testament scholar, Reginald H. Fuller, when he comments that 'Robinson's basic definition of Jesus as a man emerging from the nexus of human history yet fully embodying the divine is entirely acceptable to the New Testament, shocking though it may be for traditional orthodoxy'. See his review of *HFG*, *Journal of Biblical Literature*, 93 (1974) 138. 108 *HFG*, 144.   109 It is a basic presupposition of Robinson's thought, repeatedly stated, that the New Testament always upholds the genuine humanity of Christ. Thus, for example, the Fourth Gospel, which is often (falsely) accused of being docetic, speaks frequently of Jesus as a 'man': indeed he notes that 'no other gospel uses the word "man" anything like as much of Jesus': the figures for *anthropos* are as follows, Matthew once; Mark once; Luke six times; John sixteen times and for *aner*, Luke once; John once. Ibid., 171 and n. 136.   110 Ibid., 146.   111 Robinson has commented, however, that 'this is not, of course, to say that we are committed to the language of pre-existence. Even if it were for us a natural way of speaking, it is probably by now too much identified, as Knox says, with presuppositions that are destructive of humanity to be rescued to say what I have argued the biblical writers were meaning by it'. Ibid., 179.

primitive christology which is found, he argues (controversially), in Acts 3 and 'whose essence may be summed up in the proclamation: "we know who the Messiah will be".'[112] Nor is this doctrine in Acts 2, where it 'is *by virtue of the Resurrection* that Jesus is Lord and Christ'.[113] He sees its entry upon the scene with the recognition that 'at the Resurrection Jesus was merely designated "with power" what eternally he was (Rom. 1:4); and his pre-existence is explicitly recognised (Phil 2:6) as equivalent in Greek terms of his "foreordination" (Acts 3:20)'.[114]

It is thus clear to Robinson that the New Testament writers had a very different understanding of what lies behind those texts (which are seen as upholding the doctrine of Christ's pre-existence) from what was to emerge soon afterwards.[115] He believes that pre-existence language grew out of the earlier language of foreordination[116] and that 'the test [of this assumption] lies in the detailed exegesis of the New Testament'.[117] This we shall attend to in due course.

Before examining what this very early (if not earliest) understanding of pre-existence was,[118] we need to recall the classical doctrine of pre-existence which was to emerge so quickly on its heels, and which was to be so influential down

112 'The Most Primitive Christology of All', in *Twelve New Testament Studies*, 142-3. The gist of this argument is the belief that Jesus did not become the Christ – even at his resurrection, but *would become* that when the time came for him to return and to function as such in the final judgement. 113 Ibid., 142. 114 Ibid., 151. 115 *HFG*, 179. 116 Robinson seems to be indicating here, as Knox points out, 'that the idea of pre-existence did not emerge until the Church had left its originally Jewish milieu'. See his *The Humanity and Divinity of Christ* (Cambridge, 1968), 11. This is a moot point: evidence coming from the New Testament and from extra-New Testament sources reveals that in first century Palestine there was already a strong Hellenistic influence. Thus H.D. Betz, for example, has commented that in 'the New Testament, even in its oldest layers of tradition, it is taken for granted that Jesus and his disciples spoke Greek in their daily life'. See his 'Hellenism', in D.N. Freedman (ed. in chief), *The Anchor Bible Dictionary*, vol. 3 (New York, 1992), 130; hereafter *ABD*. For a more detailed discussion, see J.A. Fitzmyer, *A Wandering Aramean* (Missoula, 1979). 117 *HFG*, 152, n. 18. 118 A consistent, though controversial, theme in Robinson's writings is his belief that the New Testament was written, in its entirety, before AD 70. He has advanced this view in (the technically written) *Redating the New Testament* (1976), and (in the popularly styled) *Can We Trust the New Testament?* (1977). Robinson's main argument is that the New Testament's silence on the destruction of Jerusalem in AD 70 suggests that the whole New Testament was composed before that event took place. This argument has been severely criticised. J.A. Fitzmyer who, in commenting on the first of these books, described it as 'a collection of the whimpers and niggling fears of New Testament interpreters just right of centre. And the most telling thing about it is Robinson's own admission in the small popular book that it supplies "reassuring answers" not for the wise, but for the conservatism of the committed. And that says a lot about it all'. See Fitzmyer, 'Two Views of New Testament Interpretation: Popular and Technical', *Interpretation*, 32 (1978) 313. John Knox has described Robinson's proposals for redating the New Testament as 'indubitably bold, and in my own friendly judgement, even "rash"'. See his 'Robinson and the Meaning of New Testament Scholarship', *Theology*, 92 (1989) 261.

the Christian centuries. We shall then accompany Robinson through his exegesis of those texts that traditional christology has interpreted as upholding the personal pre-existence of Christ.

The classical understanding of pre-existence (as personal)

Robinson summarises the classical position on the doctrine of Christ's pre-existence, which emerged through the patristic period, and became explicit in the doctrine of the *anhypostasia*, in the following terms:

> pre-existence meant the prior existence in heaven of an individual *hypostasis* or *persona* who was in the fullness of time to become the subject of the human nature taken from the virgin Mary. The Logos was already in the fullest sense a person (of the Trinity). At the Incarnation, he did not become an individual; he became human – without, of course, ceasing to be divine. He was a being, who did not start like us but was *made like* us by sharing our life.[119]

Robinson's reaction to this classical understanding is, as we should expect, decidedly unfavourable. The details of his argument concerning how it arose are, however, fragmentary and incomplete. If I have understood him correctly, he claims that its shape is heavily indebted to the Gnostic concept of a supernatural heavenly Man, 'not of our clay, who is celestial as *opposed* to earthly, spiritual *rather than* material'.[120] He is profoundly uncomfortable with the notion of the hypostatization of an individual heavenly person which is subsequently implied. He finds the concept of a *being, who did not start like us* 'difficult (if not impossible) to combine with Jesus being, with the rest of us, a genuine product of the evolutionary process'.[121] It is certainly incompatible, Robinson argues, with genuine

---

119 Ibid., 148.   **120** Ibid., 168. He does refer, however, to the increasing importance of Gnostic trends in first-century Judaic thought. And although Robinson comments that 'it is not part of our purpose here to go into the historical question of just how and when this change occurred ...', he does, nonetheless, counsel: 'it is generally believed that this hypostatization of the Logos in ontological terms stemmed directly, if only in part, from the personification in late Judaism of the Word of God in mythological terms - along with similar personifications of the Wisdom of God and the Spirit of God. It would be tempting to jump to the conclusion that the shift in presuppositions I have spoken of is to be located at the point of transition from the mythological categories of Jewish thought to the ontological categories of Greek thought. But this transposition, however important, I believe merely consolidated a change that had already occurred *within* late Judaism, from the more functional and historical way of thinking characteristic of the prophets and early apocalyptic to the more mythological and speculative thought-forms of later apocalyptic, mysticism and philosophy.' Ibid., 149.   **121** Ibid. Thornton, conversely, would see no such difficulty here. He resolutely argues that Christ is not a product of the organic series. See his

humanity, and since the New Testament always upholds the authenticity of Christ's humanity, is also irreconcilable with the scriptural testimony.[122]

Pre-existence in late Judaism and early Christianity

Robinson is doubtful whether Paul, John and the author to the Hebrews are really presupposing in their use of pre-existence language any more than the *personification*, already familiar in Hellenistic Judaism, of the Word, Spirit and Son of God as agencies of God's activity.[123] Thus he comments that the New Testament 'can best be read if we do *not* [italics mine] bring to it the assumption that in the Judaism in which these writers were nurtured the notion of pre-existence already involved the hypostatization of an individual heavenly person'.[124] Robinson claims that there need be no suggestion here that he was 'God by nature' and had to 'become' man; the weakness of the classical approach.[125] He is aware of christology's great indebtedness to the Wisdom Literature for so much of its language.[126] Thus he notes, for example, that the similarities between the New Testament's treatment of Christ (as Wisdom, Spirit, Word, and Son of God) and Wisdom Literature's[127] personification of *Wisdom* as God's constant companion and agent in creation, who 'tabernacles'[128] among God's people and in age after age enters into holy souls, making them prophets and friends of God. He emphasises the point that there is no suggestion in the Wisdom Literature that 'these figures were thought of as existent or pre-existent beings with a life of their own'.[129] Nor does this indwelling threaten the common humanity or connections with the human race of those who were indwelt.[130] Similarly, when we turn from the Wisdom Literature to the New Testament, Robinson argues that 'we are still in the same world of discourse'.[131] He is thus confident that he can speak of the Christ of the New Testament as only 'the divine personification', while simultaneously spurning any suggestion that he 'was not a man in every sense of the word'.[132] (Robinson is skating on thin ice here: is he suggesting that the Jews of

The Incarnate Lord, 228.   **122** Ibid., 151.   **123** *RR*, 65.   **124** *HFG*, 151.   **125** *RR*, 67.   **126** *HFG*, 152.   **127** Prov 8:22-31, Wis 7:22-8:1 and Sir 24:1-22   **128** See Sir 24:8 *LXX* with Jn 1:14.   **129** *HFG*, 150.   **130** Ibid., 152. Robinson goes on: 'nor, of course, is it ever implied that those - prophets and priests, kings and craftsmen – to whom the *Word* of God came or upon whom his *Spirit* descended were not completely normal human beings. The personification of all these functions, attributes or activities of God, which, of course, were eternal like himself, constituted no problem'.   **131** Ibid., 152. Thus Robinson can say of the prologue to John's Gospel that it presents Jesus, in whom 'the pre-existent Word became embodied in a single human individual who was so faithful a reproduction of it as to be its complete reflection and incarnation. But there is no suggestion that this individual was not a man in every sense of the word'. Ibid., 152-3. It has to be put to Robinson at this point that in saying that Christ was perfectly and fully a man, there is surely no conflict in maintaining, with the theological tradition, that he was not *merely* a man?   **132** Ibid., 153. At this stage a caveat may be in order: while it is claimed that the category of personification does not threaten the genuine

the Old Testament worshipped what was only a divine personification? Surely it is a divine Person who is worshipped?)

To do justice to both the complete humanity of Jesus and the initiative of God, Robinson argues that theology must disentangle the New Testament's understanding of the doctrine of pre-existence from the supernaturalistic form it was to develop later. In other words, the doctrine of pre-existence should be seen for what it really is: a *myth* which developed as

> the result of Christians having known Jesus as *a person*, as a real historical individual. To register the conviction that in this man was fulfilled and embodied the meaning of God reaching back to the very beginning, they proclaim him as his Word, his Wisdom, his Image, his Son, from all eternity. In so doing they read back, or retroject, his human personhood as the subject of the divine personification – just as they project it in his heavenly 'post-existence' as a person seated at God's right hand.[133]

Robinson characterises this as 'a harmless and indeed a profound myth', 'a way of speaking' that does not threaten Christ's humanity.[134] 'Whether the transition was

humanity of Christ, the question must be posed as to whether it is adequate to the task of upholding Christ's divinity.   133 *RR*, 65.   134 Robinson contends that 'the understanding of pre-existence in late Judaism and early Christianity' is close to that of 'a life, power or activity (whether divine or spiritual) which is not a person [but which] comes to embodiment and expression (whether partial or total) in an individual human being'. It is certainly an altogether more satisfactory approach, he claims, than that proffered by the classical one when it states, to quote Robinson, that 'what is pre-existent and takes flesh is "an individual substance of a rational nature" (to use a later definition of a person)'. *HFG*, 147. It is also worth noting here in passing that Robinson, in coming to this judgement, makes reference to the Hindu and Buddhist understandings of incarnation (and he does so in the most sweeping of ways: no mention is made of the different nuances in thought on this, and indeed other matters, within both of these complex traditions). Robinson asserts that the Hindu stresses the continuity of individual substance or soul, which re-enters the world in   a new body (whether of an animal or a man), retaining its identity and theoretically its memory of its previous state. The Buddhist concept, on the other hand (and through Pythagoreanism in Platonism) 'sees the individual as negated and dispersed by death - there is no continuity of that individual soul any more than there is of that individual body. Yet the spirit is no more destroyed than the matter: it is reunited with its source, and emanations of it are released into all the world to reappear in new configurations or individuals ... Thus, the Buddha can be incarnate in, and the source of enlightenment to, countless other individuals, and a lama can become incarnate in a particular successor ... in the sense that a special portion of his spirit ... finds embodiment in the one designated, and discerned by revelation, to be the inheritor of it. This concept as the phrase "portion of his spirit" indicates, is not alien from the biblical notion of the spirit of Elijah resting upon Elisha [2 Kings 2:9-15] or of John the Baptist being Elijah's *redivivus* ... One could even say that this is how Paul and John see the spirit of Christ released by the death of the individual Jesus to become incorporated, as his *alter ego*, in the body of his followers.' Ibid., 147-8.

made in the New Testament or after it', Robinson asserts that it was not long until the pre-existence language of the Wisdom Literature and the New Testament came to be interpreted to mean that a divine Being, subsequently designated the Second Person of the Trinity, came down from heaven, walked the earth as a man, before returning whence he came. The lamentable consequence of this for christology, according to Robinson, was that all too soon the order of the New Testament testimony is reversed and the divine Person becomes the subject of Jesus' human experience. The myth is transformed into a metaphysical riddle and 'thereby his humanity is rendered questionable, as it never is in the New Testament ...'[135]

In the next section we shall see Robinson scrutinise some of the texts which are associated with the doctrine of pre-existence; for now it is enough to note that he holds that none of the various New Testament affirmations of Jesus (whatever they may be)[136]

> is intended to suggest that Jesus was not fundamentally a *man*, with all the antecedents of every other man, who was yet called from the womb to embody his unique role. *Qua* Son, indeed, he is not of this world and

135 Ibid., 65. Robinson, elsewhere, speaking specifically about John's Gospel, notes a similar process at work in relation to the doctrine of the Trinity: he claims that 'patristic and medieval theology misused the Fourth Gospel by taking its christological statements out of context and giving them a meaning which John never intended. Functional language about the Son and the Spirit being sent into the world was transposed into that of eternal and internal relationships between Persons of the godhead and words like "generation" and "procession" given technical meanings which New Testament usage simply did not sub-stantiate ...' He notes Schillebeeckx's utterance (in his *Christ*, [London, 1977], 875, n. 57) that 'there is no basis in Johannine theology for the later scholastic theology of the pro-cession of the Son from the Father within the Trinity per modum generationis (birth)'. See Robinson, *The Priority of John* (London, 1985), 397, n. 156; hereafter *PJ*. This is a highly controversial assertion: it can be argued, for example, that the language of *sending* in John represents economically what happens eternally. 136 Thus to mention some of the New Testament affirmations about Jesus that Robinson refers to: the agent of God's purpose from the start (Jn 17:24; 1 Pet 1:20); the Son who is uniquely the reflection of God's person and character (Heb 1:3); the Son who, as such, occupies the place of the Wisdom of God (Wis 7:25f.). See *HFG*, 154. Robinson goes on to say that 'it is a matter of indifference whether he [Christ] is represented as saying, with Luke, The Wisdom of God said "I will send them prophets and messengers" [11:49] or, with Matthew, "I send you ... prophets, sages, and teachers" [23:34]. For in issuing the invitation, "Come to me ... and I will give you rest" [Mt 11:28-30], he is echoing the call of God [Ex 33:14] and Wisdom [Sir 24:19; 51:23-27]. It is thus entirely natural that Paul should see in Christ the pre-existent wisdom and image of God, with primacy over all created things, and the power of nature and history [1 Cor 1:24; 10:4; 2 Cor 4:4; Col 1:15-20]. Natural, too, that John should view him as the creative Logos who was from the beginning with God [Jn 1:1-3], and portray him as speaking as one who was before Abraham [Jn 8:58], and indeed shared the Father's glory before the foundation of the world'. Ibid.

does not have his origin in space and time, where anyone can know and locate it [n. 44: Jn 8:14, 23]. And yet as the man from Nazareth he is born and bred completely within the local human situation, with a parentage that is open to anyone's inspection – and insinuation [n. 45: 1:45f; 6:42; 7:27, 40-42; 8:41].[137]

Robinson's exegesis of the pre-existence texts
Robinson is chiefly a New Testament scholar,[138] and before looking at his treatment of the Epistle to the Hebrews, we do well to recall that the prime purpose of his exegesis of this text, along with the writings of Paul, and the Fourth Gospel, is to advance his thesis that none of these writers intended to promote a doctrine of the personal pre-existence of Christ.

The Epistle to the Hebrews   Robinson asserts that in this book there is to be found, more than anywhere else in the New Testament, the juxtaposition of the language of eternal pre-existence (and post-existence)[139] with that of adoptionism,[140] and apparently without any sense of discomfort or discrepancy.[141] This is so, runs Robinson's now familiar argument, because the author 'is starting from a different set of presuppositions from those which prevailed later'.[142]

In alluding to the author of Hebrews' understanding of pre-existence, Robinson refers to the following texts: 1:1-3, 9; 2:7, 9, 10, 17; 3:14, 5:7-9; 7:3, 5, 10, 14, 13.[143] A brief look at Robinson's treatment of 1:1-3, 2:17 and 5:7-9 will be

---

137 Ibid., 154.   138 This is the expressed opinion of the following scholars: J. Knox in 'Robinson and the Meaning of New Testament Scholarship', *Theology*, 92 (1989) 251-2, and O. Chadwick in *Michael Ramsey: A Life*, 370.   139 5:6; 6:20; 7:3, 16f., 21, 24, 28; 9:24, 28 and 10: 12-14.   140 See 1:4, 9, 13; 2:9f, 12f, 16; 3:2; 5:1-6, 8, 10; 6:20 and 7:28.   141 He thus comments that 'all this is astonishing language' and notes his surprise that this fact is overlooked by O. Cullmann, in his *Christology of the New Testament* (London, 1959) and by F. Hahn, in his *The Titles of Jesus in Christology* (London, 1969). See *HFG*, 157.   142 Ibid., 157.   143 It is interesting to note here that Robinson, in his analysis of this New Testament book, makes reference only once to a specific study of the Epistle, that by B.F. Westcott (1825-1901): *The Epistle to the Hebrews* (London, 1889). Westcott was a sometime Regius Professor of Divinity at Cambridge. With this point in mind, we can note that Canon Leslie Houlden (lecturer in New Testament Studies, King's College, London) wrote in the course of a review of Robinson's posthumous *PJ*: 'to see Robinson as *par excellence* the thrillingly shocking radical was a misconception. The essence of the man lay less in any consistent espousal of heterodox views and reformist policies in the church than in a constant independence of mind. He hunted with no pack for long but went his own way. His chief debts were not to the purveyors of novelty in his own day, but to figures in his past (mostly family or Cambridge) to whom his loyalty was assured. His books are liable to be as full of references to nineteenth century scholars as to those more recent and are inclined to dig up names long forgotten by everyone else and never much attended to even in their own day. Those who have seen him as a late Victorian radical born out of due time are perhaps the most discerning. The many who failed to grasp

enough to acquaint us with the direction and flavour of his exegesis of the Epistle to the Hebrews.

1:1-3 Robinson begins his treatment of Hebrews by noting how the book opens 'with the most stupendous affirmation of Christ' in 1:3. He is the complete representative and plenipotentiary of God, the agent of his purpose alike in creation and redemption. Yet, Robinson counsels, 'if we ask who it is that fills this role, the whole point of the argument of the first chapter is that it is no angelic being but a *man*'.[144] He goes on to say that 'the language here is almost certainly intended not to have reference to a divine or to a semi-divine being but to the biblical account of the nature and glory of man.' For to be the stamp (*charactēr*) [χαρακτήρ] of God's very being is truly to be in his image.[145] In a similar vein, he argues that the word *apaugasma* [ἀπαύγασμα] should be translated as the reflection (rather than the radiance) of his glory, as the other metaphor of Wisdom 7:26 (from which it evidently derives), would suggest.[146]

2:17 Robinson advances a similarly critical argument in respect of the traditional interpretation of this text: 'Therefore he had to be made like (*homoiothēnai*) [ὁμοιωθῆναι] these brothers of his in every way. This has traditionally been interpreted to mean that the Logos had to be made like men from being something very different (heavenly being). I believe that the whole context of this argument shows that our writer intended no such thing. Jesus was never anything but like his brothers. For it is essential that a consecrating priest and those whom he consecrates should be all "of one stock" (2:11) ...'[147]

these things about him were bewildered when, in *Redating the New Testament* (1976), he emerged as the champion of an unlikely and undeniably conservative cause – the dating of the New Testament books to the period before AD 70 and so the strengthening of their claims to historical accuracy.' *Times Literary Supplement* (4 October, 1985); quoted by James, *A Life of Bishop John A.T Robinson*, 323. **144** This is a controversial assertion: surely Christ is considered here to be something 'more' than a man, not least in terms of his being the agent of creation? There is a strong body of biblical scholarship that holds that the references in the catena of 1:5-13 to Ps 2:7 and Ps 110:1 are to be taken as divine oracles directed at Christ. See H.W. Attridge, 'Hebrews, Epistle to the' in *ABD*, vol. 3, 102. Similarly, it is argued that the exordium (1:1-3), for example, 'contains a festive celebration of a "high" christological perspective, and affirms clearly the divine character of the Son and his role in creation'. See also Attridge, *The Epistle to the Hebrews* (Philadelphia, 1989), 25. **145** *HFG.*, 155, **146** Robinson strains our credulity by commenting that 'the language of Heb 1:1-3 is also remarkably reminiscent of the parable of the wicked Husbandman in Mark. Whereas the previous messengers, the prophets, were servitors, like Moses, God has now finally spoken through a son, who is heir over everything and set over his household. There is no more suggestion in Hebrews than in Mark that the servants and the son are not equally human: it is the relationship, the function that is decisively different'. Ibid., 156. **147** Ibid., 158.

5:7-9 Turning to this text, we find Robinson rejecting the premise that it describes a heavenly figure coming in from outside, who, despite the fact that he was the Son of God, condescended to suffer. Robinson proposes a different interpretation when he says: 'on the presupposition with which I believe our author is working, it [Heb 5:7-9] means that Jesus' call to the unique role of living as God's son or personal representative did not exempt him from having to go through it to the end: precisely the contrary, it requires this of him without remission'.[148]

In drawing to a close this brief examination of Hebrews, it will suffice to note that Robinson believes that the letter cannot be used to support a doctrine which suggests the notion that Jesus started from a superior position, came down for a time to human level and was once more exalted above humankind. It must be said that it is far from clear that Robinson has convincingly argued his case here. The paucity of his references to the works of other biblical scholars familiar with the Epistle is striking (with the notable exception of F.D. Wescott). He has not dealt with the evidence that suggests that the author to the Hebrews did think of the pre-existent Christ as active in Israel's history, just as Paul did.[149] It is certainly clear that many scholars would dispute the thrust of his analysis; not least in relation to his argument that *apaugasma* and *charactēr* (Heb 1:3) do not denote a divine being of some sort. A.T. Hanson has drawn attention to the facts that the Book of Wisdom applies *apaugasma* to the divine Wisdom, and Philo uses both of these terms of the Logos.[150] H.W. Attridge has commented that the image employed in 1:3 serves 'to affirm the intimate relationship between the Father and the pre-existent Son, through whom redemption is effected' and that 'the Son is also the imprint or stamp ($\chi\alpha\rho\alpha\kappa\tau\dot{\eta}\rho$) of the divine reality.'[151]

Paul When Robinson turns to an examination of the Pauline Epistles, he finds there a strong preponderance of both high pre–existence and apparent adoptionist language. In Romans 1:3f., for example, he finds much that re-echoes what has just been noted about the Epistle to the Hebrews:[152] 'the pic-

---

148 Ibid., 158-9. **149** This is a charge levelled against Robinson by Anthony Tyrrell Hanson as he notes that Robinson has apparently not read his (earlier) discussion of this matter in his *Christ in the Old Testament* (London, 1965), 48-82. See ibid., 67 and 119, n. 9. **150** Hanson, *Grace and Truth*, 67. **151** Attridge, *The Epistle to the Hebrews*, 43. **152** Thus he finds 'the same paradox of the pre-destined Son, in succession to the prophets, who is yet a man, with all his human background, installed in power by virtue of the resurrection. It is not a heavenly being who becomes human, so much as a man who enters into the office of Son of God marked out for him for all eternity. From the point of view of God, the Son, God's "own" or only one, waits to be sent to his people: the role of perfect obedience and representation stands ready to be revealed until he for whom it is prepared is due to be born. From the point of view of man, the faithful one waits to be brought forth, by human seed, from within the womb of Israel.' Robinson argues that it is with these presuppositions that the following typical Pauline texts

ture is not of a divine being arriving to look like a man, but a man born like the rest of us, from within the nexus of the flesh, law and sin, who nevertheless embodied the divine initiative and saving presence so completely that he was declared at his baptism and confirmed at his resurrection to be everything God himself was – his Son, his power and his wisdom, his image, his fullness'.[153]

Robinson spells out his interpretation of Paul on Christ's pre-existence by delaying on two particular passages, Philippians 2:5-11 and 1 Corinthians 15:45-47, which we shall now consider briefly. Criticism of the validity of his assertions will come later.

Philippians 2:5-11 More ink has probably been spilt on this passage than on any other set of seven verses in the Epistles, prompting one scholar, Marcus Bockmuehl, to term it 'one of the most over-interpreted texts of the New Testament'.[154] Robinson attests that traditional christology[155] has usually interpreted this as the *locus classicus* in the New Testament for the myth of the supernatural, heavenly Redeemer visiting the earth in the form of a human being.[156] He asserts (*contra* Bultmann) that its origins were not as a pagan myth which Paul (and John) Christianised, but a Gnosticising version of the distinctively Christian message.[157] He claims that 'if any pre-Christian myth lies behind Phil 2 it is more likely that of Adam, with whom Christ is fairly clearly being compared and contrasted'.[158] He thinks that Rabbinic Judaism is its probable background.[159] Thus Christ is not being celebrated as a pre-existent being, but as a human counterpart to Adam. Robinson's opinion here is highly contentious.

should be read: Gal 4:4, 'God sent his own Son, born of woman, born under the law'; and Rom 8:3, 'What the law could never do ... God has done: by sending his own Son in a form like that of our own sinful nature.' Ibid., 161. (Robinson's exegesis here is open to question: surely the prophets are never sent, as in these two passages, as the Son of God [Rom 8:32 implies that he already was Son at his sending]?). **153** Ibid., 161-2. **154** M. Bockmuehl, '"The Form of God" (Phil. 2:6): Variations on a Theme of Jewish Mysticism', *Journal of Theological Studies*, 48 (1997) 1. **155** John T. Fitzgerald has commented that traditional exegesis has 'usually assumed that the beginning of the hymn (2:6-8) refers to Christ prior to the Incarnation, so that his preexistence is presupposed'. He notes that a good example of this approach is G. Bornkamm, 'On Understanding the Christ-Hymn: Philippians 2:6-11' in his *Early Christian Experience* (London, 1969). See Fitzgerald, 'Philippians, Epistle to the', in *ABD*, vol. 5, 318-26. **156** *HFG*, 162. **157** Ibid., 162-3. In making this judgement Robinson appeals to the following works: E. Percy, *Untersuchungen über den Ursprung der johanneischen Theologie* (Lund, 1939); to the discussion in R.P. Martin, *Carmen Christi: Philippians 2:5-11 in Recent Interpretation and in the Setting of Early Christian Worship* (Cambridge, 1967), 121-8 and L.E. Keck, *A Future for the Historical Jesus* (London, 1972), 112-9; 144-51. **158** *HFG*, 163. Macquarrie has commented that 'Robinson anticipated the interpretation which James Dunn gave to the Christ-hymn of Philippians 2, an interpretation which does not entail pre-existence' and instead calls for it to be interpreted in terms of Adam christology. See his *Jesus Christ in Modern Thought*, 334. **159** *HFG*, 163. In arriving at this opinion he cites the work of W.D.

The Evangelical Anglican exegete, N.T. Wright, has noted that the 'contention that Christ [in Philippians 2:5-11] is being contrasted with Adam is a controversial one' and that it is 'by no means settled' whether or not Adam christology is to be detected in Philippians.[160] Since the claims of Adam christology will be set out and critically examined at length below (it plays a central role in John Macquarrie's christological proposals), we shall not delay here on a discussion of it.[161]

When it comes to the exegesis of this passage from Philippians, Robinson believes that Cullmann's interpretation is on the mark. The latter claims that the opening statement of the passage that Jesus was 'in the form of God [ἐν μορφῇ θεοῦ] does not refer to Jesus divine nature, but rather to the image of God which he possessed from the beginning'.[162] Robinson notes that Cullmann, in common with other scholars before him,[163] views *morphē* (form) and *eikōn* (image) as representing variant renderings of the idea that goes back to Genesis 1:26 of man being made in the image of God. Jesus, as the *proper* man, is the exact image or true son of God that Adam was created to be. As such, he could have enjoyed as of right all the divine glory of which humanity since the Fall had been deprived.[164]

Moving along the text to verse 2:9, we have the statement: 'Therefore God highly exalted him and graciously bestowed on him (*echarisato*) the name above every name'. Yet again, and supremely here, we are faced with the combination of pre-existence and adoptionist language. Robinson comments, however, that

> the picture is not of a celestial figure lowering himself to become a man, to be exalted higher than he was before. Rather, it is that the entire fullness of God was enabled by divine grace and human obedience to find embodiment in one who was as completely one of us as any other physical descendant of Abraham. Thereby, he 'broke the barrier' between man and God. Jesus was not, I believe, for Paul, as he became for later dogmatics, a divine being veiled in flesh or one who stripped himself of superhuman attributes to become

Davies, *Paul and Rabbinic Judaism* (London, 1948), 45-9. See ibid., n. 77.   **160** N.T. Wright, *The Climax of the Covenant* (Edinburgh, 1991). 49. He goes on to comment that it is not yet clear 'what the results would be if it were agreed that Adam is to be found there'. Ibid., 86. **161** It will suffice for now to note that numbered among those scholars who believe that the Philippians Christ-hymn does not point to pre-existence but, rather, represents an attempt to define the uniqueness of Christ considered (merely) as a man are: S. Kim, J.D.G. Dunn, M.D. Hooker, G.B. Caird, P. Bonnard, O. Cullmann, J. Héring, J. Murphy-O'Connor. Against the thesis: B. Byrne, G. Howard, I.H. Marshall, L.D. Hurst, C.A. Wanamaker. **162** Ibid. and see O. Cullmann, *The Christology of the New Testament* (London, 1959), 176. **163** Especially J. Héring, *Le Royaume de Dieu*, 2nd ed. (Paris & Neuchâtel, 1959), 146ff.; A.M. Hunter, *Paul and his Predecessors* (London, 1940); F.W. Eltester, *Eikon im neuen Testament* (Berlin, 1958), 10; J. Jervell, *Imago Dei* (Güttingen, 1960), 228 and R.P. Martin, *Carmen Christi*, 102-19. **164** *HFG*, 163-4.

human; he was a man who by total surrender of his own gain or glory was able to reveal or 'unveil' the glory of God as utterly gracious, self-giving love.[165]

N.T. Wright is not impressed with the burden of Robinson's interpretation of Philippians 2:5-11 which he characterises as 'a non-incarnational reading'.[166] Though Wright does not expand upon this criticism of Robinson (made in passing), it is clear from his appraisal of J.D.G. Dunn's interpretation of this passage in his *Christology in the Making* (1980) that Wright believes there is insufficient evidence to support the thesis that the development of christology moved firstly from a non-incarnational reading of Philippians 2 to a Gnostic view of the passage (and/or passages) and hence to the orthodox view of Christ's pre-existence.[167]

1 Corinthians 15:45-47　This is another Pauline text, closely associated with the doctrine of pre-existence that Robinson feels is in need of reinterpretation. He explains that the passage has normally been taken to suggest that 'the manhood of Christ, unlike ours, was "spiritual" rather that "natural", and had its origins not on earth but in heaven'. He goes on to say that 'if the implications of this were pressed, we should have an entirely eccentric, and indeed heretical, Christology – of a Christ-figure whose humanity as well as whose divinity was of a heavenly substance'.[168]

Robinson proposes a very different interpretation, arguing that the reference in this text is

> not to Adam and Jesus Christ as individuals, but to two different bodies or conditions of humanity, *adam* and *anthrōpos* being ways, in Hebrew and Greek, of referring to man with a capital M. Our primary manhood is that in which we share by virtue of the natural creation. This humanity may be comprehended entirely in physical and psychological terms; it is *choïkos* and *psychiksos*. But the second can be comprehended only in spiritual or heavenly categories: it is *pneumatikos*, *epouranios*. It is spirit – not 'a spirit' – and it

---

165 Ibid., 165-6. Robinson offers the following as a paraphrase of what Paul is saying of Christ in Phil 2:6-11: 'God shaped his entire being. He was the perfect reflection of his glory. He might have lived completely in that unclouded glory. But he did not think being God-like a state to be selfishly enjoyed (or grasped at). Instead he emptied himself of everything. His life took the shape of a slave. He was found living exactly as other men, accepting the common pattern of the human lot. This utterly humble obedience of his led him all the way to his death, to a criminal's death at that. This is why God exalted him higher even than he had been before (or to the very heights), bestowing upon him the title of his own supremacy, so that at the name of Jesus everything in heaven and earth and the world below should bow the knee and openly confess Jesus Christ as "Lord" - though always to the glory of God the Father.' *RR*, 68.　166 Wright, *The Climax of the Covenant*, 86, n. 120.　167 Ibid., 95.　168 *HFG*, 166.

is life – real life, in contrast with mere animation. For it is spirit alone that gives life, as John and Paul both insist. The first level of life Paul sees as having been initiated in Adam, the second as having been opened up through Christ.[169]

Thus Robinson contends that the real contrast is not between Adam and Jesus as individuals, but between, the *sōma psychikon* (the natural body) and the *sōma pneumatikon* (the spiritual body), the two solidarities or states of humanity, *both* of which Jesus shared and both of which we shall therefore share.[170]

It is clear, then, that Robinson has tried to prove that Paul did not uphold the personal pre-existence of Christ. To achieve this purpose he has attempted to present an alternative, more functional interpretation of certain texts which are regarded as central to the doctrine. The kernel of his argument here is that Paul never intended that such a doctrine should arise: it emerged, Robinsons claims, in a striking phrase, as a 'scribal gloss'. And so pervasive was this gloss, Robinson adds, that it has coloured christology down to the present day by providing the 'scriptural anchorage for the Gnostic concept of a supernatural heavenly Man, not of our clay, who is celestial *as opposed to* earthly, spiritual *rather than* material. It is difficult to believe that Paul entertained any such notion'.[171]

It is far from obvious that Robinson has proved his thesis with respect to Paul's writings. He has not dealt, for example, with the meaning of 1 Corinthians 10:1-11[172] and has only touched upon 2 Corinthians 8:9[173] in the most fleeting of ways. In the first of these passages Paul speaks of the pre-existent Christ as the source of the manna and water in the desert and implies that Christ journeyed with the Israelites in their wanderings, probably in the form of the angel in the pillar of the

---

169 Ibid., 167.   **170** Robinson comments further that '"the first man", "the old man", "the outer man", "the natural man" are for Paul equivalent terms, so too are "the second man", "the last man", "the new man", "the inner man", "the spiritual man". They refer to collectives in which the individual participates – as also does "the perfect man". In the same way, "the man from heaven" corresponds to "the habitation from heaven" – the new corporeity.' Ibid., 168-9. **171** Ibid.   **172** H. Conzelmann, in his commentary on First Corinthians, argues that verse 4b [the rock was Christ] upholds 'a real pre-existence, not merely symbolic significance'. See his *I Corinthians* (Philadelphia, 1975), 177.   **173** V.P. Furnish has commented that this passage seems to be based on the kind of christological affirmation present in the creedal fragments of 1 Tim 3:16 and in the hymn Phil 2:6-11. All three texts, Furnish goes on, 'presume that Christ enjoyed a heavenly existence with God before the incarnation' and that in 2 Cor 8:9 'Paul characterizes the grace of *our Lord Jesus Christ* ... a phrase familiar from the Christian liturgy; as his divesting himself of his riches and becoming *poor*'. Furnish insists that there can be no question here (*pace* Bultmann) of a reference to the literal poverty of the historical Jesus. See his *II Corinthians*, The Anchor Bible (Garden City, New York: 1984), 417. On the other hand, an interpretation close to that of Robinson is offered by J. Murphy-O'Connor when he, following J.D.G. Dunn, asserts that the text does not imply pre-existence. See his 'The Second Letter to the Corinthians', in *NJBC*, 824.

cloud. If this is not the conception of a distinct divine being, the burden of proving such a thesis, as A.T. Hanson has said, lies with those who propose it.[174]
Robinson does not allude to this passage at all. Nor does he ever come to terms
with the issues raised by 2 Corinthians 8:9: ('You know the grace of our Lord
Jesus Christ, that though he was rich, yet for our sake he became poor, so that by
his poverty you might become rich.')[175] At first sight, at least, this looks like a presentation of Jesus as a pre-existent divine being who humbled himself to accept
our condition. We can also point to the implications of the reference to Isaiah
40:13 and Job 41:11 in Romans 11:34-35. Hanson claims that most scholars who
have probed this text are of the belief that behind it lies the idea of the pre-
existence of Christ as the divine counsellor mentioned in Isaiah.[176] Joseph A.
Fitzmyer, however, in his recent commentary on Romans does not claim that this
passage implies pre-existence.[177] Finally, it is questionable whether Robinson has
successfully demonstrated that Philippians 2:6-7 ('being in the form of God')
does not imply pre-existence in a divine status. We must now move, with
Robinson, to an exegesis of the salient parts of the Fourth Gospel.

John The battle that ensues here can easily be designated his most daring:
A.T. Hanson has spoken of it as 'his Herculean task of proving that there is no
doctrine of [personal] pre-existence in the Fourth Gospel'.[178] (Robinson argues a
highly debatable thesis: it is not shared by Rudolf Schnackenburg[179] and Raymond

174 A.T. Hanson, *Grace and Truth* (London, 1975), 67   175 Save for the unexplained
judgement that it 'does not refer simply to a pre-incarnate state but to the wealth of his
continuous inner relationship to God'. *RR*, 68.   176 Hanson, *Grace and Truth*, 68.   177
J.A. Fitzmyer, *Romans*, The Anchor Bible (New York, 1993). Indeed his only direct
reference to the theme is contained in the following remark: 'Although Paul never speaks of
Jesus as his incarnate Son (cf. Jn 1:14-18), his use of *huios* may imply some sort of pre-
existent filiation. Cf. 5:10; 8:3, 29, 32; I Thes 1:10; Gal 1:16; 2:20; 4:4; 1 Cor 1:9; 15:28; 2
Cor 1:19'. Ibid., 234. It should be noted that Fitzmyer is interested here in the use of *huios*;
hence he does not refer to Rom. 11:34-35, because it does not include this title. Also note
that one of the *huios* texts included by Fitzmyer appears precisely because it refers to *huios*,
even though it really has no direct relevance to pre-existence (1 Cor 15:28).   178 A.T.
Hanson, *The Prophetic Gospel* (Edinburgh, 1991), 310. Robinson is not helped in this task by
his over-reliance on earlier English biblical scholarship: not least the writings of J. B. Lightfoot
and P. Gardner-Smith. This has led Ernst Bammel to contend that 'Robinson sees himself
in a long line of English scholarship now extinct. It is moving to notice his devotion to those
whose work he rescues from oblivion'. Bammel goes on to assert that Robinson 'falls into the
trap of referring to material of ephemeral quality, whereas most of the German masters are
not even known to him by name (German was a language, which, unfortunately, he did not
read with ease). This is a serious deficiency'. See his review of *PJ*, *Journal of Theological
Studies*, 39 (1988) 201-4.   179 Schnackenburg has asserted, for example, that 'John speaks
unambiguously of Jesus' pre-existence' and has commented that 'the pre-existence of the
Johannine Christ is affirmed in the prologue and in the testimony of the Baptist (1:30) ..., by
Jesus himself in 6:62 ('where he was before'), 8:58 ('before Abraham was, I am'), in the high

E. Brown[180] – two leading Johannine scholars. Nor indeed is it held by the British exegete, J.D.G. Dunn, who, as we have reported, has strongly opposed the presence of the doctrine of personal pre-existence in Paul).[181] Robinson takes up the cudgels on this issue, not only in *The Human Face of God* (1972), but in his *magnum opus* as a New Testament scholar,[182] *The Priority of John* (1985).[183] His main points concerning John are as follows:

priestly prayer (17:5, 24) and indirectly in many other texts where his pre-existence is assumed (cf. 6:33, 58f; 7:28f.; 8:14, 23, 26, 42; 10:36; 16:28)'. See his *The Gospel according to St John*, vol. 1 (London, 1968), 511, 504. In addition, it should be noted that Schnackenburg is resolute in the belief that, whatever the seeming similarities between the Johannine treatment of Christ's pre-existence and the Gnostic notion of a pre-existent redeemer, 'the impression is illusory, as is apparent when one observes the real facts'. Ibid., 504.   180 Brown states unambiguously his conviction that the theme of pre-existence is to be found in John's prologue; 8:58 and 17:5. Turning to a detailed exegesis of the prologue, he cautions: 'we find unacceptable the attempts to avoid an implication of pre-existence here'. See his *The Gospel according to John* (I-XII) (London, 1971), 63. Brown contends that the Fourth Gospel holds 'a uniquely high christology ... the highest in the New Testament' and that this was a product of the type of belief in Jesus that came to be accepted by the Johannine community. See his *The Community of the Beloved Disciple* (London, 1979), 45. He argues that 'a belief in the pre-existence of God's Son was the key to the Johannine contention that the true believer possessed God's own life; and the Fourth Gospel had been written to bolster the faith of the Johannine community on that very point (20:31)'. Ibid., 109-10. This uniquely high Johannine christology of pre-existence, Brown's argument proceeds, was 'so high that Jesus can use the divine name "I AM" and the Jewish opponents accuse him of making himself God'. Ibid., 114. The baptism of Jesus administered by John the Baptist 'is no longer seen as a baptism of repentance for the forgiveness of sins (Mk 1:4); it now confirms the revelation of pre-existence found in the Prologue hymn'. Ibid., 117-8.   181 Robinson notes that he must part company with Dunn at this point. For Robinson's treatment of Dunn's handling of John see his 'Dunn on John', *Theology* 85 (1982) 332-8; which is expanded upon in *PJ*, 379-94. Hitherto both authors have been in agreement that neither Paul nor the Synoptics uphold the personal pre-existence of a heavenly being. When it comes to the Fourth Gospel, however, Dunn contends that the *combination* of the wisdom christology of the Logos-hymn (which he considers to be pre-Johannine – Robinson feels this is improbable, but both agree that it does not in itself need to be read as speaking of a pre-existent divine Person), with John's dominant Son of God christology produces an entirely different situation. And in fact it is the latter Son of God language as such which compels him to this conclusion. Ibid., 382-3. Thus Dunn comments that it is 'clear that for John the pre-existent Logos was indeed a divine personal being'. See his *Christology in the Making*, 2nd ed. (London, 1989), 244. For a discussion of Dunn's interpretation of Paul on pre-existence see the relevant section of the Macquarrie chapter below.   182 This is the description of *PJ* proffered by John Knox in his 'J.A.T. Robinson and New Testament Scholarship', *Theology* 92 (1989) 262.   183 Incidentally, this work (of over 440 pages) draws together and goes beyond, the ideas contained in a smattering of articles concerning the Fourth Gospel, written over his lifetime. The principal thesis of the work is Robinson's

i) *The Fourth Gospel upholds the genuine humanity of Christ* For our purposes here, we shall begin by noting Robinson's stern rebuttal of any suggestion, (*contra* Käsemann),[184] that this Gospel presents a quasi-docetic picture of the humanity of Christ. Robinson dismisses any suggestion that Christ 'does not start where we start', that he is, so to speak, 'a cuckoo in the human nest'.[185] He acknowledges that the portrait offered by John differs from those of the author to the Hebrews and Paul: 'there is none of the more obviously "adoptionist" language; nor is there any suggestion that Jesus himself grew in awareness'.[186] At first glance Robinson is prepared to concede that 'if ... we apply the standards of psychological veri-similitude rather than of theological verity, then not only does this gospel *look* docetic, static and unhistorical: it is docetic. And it is not in the least surprising that this has been the charge it has invited from the beginning'.[187]

Be that as it may, however, Robinson is convinced that such an ontological, supernaturalistic interpretation of John is erroneous: 'the picture of Christ as a divine visitant is not what he [John] meant at all, however unsuccessful he has been at guarding against its being so understood'.[188] Robinson bases this judgement on two factors. The first is his by now familiar premise that the 'notion of a fully individuated heavenly person, as distinct from personifications of God's attributes and agencies, cannot be demonstrated, ... in pre-Christian Judaism or in the rest of the New Testament'. And, secondly, he contends that 'careful study of his [John's] language' does not support the belief that 'this is the real point of difference between Jesus and the rest of mankind'.[189] If we are to pin-point where

conviction that John is the foremost witness to the life of Jesus. M. Hengel, however, like the great majority of scholars, has stated that Robinson's labours here were 'not enough to make his theory really convincing'. See his *The Johannine Question* (London, 1989), n. 9, 139. **184** Käsemann classes the Gospel as 'naïve docetism' and goes on to claim 'that the Church committed an error when it declared the Gospel to be orthodox'. See his *The Testament of Jesus* (London, 1968), 13 (referred to in *HFG*, 169). **185** *PJ*, 366. **186** *HFG*, 170. Whereas in Hebrews Jesus was subject to *teleiosis* (maturation), in the Fourth Gospel, however, one finds *tetelestai* ('it is finished'). **187** 'The Use of the Fourth Gospel for Christology Today', in B. Lindars & S.S. Smalley (eds), *Christ and Spirit in the New Testament: Studies in honour of C.F.D. Moule* (Cambridge, 1973), 61-78 and *HFG*, 171. **188** *PJ*, 366. **189** *Ibid.*, 366. Thus Robinson notes elsewhere that 'come into the world' is used identically of Jesus (9:39; 12:46; 16:28; 18:37), of 'the prophet' (6:14), of the Messiah (11:27; cf. 4:25; 7:27, 31, 41f.,), of 'every man' (1:9). 'It is the equivalent of being "born" (18:37) or being "born into the world" (16:21), which again is applied indifferently to Jesus and to any woman's child. Similarly, not only Jesus but John the Baptist is "sent from God" (1:6; cf. 3:28); and even Nicodemus acknowledges Jesus as a teacher "come from God" (3:2) ...'. Robinson has a similar interpretation of the estimate of Jesus as 'a man of God' (*para theou*, 9:16, 33), which in its general sense is equated with 'a prophet' (9:17), and indeed with 'anyone who is devout and obeys his will' (9:31). 'There is a continuum, too,' he argues, between the very distinctive language which John uses to describe Jesus' sonship and that which ought to apply to every man [it is clear here that Robinson has not dwelt adequately

precisely this difference lies, Robinson argues that we must explore the concept of Jesus' unique sonship in the Fourth Gospel since 'the overwhelming Johannine answer to why Jesus alone is privy to the Father's secrets and has been given his "glory" and his "name" to reveal to others is not that he is "God" but that he is "the Son"'.[190] The task we thus face now is to understand what 'Son' means for John.

ii) *The unique sonship*   To begin, it is necessary to note that Robinson claims that sonship is best viewed in functional, rather than ontological, terms. This is because 'sonship is *most really*, at the level of spirit and of truth, to do with relationships rather than status, with verbs rather than substantives (let alone substances)'.[191] Thus he comments that

> to be son is ... to allow God wholly and utterly to be the Father. But in the case of only one man can that truly be said to have been done. This is why the designation 'son' is reserved by John (unlike Paul) for Jesus alone: others, however close, are only 'children' of God, and that through him. Yet this is not because he is divine and they are not, but because only he 'always does what is acceptable to him' (8:29). He is unique because he alone is truly normal, standing where every son of Adam should stand, not because he is abnormal.[192]

In spite of this, Robinson is certain that there is no more suggestion in John than in the Epistle to the Hebrews that, because Jesus is son he does not stand in the same human relationship to God as every other man. Jesus is, on the contrary, 'the only completely obedient man, who "always" does his Father's will, right to "the end"'.[193] There is no hint, Robinson goes on, of this implying that 'he is more than a man'. The truth, rather, is that

upon the difference between υἱὸς and τέκνα in John: τέκνα indicates the type of sonship that Jesus communicates to those who believe in him (1:12); while υἱὸς refers to Jesus' own divine Sonship which remains unique to him (1: 14). See G. O'Collins, *Interpreting Jesus* (London, 1983), 171]. To have God as Father, Robinson asserts, is what should be true of the Jews, as they themselves claim (8:41). But morally they have forfeited that claim. However, it is not superhuman presumption for Jesus to claim sonship of God, since as John teaches, 'Those are called gods', quoting Ps. 82:6 'to whom the word of God was delivered – and Scripture cannot be set aside. Then why do you charge me with blasphemy because I, consecrated and sent into the world by the Father, said, "I am a son of God"? (10:35f)'. *HFG*, 172-3.   **190** *PJ*, 373.   **191** Ibid., 375.   **192** Ibid., 378. Robinson goes on to appeal to an assertion by the little known author, W.F Lofthouse, that 'if we could tolerate the paradox, we might say that he was a man because he had what no man has ever had before ... Christ did not become what men were; he became what they were meant to be, and what they too, through accepting him, actually become.' See his *The Father and the Son: A Study in Johannine Thought* (London, 1934), 115, 118.   **193** *HFG*, 176.

he allows the Father to be everything, all that the Father has is his and all that he has is the Father's (16:15; 17:10). As a truly and totally human being he is utterly transparent to and therefore of the Father, so that to see the Son is to see the Father (8:19; 12:45; 14.9). And the nature of this moral and spiritual union is mutual love (3:35; 10:17; 14:31; 15:9f.; 17:23f.,26), the fully personal relationship of reciprocal indwelling – exactly analogous to what is to be shared by believers.[194]

Robinson thus claims that the basis of Christ's unique sonship in the Fourth Gospel is a moral one: it cannot be established on an 'ontological as *distinct from* a moral basis'. This sonship, his argument proceeds, 'is one of its kind ($\mu o\nu o\gamma \varepsilon \nu \dot{\eta} \varsigma$) because of his total moral unity, and the moral unity is for John that which is most really real. The (later) Greek distinction and debate about whether he is with the Father by "nature" or "will" is not only anachronistic but distortive for the interpretation of John'.[195] This prompts A.T. Hanson to comment that 'Robinson denies all metaphysical unity between the Father and the Son in the Gospel' and again that 'the basis of the unity is love not metaphysics'.[196] We must now investigate Robinson's understanding of the doctrine of pre-existence in John.

iii) *A pre-existent purpose*   Robinson does not deny the presence of pre-existence language in John. In common with G.B. Caird, he discerns the fourth evangelist as maintaining a 'pre-existent purpose'.[197] There can be no question, however, of a pre-existent person: such would be to give 'the impression ... that Jesus is not truly an earthly, historical human being at all';[198] that he is 'an invader from another world'.[199] Thus Robinson tries as best he can to interpret the Johannine pre-existence language in terms of eternal presence in God's intentions rather than in terms of personal activity in Israel's history. He tells us that the language of pre-existence arose in John because of the need to tell 'two stories, two histories' about Jesus.[200] The first is

---

194 *PJ*, 378. As Robinson states: 'Jesus, in Whitehead's language, is not the metaphysical exception, but the supreme exemplification – unique, but representative not exclusive'. Ibid. 195 Ibid., 375-6.   196 A.T. Hanson, *The Prophetic Gospel* (Edinburgh, 1991), 312, 312-3. 197 *HFG*, 179, n. 182. Robinson quotes G.B. Caird approvingly: 'Neither the Fourth Gospel nor Hebrews ever speaks of the eternal Word or Wisdom of God in terms which compel us to regard it as a person. If we are in the habit of crediting them with such a belief in a pre-existent person, and not just a pre-existent purpose, it is because we read them in the light of Paul's theology.' And as we have become aware, Robinson believes that traditional christology has hitherto misinterpreted Paul. See Caird, 'The Development of the Doctrine of Christ in the New Testament', in N. Pittenger (ed.), *Christ for Us Today* (London, 1968), 79.   198 *PJ*, 383. He notes that to say 'that the Logos came into existence or expression as a person does not mean that it was a person before'. Ibid., 360.   199 Ibid., 365.   200 *HFG*, 176.

the story of the Logos, the history of the wisdom, and light and love of God. This history comes to its climax in Jesus and is so totally incarnate in him that he can speak directly in the name of God and utter the divine 'I am'. ... Its source and ground are not 'of this world' but 'with God' [1:1, 18]. Indeed it is God speaking and acting. Consequently, its *archē* or origin is not just the moment of Jesus birth, but is before Abraham (8:58), before the world (17:5, 24), and indeed at the beginning of all things (1:1f.). As the embodiment of this 'I am', Jesus does not speak 'of himself'. It is no wonder, therefore, that he sometimes sounds like a ventriloquist's dummy.[201]

For John, therefore, he is the Word, which was θεὸς (1:1), God in his self – revelation and expression, σὰρξ ἐγένετο (1:14), was embodied totally in and as a human being, became a person, was personalized not just personified'.[202]

The second story which the Fourth Gospel tells, Robinson asserts, concerns 'the history of a human being who comes from nowhere more exalted than Nazareth in Galilee and whose connections are known to all. There is no mystery about his origin, and it is absurd to say of this historical individual that he is pre-existent'.[203] Robinson is thus acknowledging that there is a way of having the language both of 'pre-existence' and of 'humanity', if we can understand what each is doing 'without separation' and 'without confusion'. This is difficult, he readily admits, owing to the way the narrative of the Fourth Gospel so often presents these different stories 'by deliberately superimposing them rather than laying them side by side (as the author to the Hebrews tends to do)'.[204]

The subsequent unfolding of Johannine exegesis soon lost sight of the distinction between the two stories: Robinson maintains that 'he [John] was taken over by the gnosticizers'.[205] Soon the fourth evangelist's intentions in writing his Gospel were lost sight of, a development that Robinson characterises as 'entirely explicable' because of the intellectual and cultural influences then bringing themselves to bear in Judaism and Gnosticism. Thus Robinson speaks of the beginnings of 'the retrojective process',[206] a process which he believes 'happened to John rather than in John',[207] and which he defines as 'reading back the revelation of the Logos

201 Ibid., 177.   **202** *PJ*, 380. Robinson is influenced here by the arguments of Piet Schoonenberg in his *The Christ* (New York, 1972). He comments: 'but that the Logos came into expression or existence as a person does not imply that it was a person before. In terms of the later distinction, it was not that the Logos was hypostatic (a person or hypostasis) and then assumed an impersonal human nature, but that the Logos was anhypostatic until the word of God finally came to self-expression not merely in a nature and in a people, but in an individual historical person, and thus became hypostatic.' Ibid., 380-1.   **203** *HFG*, 176.
204 Ibid., 178.   **205** *PJ*, 381.   **206** Ibid., 382. A concept which he borrows from G.W.H. Lampe, *God as Spirit* (Oxford, 1977), 39f.   **207** *PJ*, 381.

as "a son", as a human being, that is, who at last perfectly imaged God as an only son [*sic*] [of] his father, onto the revelation of "the Son", a pre-existent heavenly being, later the Second Person of the Trinity, who became man ...'.[208] In due course, supremely at the hands of what the theological tradition would come to term the Alexandrian model of christology,[209] this retrojection of the personhood of the human Jesus onto the divine Logos to make him a heavenly being prior to the incarnation, would be taken to be the mainstay of John's theology.

To draw this discussion of Robinson's reading of John to a close, it is enough to say that the burden of his argument is that the time has come for the real Johannine Christ to stand forth, from under what orthodox Christianity has made of him.[210] He is not to be considered a pre-existent person who became man but, rather, a genuine man of history who is uniquely his Father's son. Hanson pithily encapsulates the thrust of Robinson's Johannine project when he comments that the latter 'would like to substitute a "designation" from the beginning instead of pre-existence'. Hanson, however, is entirely unconvinced by Robinson's proposal and in fact dismisses it as an unattainable goal since he is convinced that 'designation' is 'a phrase for which there is no justification in the Fourth Gospel. We have ὁρισθέντος in Romans 1:4 (designated) and κεκληρονόμηκεν in Hebrews 1:4 (obtained), but nothing of the sort in John'.[211] This leads Hanson to utter the following stinging assessment of Robinson's thesis: 'in a word, it is difficult to imagine a more unconvincing defence of the incredible proposition that Jesus does not claim personal pre-existence in the Fourth Gospel'.[212] And he is similarly dismissive when he declares that 'Robinson's attempt to show that the Jesus of John did not claim pre-existence collapses when submitted to the lightest scrutiny'.[213]

Some observations may be in order here. Does not 8:56, where Jesus is represented by John as saying: 'Your father Abraham was overjoyed to see my

---

208 Ibid., 382. There can be no question for Robinson of Jesus having been personally conscious of his pre-existence. Thus, even though he concedes, for example, that Jn. 8:58 (Jesus said to them, 'Truly, truly, I say to you, before Abraham was, I am') 'certainly asserts pre-existence' (ibid., 386), he argues that the 'I' here refers to the totality of the self. Thus he comments: 'the "I" with which Jesus speaks is neither that simply of the individual ego nor of the divine name ... I suggest that it is to be understood as the totality of the self, of which Jung spoke in contrast with the ego. As he [Jung] saw it, the Christ-figure is an archetypal image of the self, the God-image in us, "consubstantial" alike with the ground of our being and with our own deepest experience.' Relying on the arguments offered by Bede Griffiths in *The Marriage of East and West* (Springfield, 1982), 189, Robinson adds that 'it is the "I" of the mystics, who make the most astonishing claims to be one with God, the "I" of Master Eckhart and Angelus Silesius, of the Sufis and the Upanishads, where atman and Brahman are completely "one", as in Jn 10:30'. Ibid., 387. 209 Ibid., 394. Robinson notes how the Fourth Gospel has traditionally served as the foundation for the Alexandrian school of christological thought, be it at Nicea or Chalcedon. He identifies Athanasius and Cyril as among the leading exponents of this view. Ibid.. 210 Ibid., 397. 211 Hanson, *The Prophetic Gospel*, 314. 212 Ibid. 213 Ibid.

day; he saw it and was glad,' imply that Abraham saw the pre-existent Christ? This was certainly the understanding of the enraged Jews when in the next verse they retort: 'You are not yet fifty years old, and have you seen Abraham?' It is hard to conclude anything other than that according to the Fourth Gospel Christ had appeared to Abraham. And should we wish to know where, the answer may be hinted at in 8:40, where Jesus says: 'you seek to kill me, a man who has told you the truth which I heard from God; this is not what Abraham did'. And finally, there is another passage in which John seems quite explicitly to link the pre-existent Christ with an Old Testament theophany. This is John 12:41, where Isaiah 6:10 is first cited and then John comments: 'Isaiah said this because he saw his glory and spoke of him'. That is to say John clearly was of the opinion that Isaiah's famous vision in the temple was a vision of the pre-existent Christ. Thus to conclude, it will suffice to say that there is much evidence to indicate that Son/Father talk cannot be merely *moral* and not ontological.

At this point, we might usefully consider whether Robinson's treatment of Christ's pre-existence parallels his treatment of the resurrection. Gerald O'Collins observes that 'the progressive recognition of Jesus Christ's identity and destiny ... began at the end with the risen "post-existence" and finished at the beginning with the eternal "pre-existence".'[214] Bearing in mind, then, this close relationship between the post-existence and pre-existence of Christ, we should not be surprised, in light of what we have seen of his interpretation of pre-existence, if Robinson were to adopt a similarly critical stance towards the orthodox notion of the resurrection. (As we shall see later there is a strong parallel in Macquarrie's treatment of these two issues). When we examine Robinson's handling of the resurrection,[215] what emerges is a curious mix: it is only at the end of his treatment of the resurrection in *The Human Face of God* that he posits an interpretation similar to his already discussed radical reading of the doctrine of Christ's pre-existence; the general thrust of his version follows the orthodox pattern. Thus in beginning his deliberation on the matter in his article of 1962, he speaks of the resurrection as 'a unique event'. It is 'the watershed of New Testament history and the central point of its faith'.[216] Whatever the difficulties involved in speaking of an empty tomb (was the body stolen?), Robinson feels that 'there can be no doubt that they [the appearances] were an essential part of the earliest witness [see 1 Corinthians 15:5-7]'[217] and that they were not hallucinations.[218] He is clear that 'the Resurrection remains for the New Testament, not primarily an experience but an event'. And the event is 'the identity between the risen Christ whom they [the witnesses] had seen and the man with whom they had companied ...'.[219]

---

214 O'Collins, *Interpreting Jesus*), 198.   215 His two major examinations of the resurrection are: 'Resurrection in the NT', in G.A. Buttrick (ed.), *The Interpreter's Dictionary of the Bible*, vol. 4 (New York, 1962), 43-53; and *HFG*, 128-41.   216 'Resurrection in the NT', 43.   217 Ibid., 47.   218 *HFG*, 130.   219 'Resurrection in the NT', 49.

Towards the end of his treatment of the resurrection in *The Human Face of God* Robinson's mood changes. In keeping with the anti-supernaturalistic theme of that book (as discussed above) he shows a curious ambivalence towards the truth of the bodily resurrection. In relation to this issue he says that he wants 'to argue for retaining the possibility of ambiguity and openness, and therefore for agnosticism rather than dogmatism'.[220] Robinson's argument is fragmentary and incomplete here, but if I have understood him aright, he suggests that one alternative explanation for the empty tomb is that it came about through a total molecular transformation of the body of the dead Christ.[221] Robinson then proceeds to illustrate this point by recalling a story about a Buddhist holy man whose body was transmuted in death so that all that remained was nails and hair.[222]

Robinson is silent here on the personal fate and identity of the risen Christ: rather he insists that, if 'such [molecular] transformation without remainder is to be affirmed of him [Jesus], it cannot be because he is an exceptional anomaly, but because he is a typical representative'. Jesus is thus characterised 'as the leading shoot of a coming, spiritual humanity, in which we shall all share ...'[223]

Although Robinson's treatment of the resurrection followed orthodox patterns at the beginning of his career, it later moved beyond those categories. In so doing, it parallels his interpretation of Christ's pre-existence. In summary, then, we can say that Robinson (at least in *The Human Face of God*) is no clearer about the personal existence and identity of the risen One than he is about the personal existence and identity of the One who became incarnate in Jesus of Nazareth around 5 BC.

To conclude, we can observe that Robinson has clearly raised many radical questions. Whatever the merits of his New Testament exegesis and his ambition to fashion a christology which would stir modern humanity to a greater faith in Jesus Christ, one is left with the impression that, in the course of his argumentation, he has not dealt adequately with certain central philosophical and theological issues. His 'degree christology' with its functional insistence on the complete humanity of Christ and disavowal of the traditional metaphysics of christology, has reduced Jesus to an ordinary man in whom God is present in an extraordinary degree. It must also be stated that it is indeed doubtful whether humanness may be defined solely in terms of one's being a product of the evolutionary process. Also, we must ask whether is it valid to reject the doctrine of the pre-existence of a divine Person without first of all exploring the language of 'before' and 'after' in God. Moreover, we may question the meaning of his assertion that Christ has two equal natures. And finally, though he criticises the traditional christological formulations based on Greek metaphysics, he has not suggested how a modern restatement of the doctrine might make use of contemporary philosophy.

---

220 *HFG*, 138.　**221** Ibid., 138–9.　**222** Ibid., 139, n. 187.　**223** Ibid., 140.

5

John Macquarrie's interpretation of Christ's pre-existence

INTRODUCTION

John Macquarrie was born in Renfrew, Scotland, in 1919, the son of a Scottish Presbyterian family. Having attended Paisley Grammar School, he went to the University of Glasgow in 1936 as a student for the Church of Scotland ministry, where he earned an MA (with first class honours) in Mental Philosophy in 1940. In an autobiographical article, Macquarrie has recalled that the first four of his seven years of studies for the Church of Scotland ministry at the University of Glasgow were 'spent on the rigorous course of study leading to the MA with honours in mental philosophy'.[1] He recounts that during this time he was particularly attracted to the ideas of the English idealist F.H. Bradley.[2] Having completed his philosophical studies, Macquarrie was in a position to begin his theological ones; this was not, however, to prove to be the most felicitous chapter of his life:

> the three years that I spent in the formal study of theology were not the happiest in my life! Biblical criticism and church history I found interesting, and we did a limited amount of philosophy of religion, but dogmatic theology I came to regard as little more than systematic superstition. Calvin and Barth (who were the big names at that time) I found especially insufferable. Theories of atonement and incarnation seemed to me a waste of time.[3]

When his undergraduate studies ended in 1943, Macquarrie refused the offer of a scholarship to pursue graduate studies in theology at Cambridge University: 'I politely declined, and for the next seven years I never opened a book of theology'.[4] Instead, he embarked upon seven years of pastoral ministry: three of them as a chaplain in the British army in the Middle East where he

---

1 *Theology, Church and Ministry* (London, 1986), 1; hereafter *TCM*. 2 Ibid., 2 3 Ibid. Elsewhere, he writes: 'I found the theology courses boring, and much less satisfying than philosophy.' *On Being a Theologian: Reflections at Eighty* (London, 1999), 13. 4 *TCM*, 3

worked in various prisoners of war camps among German detainees; the remainder were spent as a parish minister in Scotland. Macquarrie's 'almost accidental' return to theology on the invitation of one his former theological professors led to a PhD from the University of Glasgow in 1954.[5] Macquarrie's first academic post was a lectureship in systematic theology at the University of Glasgow which he held from 1953–62. He then took a professorship in systematic theology at Union Theological Seminary, New York. In 1970 he returned to Britain to fill the Lady Margaret Chair of Divinity at Oxford. He held that post until his retirement in 1986.[6] During his time in the United States, Macquarrie converted to Anglicanism and was ordained to its ministry in 1965. He still lives in Oxford with his wife, Jenny Fallow Welsh. The couple has three children: two boys and a girl.

Macquarrie's main publications
During the course of his long academic career, Macquarrie has been a prodigious writer. His first book, *An Existentialist Theology* (1955), came from his doctoral work on Heidegger's influence on Bultmann's interpretation of the New Testament. Macquarrie's existentialist interests are further evident in *The Scope of Demythologizing* (1960) and *Studies in Christian Existentialism* (1965).[7] He also co-translated Heidegger's *Being and Time* (1962).

Macquarrie distinguished himself as a critical reporter of modern thought with his *Twentieth-Century Religious Thought* (1963) – which is now in its fourth edition (1988). His *Principles of Christian Theology* (1966) was a one-volume systematic theology that saw him propose his 'existential-ontological' method in theology; a revised edition appeared in 1977.

The debate that followed upon John A.T. Robinson's *Honest to God* (1963) provoked Macquarrie to publish *God-Talk* (1967) and *God and Secularity* (1967). The first of these was to turn out to be one of his most influential books and has been translated into several languages.

The books that emerged since his return to Britain in 1970 are mostly 'expansions of topics that could be treated only briefly in my *Principles [of Christian*

---

5 The same university bestowed a DLitt on him in 1964. He received an MA (by decree) from Oxford in 1970 and a DD in 1981. He holds the following honorary degrees: a DD from the University of the South, 1967; a DD from General Theological Seminary, 1968; a DD from the University of Glasgow, 1969; a DD from the Episcopal Seminary of the South-West, 1981; a DD from Virginia Theological Seminary, 1982; and a DCL from Nashotah House, 1968.   6 Macquarrie's *curriculum vitae* has been set out in the *Festschrift* published in his honour. See A. Kee, & E.T. Long (eds), *Being and Truth: Essays in honour of John Macquarrie* (London, 1986), 453.   7 He had long felt an attraction to Anglicanism on the grounds that it 'had preserved some things of great value that had been lost by the majority of Protestant churches; namely, a liturgy which was continuos with the worship of the early church, and a ministry of bishops, priests and deacons which stood in historic succession to the ministry of the apostles who had been appointed by Christ himself'. *On Being a Theologian*, 38-9.

Theology]'.[8] Thus *Three Issues in Ethics* (1970) and *The Concept of Peace* (1973) develop further the question of the Christian's conduct in the world. *Christian Hope* (1978) explores eschatological themes. Engagement with the ecumenical movement led to *Christian Unity and Diversity* (1975). *Thinking about God* (1975) and *The Humility of God* (1978) mark a return to the God question. Macquarrie's conviction that the Church needs theologically educated laity was the inspiration behind *The Faith and the People of God* (1972).

In *In Search of Humanity* (1982) and its companion volume, the Gifford Lectures at St Andrews (1983-84), *In Search of Deity* (1984), Macquarrie has explored his contention that the doctrine of humanity is the right starting-point for a contemporary theology. What had originally been intended as a third part of a trilogy, associated with these two books on humanity and deity, has turned out to be a much bigger christological study, *Jesus Christ in Modern Thought* (1990). He has returned to christology in *Christology Revisited* (1998), where he reaffirms the position set out in *Jesus Christ in Modern Thought*.

That Macquarrie has maintained his more strictly philosophical interests is evidenced by the publication of *Martin Heidegger* (1968) and *Existentialism* (1972). *Heidegger and Christianity* (1994) explores one important interface between contemporary philosophy and theology. The breadth of his theological interests has not diminished in recent years as shown by his attentions to mariology in *Mary for All Christians* (1991), to world religions in *The Mediators: Nine Stars in the Human Sky* (1995), and to sacramental theology in *A Guide to the Sacraments* (1997). His most recent book, *On Being a Theologian: Reflections at Eighty* (1999) brings together Macquarrie's personal reflections on what it is like to live and work as a theologian and a selection of lectures marking important milestones in his academic life.[9]

The influences of Scottish Presbyterianism and modern philosophy

Having noted the main details of Macquarrie's biographical history and his main publications, we shall now attempt to lay the basis for an understanding of his christological endeavours in general, and of his interpretation of the doctrine of Christ's pre-existence in particular. To achieve these goals, it will be necessary first of all to indicate (albeit briefly) the principal characteristics of his overall theology and the formative factors that shape it. Prominent among those early influences, as we have already indicated, are his Scottish Presbyterian background and education, his interests in the existentialist thought of Heidegger and Bultmann, and his subsequent exposure to ideas from process philosophy.

---

8 *TCM*, 1.   9 While most of the material for this book has been provided by Macquarrie himself, it has been edited by John Morgan.

Scottish Presbyterian background Born into a Scottish Presbyterian family and educated at the University of Glasgow for the Church of Scotland ministry, his background is quite different from that of the other three authors seen above. Despite his conversion to Anglicanism in 1965 and his holding of theological posts in the United States and England, he never lost that attachment to systematic theology so characteristic of Scottish theology.[10] Thus it may come as no surprise to read that one writer on the history of British theology, Daniel W. Hardy, has claimed that Macquarrie does not conform to what he terms 'the typical English vision in theology'[11] in that he tends (unlike, Robinson, for example) to examine issues more from a philosophical rather than an historical vantage point.[12] Thus, as we shall see below, of the four christologies under review in this study, only Macquarrie's involves a prolonged dialogue with the leading figures of post-Enlightenment, Continental philosophy and theology.

Exposure to existentialism Macquarrie's doctoral thesis studied the influence of Heidegger's philosophy on Bultmann's theology. This exposed him to existentialist ideas, and while we cannot delay here on the detail of his findings on the relationship between these two highly significant thinkers, it seems fair to suggest that this experience pre-disposed him favourably towards an openness to other currents of contemporary thought which stress human transcendence and which would be important in his later writings.[13]

10 The faculties of the Scottish universities are considered to be ministerial training institutions, many of whose appointments committees have chiefly Church of Scotland representation. There is thus, as in the Continental universities, an institutional base for the advancement of systematic theology. See S.W. Sykes, 'Theology through History', in D. Ford (ed.), *The Modern Theologians*, 2nd ed. (Oxford, 1997), 230. In England, by contrast, Sykes reports elsewhere, the universities have neglected the study of systematic theology. A similar situation pertains, he adds, in the Anglican theological colleges, where candidates prepare for the ministry. Thus Sykes concludes: 'there [is] no tradition of systematic theology in the Church of England'. See his *The Integrity of Anglicanism* (London, 1978), 82. 11 It should be recalled here that Macquarrie has lived in England since 1970 when he took the prestigious post of Lady Margaret Professor of Divinity in the University of Oxford. 12 D.W. Hardy, 'Theology through Philosophy' in D. Ford (ed.), *The Modern Theologians*, vol. 2, 1st ed. (Oxford: Basil Blackwell, 1989), 54. Hardy goes on to note that by comparison with English theology in general 'Macquarrie's work is both more grounded in general religion interpreted through particular symbols and common life, which are examined philosophically more than historically, and less directed to the judgement and improvement of current practice'. Ibid. A revised version of Hardy's article is to be found in the new, single-volume second edition of *The Modern Theologians* (1997), 252-85. 13 This openness is evident, for example, in his later christological work, *Jesus Christ in Modern Thought* (London, 1990), 362; hereafter *JCMT*. It is also worth noting that Macquarrie comments that one consequence of his exposure to the influence of Heidegger's philosophy upon Bultmann's theology was that he was forced to re-examine his attachment to the ideas of F.H Bradley. Thus, he notes, he was brought 'much closer to

The publication of a book based on his thesis under the title, *An Existentialist Theology* (1955), established him as a scholar of international repute.[14] In it (and indeed in subsequent works) he showed himself to be a mediator of Heidegger[15] and a profound interpreter and critic of Bultmann. Bultmann declared that the book showed Macquarrie 'to be a thinker of high rank, with outstanding power of exposition'.[16] Macquarrie has proved to be of particular significance in that he has been, in the words of the Swedish scholar, David Jenkins, 'one of the few existentialist thinkers who has not been reluctant to identify himself as both Christian and existentialist'.[17] Be that as it may, Macquarrie was never an uncritical adherent of existentialism. Thus in the autobiographical article of 1981 already mentioned above, he could say that even during the heights of 'my existential phase ... I was never, however, quite happy with Bultmann's almost pure existentialism. It seemed to me in danger of becoming quite subjective. I noted too that although Bultmann relied heavily on the early Heidegger, he took no notice of the later ontological work. I felt that I had to broaden the base of my theology.'[18]

The opportunity to begin to do just that presented itself when Macquarrie was gathering material for his *Twentieth-Century Religious Thought* (1963):

reconciling religious faith with intellectual integrity than had been possible when Bradley's philosophy still held sway in my mind'. *TCM*, 3. **14** An indication of the importance of existentialism to Macquarrie's thought throughout his long academic career is the opinion proffered by John O'Donnell, a former doctoral student of his at Oxford, that Macquarrie 'feels more at home with existentialists than with Anglo-Saxon philosophers'. See O'Donnell's review of Macquarrie's *In Search of Humanity* (1982), *Heythrop Journal*, 25 (1984) 373. **15** The English-speaking academic community is also much indebted to him for his co-translation of Heidegger's *magnum opus, Being and Time*. Evidence of Macquarrie's enduring interest in Heidegger is seen in the fact, that when the Board of the Faculty of Theology at the University of Oxford honoured him with the invitation to give the Hensley Henson Lectures for 1993-94, he chose to devote them to Heidegger's concepts of time and history. They have since been published as *Heidegger and Christianity* (London, 1994). We can thus, on the face of it, readily concur with the Swedish scholar, David Jenkins (not to be confused with the English theologian and former Bishop of Durham), when he comments that Macquarrie 'has written most of his works with the aim of incorporating much of what he deems of Christian value in Heidegger's philosophical anthropology into Christian theology'. See his *The Scope and Limits of John Macquarrie's Existentialist Theology* (Uppsala, 1987), 7. **16** See Bultmann's foreword to *An Existentialist Theology: A Comparison of Heidegger and Bultmann* (London, 1955), viii. **17** This is a judgement given by Jenkins in his doctoral dissertation, *The Scope and Limits of John Macquarrie's Existentialist Theology*, 7. **18** *TCM*, 4. A similarly critical evaluation of existential theology made elsewhere by Macquarrie notes that 'this particular style of theology is very illuminating for the human side of the divine-human relationship and for the explication of such phenomena as sin, faith, and salvation. It may be claimed further that it does not permit theology to become a disinterested academic exercise divorced from the actual problems of life. But it fails to provide the critical ontological inquiry which is also necessary to an adequate theology.' See his 'Existentialism and Theological Method', *Communio*, 6 (1979) 15.

'That survey, which expanded far beyond what I had originally envisaged, was in part due to my desire to break out of a narrow existentialism and ... even if no one else were to benefit from it, I would have educated myself in the writing of it.'[19] This book was to prove very popular and through it Macquarrie gained recognition as a critical reporter of contemporary thought.[20] Macquarrie claims that the author who made the greatest impression on him at this time was Karl Rahner,[21] who, he states

> was untranslated and virtually unknown in Britain. The first thing I read was his little work on death. He had been a student of Heidegger, but he takes up the study of death where Heidegger leaves off, and the result seemed to me to be that synthesis of catholic faith and philosophical thought for which I had been searching. I eagerly read other works of his, and found his writings on christology especially illuminating.[22]

Macquarrie claims that the publication of his well received work in philosophical theology (fundamental theology),[23] *Principles of Christian Theology* (1966),[24] marked a very significant moment in his own theological pilgrimage, since 'though it set out from man's existential situation, [it] broke out of narrow existentialism and treated the theme in what I called clumsily enough the "existential-ontological manner"'.[25]

Alongside Macquarrie's debt to existentialism, another set of dynamic philosophical ideas was to have a significant influence on his theological thought (as on Thornton's): process thought.

---

19 *TCM*, 5. **20** It is now in its fourth edition (1988). It is worth noting also that it has not been without its critics. Donald M. MacKinnon, in the course of a review of another of Macquarrie's books, termed it an 'over praised study' and called upon Macquarrie to 'deepen and enlarge his philosophical perception'. See his review of *Studies in Existentialism* (London, 1966), *Journal of Theological Studies*, 18 (1967) 296. **21** Macquarrie notes that he preferred Rahner to Paul Tillich saying that, even though he was attracted by Tillich's *Systematic Theology*, which began to appear in 1953, 'I think that most of what is of value in its philosophical structure has been better said by Heidegger.' *TCM*, 4. **22** *TCM*, 4. He also notes that he came across Hans Urs von Balthasar at this time. **23** Gerald O'Collins concurs with the view that Macquarrie's philosophical theology coincides with what Catholic theology normally speaks of as fundamental theology. See his 'Fundamental Theology', in A. Richardson & J. Bowden (eds), *A New Dictionary of Christian Theology* (London, 1983), 224. **24** J.N.D. Kelly, in his review of the revised edition (1977), has written that the book has been aptly called a 'one-volume *Summa*' and that 'its most remarkable feature was its ingenious and highly successful restatement of traditional Christian beliefs within the framework of a new-style natural theology mainly inspired by the writings of Martin Heidegger'. See *Journal of Theological Studies*, 29 (1978) 617. **25** *TCM*, 6. Macquarrie does not conceal his delight that Eric Mascall, 'a severe critic of existentialism, reviewed the book generously, and agreed that the usual criticisms of existentialism did not affect it'. Ibid.

Process thought Macquarrie's appointment to a teaching post at Union Theological Seminary, New York City, in 1962 brought him into direct contact with
process ideas. He recalled in his Gifford Lectures of 1983-84 that, throughout the
course of his time there he 'taught alongside an eminent process theologian, Daniel
Day Williams'.[26] Elsewhere Macquarrie has noted that 'I was his [Williams'] close
colleague for eight years, and we often discussed theological questions.'[27]
Macquarrie recounts that Williams 'looked to Whitehead for his categories of
theological explanation, while I looked to Heidegger, and we used to compare the
merits and demerits of the use in theology of these two philosophers. I had to
concede that Whitehead provided a much more adequate theology of nature, but
Williams in turn admitted that Heidegger had the more profound understanding
of the human person ...'[28] We cannot delve deeper into Macquarrie's appreciation
and critique of Whitehead and process thought.[29] It is enough to note that,
whatever the detail involved in this realist metaphysics, its main theological contributions are twofold. Firstly, it involved the proclivity to bring God into time, to
make him a natural rather than a supernatural God, perhaps a finite and evolving
God[30] and, secondly, the tendency to regard the human being as an entity not fixed
in character but in the process of self-creation.[31] It must be said, however, that any

---

26 *In Search of Deity* (London, 1984), 146.   27 See Macquarrie's appreciative essay in tribute to
Daniel Day Williams following his death, 'Process and Faith: An American Testimony' in
Thinking about God (London: SCM Press, 1975), 215. Incidentally, this book is dedicated to the
memory of Williams.   28 *In Search of Deity*, 146.   29 An extended treatment of this relationship is to be found in P.J. Connell, *The Theology of John Macquarrie: Becoming as a Hermeneutical
Principle* (Rome, 1989), 84-124. It is to be remarked, however, that the author offers the
somewhat hesitant suggestion at the end of his discussion that 'a fair claim that process thought
may indeed be counted a formative factor in John Macquarrie's theology' can be made. Ibid.,
124. Nor have we the space to explore the ecumenical dimension of Macquarrie's thought.
Evidence of this is his *Mary for All Christians* (London, 1991). For a discussion of his treatment
of Marian themes within an ecumenical perspective in this volume, and for an acknowledgement
of the striking points of convergence between it and the interpretation offered by Karl Rahner,
see J. O'Donnell, *Introduction to Dogmatic Theology* (Casale Monferrato, 1994), 110-4. Louis
Bouyer has seen in Macquarrie, a Presbyterian convert to Anglicanism, one who is very open to
the Catholic dimension: 'Macquarrie qui est paseé du presbytéranisme à l'anglicanisme et à un
anglicanisme trés catholicisant.' See Bouyer, *Le Metier De Theologien* (Paris, 1979), 157. Evidence
of Macquarrie's commitment to dialogue with the other great world religions is his *The
Mediators: Nine Stars in the Human Sky* (London, 1995); published in the United States under
the title *Mediators between Human and Divine: From Moses to Muhammad* (New York, 1996),
where he provides portraits of nine 'really outstanding spiritual geniuses who have deeply
effected the lives of millions'. Taking them in chronological order, in addition to Moses and Jesus
these 'stars' turn out to be: Zoroaster, Lao-zu, Buddha, Confucius, Socrates, Krishna and
Muhammad'. Ibid., 9-10.   30 *Twentieth-Century Religious Thought*, 4th ed. (London, 1988),
259.   31 *JCMT*, 368. Macquarrie notes that it differs from existentialism in that it does not set
humanity over against nature but includes it within nature. Ibid.

temptation to overstress here Macquarrie's reliance on Whitehead (and his disciples) is to be firmly eschewed.[32]

MACQUARRIE'S CHRISTOLOGY

In was not until some four years after his retirement from Oxford, that he published what the dustjacket termed 'this long-awaited [christology] book', *Jesus Christ in Modern Thought*.[33] He states his hopes for the volume when he comments: 'it is my hope that the christology in this book ... stays within the parameters of catholic tradition and is entirely compatible with the governing intentions of Chalcedon and other classic Christian pronouncements'.[34] What emerges, however, in this work of over four hundred and fifty pages is an approach to christology firmly set within the parameters for theology inaugurated by the Enlightenment. The book, as we have noted above, had originally been intended as the culmination of a trilogy completing his reflections on God and humanity in two previous volumes, *In Search of Deity* (1984) and *In Search of Humanity* (1982), but is clearly intended to stand on its own.[35] And it generally exhibits more elements of exploration and inquiry than of *Systematik*.[36] It is much less (explicitly) philosophical in character than what we have come to expect from Macquarrie's pen: Heidegger, for example, only gets nine entries in the index. It breaks new ground for Macquarrie in the extent of its appeal to scripture, though he frankly admits that he is not a scriptural expert and must listen to the voices of

---

32 See D.W.D. Shaw, 'Personality, Personal and Person', in A. Kee & E.T. Long (eds), *Being and Truth: Essays in Honour of John Macquarrie* (London, 1986), 157.   33 Hitherto, Macquarrie's writings on christology had been written primarily from the point of view of philosophical theology. See, for example, his chapter, 'The Person of Jesus Christ' in *Principles of Christian Theology*, revised edition (London, 1977), 268-310. It is followed by a second christological chapter, 'The Work of Christ', 311-27.   34 *JCMT*, 383.   35 This is because an invitation from the editors of *Theologische Realenzyklopädie* to contribute a two-part article on christology (published as 'Jesus Christus VI' and 'Jesus Christus VII', in H.R. Bael et al. (eds), *Theologische Realenzyklopädie*, Band 17, [Berlin, 1988], 16-42 and 42-64) necessitated that, in addition to fulfilling the wish to write a systematic or dogmatic statement on Jesus Christ for our own time, he also had to make a historical study of the major christologies from the Enlightenment to the present day. And when he had done that it became clear to him that, since post-Enlightenment christology was constantly in dialogue with those of earlier times, both scriptural and patristic, it would be necessary to engage with them as well. *JCMT* is the fruit of these considerations and it thus falls into three parts: 'The Sources and Rise of Classical Christology'; 'The Critique of Classical Christology and Attempts at Reconstruction'; 'Who Really is Jesus Christ for Us Today?' See *JCMT*, ix-x.   36 This is a judgement of the book advanced by B.R. Brinkman in the course of a review. See his 'Notes and Comments on Christ and the Church: Macquarrie, Schillebeeckx and Moltmann', *Heythrop Journal*, 32 (1991) 539.

his colleagues.[37] Some one hundred and twenty pages are devoted to a discussion of biblical interpretations of the person of Jesus Christ. Significantly, only twenty seven pages are devoted to the Fathers. Though Macquarrie had written some dozen articles on various christological themes during his long academic career, it is only in this tome that he offers a sustained treatment of christological issues. The following *exposé* of his christology, and more particularly of his inter- pretation of Christ's pre-existence, will have to rely heavily on this book. Let us note then some of the reviews and reactions the book has received.

Alastair H.B. Logan has described *Jesus Christ in Modern Thought* as being 'clear, scholarly, humane, judicious in judgement, illuminating in aside, ecumenical in its breath, Anglican in the best sense in its balance and sacramental concern, brim full of Scots common sense ... [U]nlike many systematicians before him, he not only insists on facing the awkward historical questions but makes creative use of the results of recent New Testament scholarship...'[38] John Hick terms the book 'lucid and comprehensive'.[39] Adrian Thatcher characterises it as 'a mine of infor- mation and scholarship'.[40] John P. Galvin describes it as 'a thoughtful recent study of traditional themes and contemporary reflection on Christ'.[41] John O'Donnell has written that the work represents 'the crowning of the contributions given to us by Prof. Macquarrie ... The major question which the author addresses is how we are to think [about] God in the wake of the challenge of the Enlightenment. The classical christology of the Church which held for over a thousand years from the end of the patristic era to the beginning of the *Aufklärung* collapsed under ... [its] weight'. O'Donnell, however, is somewhat hesitant in his criticism of his old pro- fessor, save for the comment that he wonders 'whether one can be totally satisfied' with the conclusions he offers.[42] Charles A. Wilson is more forthright in spelling- out his misgivings when he remarks that while 'Macquarrie's is a christology of "modernity" and thus it struggles with historical consciousness and Enlighten- ment freedom', the question is whether 'it is the case anymore that believers and nonbelievers alike, really anguish over the cognitive issues associated with the Enlightenment?' He concludes that Macquarrie's 'is a retrospective [christology], a comforting one, from a world that makes more sense than the [post-modern] one into which we seem to be heading'.[43] A similar estimation comes from yet another reviewer, Richard Bauckham, when he comments, in laconic fashion, that Macquarrie 'relates to that [Enlightenment] era like a late Byzantine theologian

---

37 We shall argue below that his confidence in the work of one scriptural scholar, J.D.G. Dunn, has been excessive.   38 A.H.B. Logan, review of *JCMT*, *Theology*, 94 (1991) 211.   39 J. Hick, *The Metaphor of God Incarnate* (London, 1993), 11.   40 A. Thatcher, review of *JCMT*, *Scottish Journal of Theology*, 44 (1991) 534.   41 J.P. Galvin, 'Jesus Christ', in F.S. Fiorenza & J.P. Galvin (eds), *Systematic Theology: Roman Catholic Perspectives* (Minneapolis, 1991), 323. 42 J. O'Donnell, review of *JCMT*, *Gregorianum*, 72 (1991) 582-3.   43 C.A. Wilson, review of *JCMT*, *Journal of Religion*, 73 (1993) 272.

relating to classical Christology, creating a peculiarly lucid and attractive synthesis of the insights of a long period of controversy and innovation ... [T]his book is a magisterial summing up of an era of Christology, but not a book which points to Christology's future'.[44] And finally, Jacques Dupuis views it as heir to that tendency which more often than not besets all christologies 'from below', when he charges that such christologies 'fail to reach out adequately to Jesus-the-Son-of-God. Christology thus becomes a "degree Christology" in which Jesus is reduced to an ordinary man in whom God is present in an extraordinary degree'.[45]

It should be clear from the tenor of these reviews what direction Macquarrie's christology takes: it is written with a firm eye on the questions raised for christology by the Enlightenment, i.e. that movement of ideas of the seventeenth and eighteenth centuries which characteristically distrusted all authority and tradition in matters of intellectual inquiry, and believed that truth could be attained only through reason, observation and experiment.[46]

Severe critique of classical christology
Macquarrie believes that modern Western thought derives its shape and direction, down to our own day, from the Enlightenment: 'it touched virtually every aspect of European thinking ... and not least did it shake to its very base our own theme of christology'.[47] It was, Macquarrie says, to prove to be a watershed in the history of Western thought and ever since

> the traditional answers have been put more and more in question. The New Testament records, considered as history, seem to have become more and more undermined. At the same time, the dogmatic pronouncements concerning the incarnation and the presence in Jesus Christ of the two natures, human and divine, begin to seem very improbable, and we even ask whether we can make sense of them, let alone affirm them as true.[48]

In the face of this 'tidal wave',[49] Macquarrie recounts that the carefully wrought structures of classical christology,[50] which had been agreed at the early Councils

---

44 R. Bauckham, review of *JCMT*, *Journal of Theological Studies*, 42 (1991) 796-7.   **45** Interestingly, Dupuis offers this as a criticism of Robinson, *The Human Face of God* (1972) as well. See Dupuis, *Who Do You Say I Am?* (Maryknoll, New York, 1994), 35 and 38, n. 31.   **46** See F.L. Cross & E.A. Livingstone (eds), *The Oxford Dictionary of the Christian Church*, 3rd ed. (Oxford, 1997), 546-7.   **47** The Enlightenment, as Macquarrie spells out, 'was deeply influential in science, history, politics, philosophy, theology, economics, as well as giving birth to new sciences which applied the principles of the Enlightenment to further areas of nature and human society'. *JCMT*, 23.   **48** 'Pluralism in Christology', in W.G. Jeanrond & J.L. Rike (eds), *Radical Pluralism and Truth: David Tracy and the Hermeneutics of Religion* (New York, 1991), 176.   **49** *JCMT*, 339.   **50** Macquarrie comments: 'Christology was in a new era, we ourselves are still in that era.' Ibid., 339.

and which had remained the norm of belief for more than a thousand years, all through the Middle Ages and even through the Reformation, now found themselves under fire.[51] Their mythological and supernatural characters were all too evident; and the new age was overtly hostile to them.

It is worth pausing at this point to observe that the direction of Macquarrie's thought here and the passion with which he argues it are clearly reminiscent of that of his theological mentor, Rudolf Bultmann (1884-1976) as the latter came to sceptical conclusions about the New Testament documents as historical facts. Moreover, Macquarrie's debt to Bultmann is evident in that *Jesus Christ in Modern Thought* carries forty-five entries under Bultmann's name in its index.[52] Whatever the historical facts may have been, Bultmann is adamant that they had undergone an irreversible metamorphosis: an ancient mythology and cosmology had turned them into a story of a divine pre-existent being who became incarnate and atoned by his blood for the sins of humankind, rose from the dead, ascended into heaven, and would, as was believed, shortly return on the clouds to judge the world and inaugurate the new age. The central story is embellished and illustrated by peripheral legends which tell of miracles and wonders, voices from heaven, victories over demons and the like. The task of critical scholarship now, Bultmann goes on, is to *demythologise* the New Testament so that the *kerygma* can be disengaged from this framework and be set free to address contemporary, post-mythical humanity.[53]

Returning to Macquarrie, we see the similarity between his and Bultmann's assessment of the task of contemporary theology when he asserts that we today 'remain inevitably children of the Enlightenment'[54] and that there are certain

---

51 Ibid., 148. Interestingly, Macquarrie claims that though Reimarus 'represents only the angry initial outburst against the long story of intellectual oppression', one sees in his so-called 'Wolfenbüttel fragments' 'a kind of religious manifesto of the Enlightenment' where 'the witness of the New Testament was read in terms of a naturalistic interpretation, the figure of Jesus was depicted not as a moral and religious leader but a failed political revolutionary, the origins of the church were seen not in a saving mission but in fraud and deception'. In due course, Macquarrie acknowledges that 'the more considered responses followed – not less radical than Reimarus, but more carefully thought out and not merely negative'. Ibid., 339.   52 Macquarrie notes that Bultmann's scriptural studies had led the German scholar to the conviction that the historical person of Jesus had been turned very soon into a myth in primitive Christianity and that it was that myth which now confronts us in the New Testament. He felt that it was impossible to get behind it to the historical Jesus. See *Twentieth-Century Religious Thought*, 4th ed, 363.   53 Ibid., 363-4. It must be said, however, that Bultmann goes too far for Macquarrie in contending that the historical-critical investigations can retrieve nothing but a theologically irrelevant 'Christ after the flesh'. *JCMT.*, 350   54 Macquarrie also acknowledges that 'there are many things in the Enlightenment [that] have been left behind. We no longer share its naive, even pathetic, belief in human perfectibility (though neither did Kant). The crude materialism of some of the French philosophers has long since been discredited by the advances of science itself. We recognise the poverty and shallowness of a merely secular lifestyle

lessons that it has bequeathed to us and these 'can never be unlearned'.[55] Thus, to underline its particular lessons for the discipline of christology, Macquarrie asserts that

> we cannot go back to the mythology of a former age, or to its super-naturalism, or to the spiritual authoritarianism of an infallible church or an infallible Bible. So if we want to ask the question about Jesus Christ and think it worth asking, we have to confront not only [exegetical and historical] difficulties and complexities ... but the equally difficult problems of making sense of it all *within the constraining framework of modern thought* [italics mine].[56]

Having identified what Macquarrie sees as the principal consequences of the Enlightenment for classical christology, we shall now examine his attempts at christological reconstruction *within the constraining framework of modern thought.* It is only by use of these means, Macquarrie believes, that christology will have any prospect of fashioning a credible reply to the question which Bonhoeffer found himself asking in prison and which has lost none of its force: 'Who really is Jesus Christ for us today?'[57] Macquarrie comments that 'we owe it to ourselves to find an answer, for only if we can give some answer can we with integrity remain Christians. And we owe it to society at large to give an answer, especially when people who have felt some attraction to Christianity or to what they have learned about the person of Jesus Christ come and want to learn more'.[58] And the Jesus Christ, to anticipate for a moment, who will emerge from Macquarrie's apologetic (like Bultmann's) is one who is divested of the mythological and supernatural trappings in which, Macquarrie asserts, classical christology had clothed him. If Jesus Christ is to be meaningful to modern humanity and its modern thought, he can only be so as one who shares genuinely and fully in humanity

The shape of Macquarrie's (post-Enlightenment) christology

Macquarrie's claim that the intellectual climate of the West in the aftermath of the Enlightenment has not been hospitable to what he has termed 'the subtle intricacies of traditional christological speculation' and, indeed, to theological and metaphysical questions in general.[59] He offers the broad outlines of a christology

...' Ibid., 25.   **55** Ibid., 26. Macquarrie also draws attention to Hans Küng's expression of a similar sentiment: 'The christological debate that has persisted since the dawn of the modern age has not yet been resolved'. See his *The Incarnation of God* (Edinburgh, 1989), 19; quoted *JCMT*, 340-1.   **56** *JCMT*, 26. Hence the second half of the title of the book, *Jesus Christ in Modern Thought.* Ibid., 23.   **57** Macquarrie refers to this question in the preface to *JCMT*, x.   **58** 'Pluralism in Christology', 177.   **59** *JCMT*, 7. Macquarrie goes on to claim that 'even those who have some interest in such questions often feel impatience on reading some of the christological debates of the past, whether from the patristic or the mediaeval or the

which he claims 'is demanded by the teaching situation in which the church now finds itself'. Macquarrie notes that, 'as the current jargon expresses it', this christology will consequently be one that begins 'from below'.[60] And since Macquarrie is aware that 'metaphysics or ontology is indispensable if one is going to give an account of Jesus Christ that is intellectually well-founded',[61] this approach 'from below' will not be devoid of a philosophical grounding. (The question of how sound this grounding is, must wait till later). It will operate within the parameters of a very different (dare he use the term?) metaphysic than that utilised by the purveyors of classical Christology:[62] one that builds upon the principles that were hammered out for christology after the Enlightenment, and the insights provided recently by certain philosophical anthropologies which stress human transcendence and which Macquarrie interprets as being 'of the highest significance for christology'.[63]

Must begin from below   When Macquarrie comes to outlining his own constructive christological proposals, he is determined, like many other contemporary

Reformation periods. Arguments about the two natures, the hypostatic union, whether Jesus had a human nature but not a human personality – these seem unreal to the modern reader'. **60** Ibid., 342.   **61** Ibid., 344.   **62** Although Macquarrie never alludes to it, there are a number of Anglo-American philosophers of religion, well informed theologically, whose publications have shown that it is far from self-evident that the concepts used by classical christology are to be repudiated as inaccessible to contemporary human inquiry. In their various writings, these authors struggle with many of the concepts that have been bequeathed by classical christology and which Macquarrie feels should now be set aside. Prominent among such authors are Richard Swinburne, Stephen Davis, Thomas V. Morris, Brian Hebblethwaite and William Alston. Macquarrie's oversight in failing to refer to them is all the greater when one notes that Swinburne, like himself, is based in Oxford. We can also note that through the pages of the English journal, *Religious Studies*, in particular, this school of thought has been bringing its ideas to a wider scholarly audience. When I had the privilege of meeting Macquarrie at his home in Oxford in September, 1994, I inquired of him as to whether he had considered referring to their ideas in his *Jesus Christ in Modern Thought*. His reply was to assert that 'I find it hard to get onto the wavelengths of these chaps.' It is worth noting that John Hick in his *The Metaphor of God Incarnate* (London, 1993), dwells, critically and at length, on the christological ideas that have been emerging from this school. Among the more important works of a christological kind that have emerged from these philosophers of religion are: Morris, *The Logic of God Incarnate* (Ithaca, New York, 1986); Hebblethwaite, *The Incarnation* (Cambridge, 1987); Davis (ed.), *Encountering Jesus* (Atlanta, 1988); Alston, *Divine Nature and Human Language* (Ithaca, New York, 1989) and Swinburne, *Revelation* (Oxford, 1991) and *The Christian God* (Oxford, 1994).   **63** *JCMT.*, 363. It seems fair to draw a parallel here between Macquarrie's disquiet with classical christology and his already well known impatience with the classical notion of the God-world relation which he has termed monarchic. This designation he deems appropriate since it involves no reciprocity of relations between God and the world. See his *Thinking About God* (London:, 1975), 111. John O'Donnell dwells briefly upon Macquarrie's treatment of this question in his *The Mystery of the Triune God* (London, 1988), 3.

theologians, to break away from the traditional pattern of beginning 'from above', and to begin his exposition of the person of Christ from an unequivocal affirmation of his complete humanity.[64] This approach is required, he asserts, by the two hundred years of critical scholarship that have followed upon the Enlightenment[65] and has already begun to bear fruit, since 'by pruning away the docetic tendencies that very early entered into the picture of Jesus, it has forced us to recognise that the one who confronts us in the gospels is no mythological demigod but a genuine human being in the fullest sense'.[66] In arguing that christology should begin 'from below', Macquarrie robustly maintains that there are, to his mind, no credible theological objections to adopting this starting-point, and indeed that 'in demanding that christology takes its departure from the human Jesus, one is simply going back to its original path in the earliest days of Christianity'.[67] In support of this

64 *JCMT*, 343. Such a starting-point will have great apologetic advantages since, as Macquarrie states, 'we live in a secular age, when the very word "God" has become elusive for many people. How can one hope to speak intelligibly of Jesus Christ if one begins by talking about his coming from God or identifying him with the divine Logos? But there is more to it than just the practical demands of the educational situation. If there is any truth in the idea of incarnation, then this must mean meeting people where they are, and in a secular age that means meeting them on the level of their everyday humanity. Perhaps they do not think very much about God or have much understanding of God-talk, but they have some understanding of humanity and even of the mystery of humanity, and if Jesus Christ is to be meaningful in such a situation, it will be as the one who shares in humanity.' Ibid. Incidentally, Macquarrie, in his dialogue with Karl Rahner on 'The Anthropological Approach to Theology' at Heythrop College to mark the latter's eightieth birthday, commented that Karl Rahner has employed the anthropological approach 'in an extraordinary fruitful way', and went on to assert that 'the estimate we make of [Rahner's] contribution to theology must in large measure depend upon our opinion about the validity of this way into theological problems'. *TCM*, 49. 65 Macquarrie has elsewhere termed the time since the Enlightenment as 'an unprecedented era of theological renewal and creativity'. See his *Mary for All Christians*, 120. 66 *JCMT*, 358. Macquarrie will have no truck with the conclusions of the 'Jesus as myth' movement. He notes the conclusions of the modern historian, E.P. Sanders, who has attributed virtual certainty to eight facts in the career of Jesus. See Sanders, *Jesus and Judaism* (London, 1985), 43; see *JCMT*, 52-3. 67 *JCMT*, 343. It should be noted that Macquarrie finds the idea of a 'Christ-event' very useful since, he writes, 'we can say that the use of this conception does to some extent relieve the problems that arise from our lack of information about the historical Jesus'. This is because it no longer matters how Jesus understood himself. It does not matter anymore, for example, whether he thought of himself as standing in a unique relationship to the heavenly Father. What is central now, Macquarrie argues, is that we realise that the incarnation consists in the existence of the Christian community, including the beliefs that it formed about Jesus. To profess the incarnation is therefore to affirm the Church and the Christian story by which it lives; and this does not require a prior or independent judgement that the story is literally true. Ibid., 21-3. John Hick has commented that Macquarrie 'uses the Christ-event concept as a way of repairing the fabric of orthodox doctrine after the effects of New Testament criticism'. See his *The Metaphor of God Incarnate*, 34-5.

contention, he refers to Peter's preaching: 'This Jesus whom you crucified, God has made both Lord and Christ' (Acts 2:36), and asserts categorically that for Paul 'Jesus is beyond any question a human being who lived and taught and suffered on this planet'.[68] In speaking of Paul's witness in these terms, Macquarrie lays great store on the significance of his 'Adam christology', which he terms the 'earliest written witness to Jesus Christ'. He finds it very appealing, since it holds to an understanding of Jesus Christ which invokes no suggestion of his being super-human.[69] Rather, Jesus is seen to be the new Adam or new man and is contrasted with the first Adam of Hebrew mythology, the fallen man who failed to attain his stature as a man.[70] Bearing in mind what we have already heard from Macquarrie by way of comment upon the task facing modern christology and upon the need to start 'from below', it comes as no surprise that he should give a favourable assess-ment of this Adam christology, as for instance, when he declares that in it 'we find a theology of his [Christ's] person which can serve as a model for our post-Enlightenment mentality two thousand years later. For, put at its simplest, the career of Jesus Christ is seen as a rerun of the programme that came to grief in Adam but has now achieved its purpose in Christ and with those who are joined with him in the Christ-event.'[71]

Macquarrie's appeal to Adam christology will arise again below when we come to discuss its significance for his interpretation of the doctrine of Christ's pre-existence.[72] What is important for our purposes here is to recognise that Macquarrie believes that christology can be rescued from the unacceptable docetic trappings in which it has for so long stagnated, if it builds upon the evident appeal of Paul's Adam christology.[73] Humanity could then take to heart that tenet of Chalcedonian orthodoxy which classical christology had, in practice, served to repress: 'Jesus Christ was a man consubstantial [*homoousios*] with ourselves.'[74]

Having indicated Macquarrie's conviction concerning the need for chris-tology to uphold unequivocally the full humanity of Christ, we must, however, note his admission that this approach 'taken by itself ... might be criticised as adoptionist'.[75] Though it 'is an important and essential part of the kerygma ...

---

68 *JCMT*, 55.   69 Ibid., 63.   70 Ibid., 359.   71 Ibid., 59.   72 We shall, however, mention here, in passing, that Macquarrie fails to note any theological or hermeneutical problems that may arise as a consequence of his wish to return to the earliest christologies and indeed offers as a theological principle the view that 'in the long history of theological controversies, develop-ment has sometimes gone astray, and that one has got to go back to the origins to check whether a particular development has any rootage in the early witness. Even so central and venerable a dogma as the incarnation is not exempt from this kind of test. We must not force the biblical text to conform to later developments which are alien to it.' Ibid., 56.   73 Macquarrie notes: 'one of the demands of a contemporary christology is that it should begin in the same way as Paul, with an unambiguous recognition of the complete humanity of Christ'. Ibid., 359. He notes Robinson's contention that the Churches are characterised by an unconscious docetism. Ibid., 343.   74 Ibid., 360.   75 'Pluralism in Christology', 179.

it is not a complete christology. To say that a christology for the present day must *begin* from the humanity of Christ is not to decide in advance that it cannot go any further'.[76] And since Macquarrie defines christology as 'the study which has for its subject-matter Jesus Christ, or, to put it in a slightly different way, who he was (or is), and what he did (or does)',[77] it must inevitably go further, since it is obvious, that there must have been something special about this man, to account for the fact that a person from such an obscure background, rejected by his own society, has risen to be the most influential person in a spiritual sense who has appeared in human history. But though he was 'obviously special', this does not separate him from the human race.[78] So special indeed was he that Paul was to speak of him in the words, 'All this is from God' (2 Cor 5:18). Macquarrie regards this declaration by Paul as 'indicating that God had the initiative in all these events, so that there is no "christology from below", set over against a "christology from above", but the two movements are joined together at every stage'.[79] Eventually the Church would speak of Jesus Christ as being consubstantial (*homoousios*) with the Father[80] (as Nicea taught). But what does it mean for us today to talk of Jesus Christ as consubstantial with the Father? Macquarrie, as we shall see, finds particularly useful certain insights offered by Friedrich Schleiermacher, one the great figures of post-Enlightenment thought. His recourse to Schleiermacher's writings is at all times governed by the overriding determination to ensure that the specialness of Jesus is not interpreted as separating him from the human race: Macquarrie argues that he differs from other human beings in degree, not in kind,[81] thus opting for what is known as a 'degree christology', though he himself never uses this term. In adopting this position, Macquarrie is aligning himself with the general thrust of post-Enlightenment thought and rejecting one of the main planks in the metaphysics of classical christology.

The contribution of Schleiermacher Macquarrie recognises in F.D.E. Schleiermacher (1768-1834), 'the father of modern liberal theology',[82] a precursor who was similarly convinced of the urgent need to uphold the full humanity of Christ[83] and whose writings were to be of the utmost significance to the realisation of that objective. Macquarrie recounts that 'his work was like a breath of fresh air blowing into

---

76 *JCMT*, 343.   77 Ibid., 3.   78 Ibid., 359.   79 'Pluralism in Christology', 179. Macquarrie has written elsewhere that 'a christology that begins with the human Jesus comes eventually to an incarnational christology, but the latter complements it rather than supersedes it'. See 'The Humanity of Christ', *Theology*, 74 (1971) 249.   80 *JCMT*, 166.   81 Ibid., 359.   82 Ibid., 193. 83 He comments: 'I have stressed the necessity of maintaining the full humanity of Christ, on the ground that if it is undermined in any way, Christ is made into an alien being and can no longer have any major significance for the human race. I believe that Schleiermacher had the same view.' Ibid., 209.

the dust-filled studies of theologians and philosophers alike', as 'it repudiated the scholastic orthodoxy of both Catholic and Protestant theology, and at the same time the dry conceptualism ... of the rationalists of the Enlightenment'.[84] Since Macquarrie considers Schleiermacher of such importance to modern christology, we shall pause to discuss his contributions.[85] Schleiermacher's christology has been the subject of many studies.[86] Macquarrie devotes some thirty pages to it in *Jesus Christ and Modern Thought*.[87] One central theme in Schleiermacher's thought has 'a strong appeal'[88] to Macquarrie, namely, his intention to expound the incarnation as a 'natural fact' by concentrating on the humanity of Christ[89] and by setting it within an evolutionary or developmental context. Thus Macquarrie comments: 'I think we must agree [with Schleiermacher's project], if we are determined to maintain the full humanity of Christ.'[90] As to an explanation of what is meant by the term 'natural fact', Macquarrie observes that for Schleiermacher

> what we may call a union with the divine was possible for Jesus of Nazareth only because this is a potency that is present in all human nature. Christ did not, so to speak, begin with a supernatural endowment that put him in a different category from all other human beings – then he would not be one of us and would have no significance for human life. Yet this is not to say that he was just a natural product of evolution. In a world created by God, the natural is not merely natural ... [T]he natural, perceived from the point of view of religion, is infused with the supernatural, while the supernatural always communicates itself in and through the

84 Ibid., 193. Macquarrie is referring here, in particular to Schleiermacher's *Reden über die Religion an die Gebildeten unter ihren Verächtern* (1799) which is entitled in English, *On Religion: Speeches to Its Cultured Despisers* (London, 1958). 85 Macquarrie says of Schleiermacher that 'his logical critique of Chalcedon is brilliant'. See his 'Foundation Documents of the Faith III. The Chalcedonian Definition', *Expository Times*, 91 (1979) 71. See also his 'Friedrich Daniel Ernst Scheiermacher', in A. Richardson (ed.), *A Dictionary of Christian Theology* (London, 1969), 306-7. 86 One example is David F. Strauss, *The Christ of Faith and the Jesus of History: A Critique of Schleiermacher's 'Life of Jesus'* (Philadelphia, 1977). Strauss comments that 'Schleiermacher's Christology is a last attempt to make the churchy Christ acceptable to the modern mind'. Ibid., 4. See also K. Barth, *Protestant Theology in the Nineteenth Century* (London, 1972), 425-73. 87 The esteem in which Macquarrie holds Schleiermacher's critique is evident when he notes that 'his critique of classical christology was one of the most acute that has been made' (*JCMT*, 209) and surpasses others (he spells out, in particular, how it betters that of the similarly influential Kant), since it has a more adequate view of what constitutes a human being'. Ibid., 192. Also see Macquarrie, 'Schleiermacher Reconsidered', *Expository Times*, 80 (1969) 196-200, where Macquarrie stresses the profound contribution that Schleiermacher's thought can make today 'towards a rediscovery of religion'. Ibid., 200. 88 *JCMT*, 206. 89 Macquarrie claims that Schleiermacher restores the humanistic christology that had been a feature of the New Testament and which had also been evident in the writings of Irenaeus and Maximus the Confessor. Ibid., 167 and 372. 90 Ibid., 203.

natural. To speak of the incarnation as a 'natural fact' is not to deny God's agency, his predestination of Jesus and his vocation of Jesus – in short, his election of Jesus to his messianic office. Schleiermacher has no wish to deny this other aspect of the matter. He is trying hard to hold together both the solidarity of Christ with all humanity, and his difference.[91]

Macquarrie goes on to note that for Schleiermacher 'the structure of this humanity that we know in ourselves and which is the same in us as it was in Christ Jesus' is the consciousness of absolute dependence upon God. And Macquarrie asserts, very importantly, that 'the more clearly a human being is conscious of his absolute dependence, then the clearer becomes its correlative, namely, his God-consciousness'.[92] What distinguishes Jesus, however, from humanity is the constant potency of his God-consciousness, which was a veritable existence of God in him. As divine, in this sense, Jesus is not to be considered as unique in kind or quality but only in the degree of his God-consciousness.[93]

It should also be observed that Macquarrie feels very drawn to Schleiermacher's doctrine of the person of Christ as epitomised by the German theologian's comments: Jesus is 'the one in whom the creation of the human nature, which up to this point had existed only in a provisional state, was perfected';[94] and again, 'the Christ even as a human person was ever coming to be simultaneously with the world itself'.[95] Macquarrie interprets 'even as a human person' here to refer to Christ not just as the eternal Logos but as the incarnate Logos. He states that for Schleiermacher the

> incarnation did not take place on a particular date but was a process that has been going on over a very long period of preparation. The suggestion seems to be that the incarnation is an aspect of world-history or an element in the cosmic process, so that even as the world was developing and assuming its form through the ages in which it had been in existence, Jesus Christ too as a physical existence was in the process of formation in these events.[96]

---

91 Ibid., 203-4.   92 Ibid., 204. Macquarrie quotes Schleiermacher directly here: 'the feeling of absolute dependence [is] in itself a co-existence of God in the self-consciousness'. See Schleiermacher, *On Religion*, 126.   93 Macquarrie comments: 'the understanding of what a human being is or can become is the clue to that particular status which Christians ascribe to Jesus as the Christ or the Redeemer or the Mediator or whatever expression may be used'. *JCMT*, 192.   94 F.D.G. Schleiermacher, *The Christian Faith*, 2nd ed. (Edinburgh, 1928), 374; quoted in *JCMT*, 204. Macquarrie recognises in Schleiermacher at this point that type of second Adam christology which he finds in Paul and Irenaeus. For Schleiermacher the second Adam is not only successful in overcoming the sin of the first Adam, but also in advancing from the immaturity of that first Adam to the perfecting of hitherto undeveloped human potentialities. Ibid., 205.   95 Ibid., 402; quoted in *JCMT*, 205.   96 *JCMT*, 205. Macquarrie remarks that evolutionary ideas were circulating since the early part of the eighteenth century

To conclude here, we can acknowledge that Macquarrie's insistence that there is no difference in kind (an infinite qualitative difference) between Christ and humanity has drawn him towards certain arguments concerning the incarnation proffered by Schleiermacher. We have seen that Macquarrie finds himself in complete agreement with Schleiermacher's claim that Christ's divinity is a variable human attribute which has reached its maximum in Jesus of Nazareth. Macquarrie thus speaks of Jesus as 'the completion of the creation of man' and, as such, the man in whom there is a 'veritable presence of God'.[97] Macquarrie, as we shall now see, continues to struggle with these and related ideas while pondering the potential offered to christology by a number of modern transcendental philosophies.[98] To his appreciation of these modern philosophical anthropologies we must now turn our attention.

The contribution of various transcendental philosophies   The thought of the younger Macquarrie was shaped by his exposure to the modern dynamic anthropologies of existentialist and process thought. In *Jesus Christ in Modern Thought,* a book published some four years after his retirement, and thus the fruits of his mature reflections, those same influences are still evident, though of course his knowledge and interests extend well beyond the confines of those two particular philosophical schools. Having gleaned what he can from the principal figures of post-Enlightenment thought (above all Schleiermacher), and having noted the critical responses that their ideas provoked among a host of thinkers from Kierkegaard down to the present day, Macquarrie turns to examine what the dynamic, philosophical anthropologies of recent decades can offer to a christological project that takes as its point of departure the humanity of Christ. What is of particular interest to him is the potential these anthropologies might afford to the task of fashioning a deeper understanding, or rather providing a language which allows for intelligible discourse about the 'other side of the God-man relationship',[99] the divine side of Jesus Christ ('All this is from God'). In doing this, however, Macquarrie has widened his inquiries beyond a consideration of existentialist and process ideas to include also two other philosophical anthropologies: Marxism (or neo-Marxism) and transcendental Thomism.[100]

Macquarrie is clearly attracted to these anthropologies because of a characteristic that they have in common: the emphasis they put on human transcendence. He defines transcendence as 'the idea that human nature is not a fixed essence but

and that it may well be that some of the speculations of Johann Gottfried Herder (1744–1803) lie behind Schleiermacher's words. Ibid., 206.   **97** Ibid., 373.   **98** Ibid.   **99** Ibid., 383.   **100** Ibid., 363. In the existentialist schools he mentions Jean-Paul Sartre and Fredrich Nietzsche (both atheists); in the (neo) Marxist one, Herbert Marcuse and Ernst Bloch; in the field of process ideas, A.N. Whitehead, Norman Pittenger and Charles Hartshorne; and in transcendental Thomism, Karl Rahner and Bernard Lonergan.

has an openness that seems to allow for indefinite development ...'[101] The potential evident in this way of thinking for christology, according to Macquarrie, is very clear:

> modern philosophical anthropologies are presenting us with a view of the human being which makes intelligible certain ideas which seem to be assumed in christology – that human 'nature' is something still taking shape and therefore capable of 'transcendence', and that it is through a transcendent anthropology that one might hope to come to some understanding of divinity, as the ultimate horizon of our transcendence.[102]

In other words, human existence is precisely transcendence towards God.[103]

Macquarrie characterise the development in recent decades of these philosophical anthropologies which stress human transcendence as 'a fact of the highest significance for christology'. He argues that 'If indeed christology should take its departure from the humanity of Christ, and if humanity contains within itself a principle of transcendence, then there may be a way here that, beginning from the total humanity of Jesus Christ, "consubstantial" with all humanity, leads to the conception of a transcendent or transcending humanity which, in an older terminology, would have been called "God-manhood".'[104] In this way, a christology beginning from below (an ascending christology), opens up to incarnational christology.

Bearing in mind Macquarrie's determination to fashion a christology which takes Christ's humanity as its point of departure, the attraction of this trans-

---

101 Ibid., 375.   102 Ibid., 365.   103 It should be noted here that Macquarrie's understanding of God involves the rejection of the 'almost exclusive stress on the transcendence of God' that is to be found in much of Christian theology. He argues that 'when God is understood in this way, it becomes very hard to see how he could enter history in the manner that is implied by the doctrine of the incarnation'. Kierkegaard and Barth are taken to task for their talk of God as 'wholly other'. Ibid., 376. In an earlier book, Macquarrie has outlined a more dynamic conception of God; one demanded by reflection on God and his creation: 'God was never an absentee God, dwelling apart from his creation. From the beginning he has been deeply involved with his creation. His spirit has been bringing forth new possibilities and healing the wounds which sin has inflicted. God's commitment to the creation has been an ever deepening commitment, and Christians believe that with Jesus Christ that commitment took on a new dimension in what we call the incarnation. God's presence and activity, which had always been in the world, were concentrated and focused in a human life which manifested on a finite level what is most central in the life of God himself.' See his *The Humility of God* (London, 1978), 19. 104 *JCMT*, 363. Macquarrie refers here to 'Rahner's claim that christology is "transcendent anthropology",' and Macquarrie goes on to state that 'that expression would seem to imply not just a humanity that transcends itself but an anthropology that transcends itself to become theology (thus reversing Feuerbach)'.

cendental approach is very strong: it involves no appeal to those special supernatural forces which are so inimical to post-Enlightenment thought. The case
is rather, as Macquarrie points out, that

> to call him the God-man (or whatever the preferred expression may be) is
> to claim that in him human transcendence has reached the point at which
> human life has become so closely united with the divine life that, in the
> traditional language, it has been 'deified'. It has not however ceased to be
> human – rather, for the first time, we learn what true humanity is. In a
> typical sentence, Rahner says: 'Only someone who forgets that the essence
> of man is to be unbounded ... can suppose that it is impossible for there to
> be a man who, precisely by being man in the fullest sense (which we never
> attain) is God's existence in the world'.[105]

Macquarrie goes on to claim that this interpretation of christology in terms
of the raising of a human being to God 'has its roots as far back as we can go',
and he points to the Genesis account of the first human couple being created in
the image and likeness of God (1:26-27).[106] Then, looking upon humanity as
imago Dei,[107] Macquarrie asks: 'If then there ever came into existence a human
being in whom the image was not defaced but manifested in its fullness, would
not that human being, precisely by being fully human, be God's existence into
the world, so far as the divine can become manifest on the finite level?'[108]

MACQUARRIE AND CHRIST'S PRE-EXISTENCE

From what we have seen already of Macquarrie's criticisms of classical christology as tending towards docetism and of his predilection for a christology that
begins from below, it should come as no surprise that the doctrine of Christ's
personal pre-existence fills Macquarrie with foreboding. Running like a red-thread
right through his treatment of the issue is the curious presupposition that the
doctrine implies the claim that the *humanity* of Christ pre-existed the incarnation;
that Jesus somehow eternally pre-existed *qua Jesus*.[109] Such a claim would

105 Ibid., 370-1. This quotation from Rahner comes from his 'Current Problems in Christology', *Theological Investigations*, vol. 1 (London, 1961), 184.   106 *JCMT*, 371.   107 The
concept of the *imago Dei* is an important one in Macquarrie's writings. See D. Pratt, 'The
Imago Dei in the Thought of John Macquarrie: A Reflection on John 10:10', *Asian Journal of
Theology*, 3 (1989) 79-83.   108 *JCMT*, 371. Macquarrie has commented elsewhere that 'if
Jesus Christ is the true man, the unveiling of the highest possibilities inherent in humanity, then
he is the best clue to the creative reality at the heart of our universe, he is the truth of God. He
is the word or meaning that has been there from the beginning and that in him has come to light
and been made unconcealed in a decisive way'. See his *The Humility of God*, 31.   109 If there

threaten the genuineness of Christ's humanity and would thus be clearly at odds with the directions for christology (in the wake of the Enlightenment) that we have seen him delineate above. Hence he unambiguously states: 'I would reject any personal pre-existence as mythological and also as undermining a genuine recognition of the humanity of Christ.'[110]

In what is to follow in this section, we shall see Macquarrie contend that Paul did not teach the doctrine of Christ's pre-existence. And where pre-existence language is found in the New Testament, especially in John, Macquarrie argues that it was never intended to be read as implying that Jesus Christ had *personally* pre-existed.[111] In an article written thirty-five years ago, Macquarrie articulated an attitude towards the doctrine that has remained with him throughout his career:

> It sees to me ... that the idea of pre-existence, like so many other ideas in the New Testament, does have a value that lies obscured beneath its mytho-logical associations, and that it would be wrong to reject pre-existence in favour of a through-going adoptionism. Rather, we ought to look more closely at the idea of pre-existence, and see whether we can restate its essen-tial meaning in a language that would be intelligible to our time.[112]

Macquarrie, as we shall see, proposes very different interpretations of those texts which have traditionally been interpreted as pointing to the doctrine of Christ's personal pre-existence. We begin with Paul.

Paul

Macquarrie insists that Paul understood Jesus Christ as someone rooted in his-tory: 'he was not a heavenly being, in the sense of an alien form of existence, but a human being, a fellow-Israelite who moreover had been humiliated and subjected to a degrading execution as a criminal'.[113] Going on to consider whether Paul thought of Jesus Christ as a pre-existent being, Macquarrie begins by recalling the words of the American Anglican theologian, W.P. DuBose, who, in the early years of the twentieth century, wrote: 'that St Paul realizes profoundly the truth of the pre-existence and the deity of our Lord, there can be no question.'[114] If similar

was any basis to this charge, it would mean that the doctrine of pre-existence would be deci-sively at odds with Chalcedon's teaching that Christ is *homoousios* with us as to his humanity (*DS* 301), since there is no suggestion that we are pre-existent in our humanity.   110 *JCMT*, 145.   111 This is his evaluation of the pre-existence language that he agrees can probably be found in Hebrews, 1 Peter, Ephesians and Revelation. He believes that 'we do not need to introduce pre-existence in some of the other important New Testament witness, notably the synoptics'. Ibid., 388   112 'The Pre-existence of Jesus Christ', *Expository Times*, 77 (1966) 199-200.   113 *JCMT*, 54. Macquarrie is unimpressed with the arguments of scholars like Wrede on this point. Ibid. 55.   114 DuBose, W.P., *The Gospel according to Paul* (London, 1907), 293. Reprinted in D.S. Armentrout, *A DuBose Reader* (Sewanee, 1984), 142; quoted *JCMT*, 55.

claims were to be made today, Macquarrie maintains that these would 'bring shrill howls of protest not only from radical theologians ... but would also call forth a demur from many moderate biblical scholars who might perhaps themselves be firm believers in a doctrine of incarnation, but whose scholarly integrity would compel them to deny that "the pre-existence and the deity" of Jesus Christ are as clearly taught by Paul as DuBose supposes'.[115]

Whether the presence of the doctrine of pre-existence in Paul is really held in such low regard by moderate scholars today, need not detain us here. We need only state that, while it is generally accepted that the notion of pre-existence is not a dominant theme in Paul, most scholars would conclude, *pace* Macquarrie, that it is to be found there (especially 1 Cor 8:6; 2 Cor 8:9; Phil 2:6-7 and Col 1:15-17).[116] And even more problematic arguably is his claim that this same 'scholarly integrity' would compel them to deny that Paul taught the deity of Christ.[117] At this point, it is sufficient to observe that Macquarrie, in pursuing his polemic against the presence of the doctrine of pre-existence in Paul, draws very heavily upon the writings of one Scottish exegete, James D.G. Dunn,[118] whom he implausibly terms a 'moderately conservative scholar'.[119] Dunn, in his *Christology in the Making*,[120] had set himself the task of discovering how and when a doctrine of

---

115 *JCMT*, 55. Macquarrie regrets that he must reject the opinion of his friend, John Knox, that Paul unfortunately upholds the notion of pre-existence. Ibid. 144-6. See Knox, *The Humanity and the Divinity of Christ* (Cambridge, 1967), 20.   116 The Pauline scholar, Joseph A. Fitzmyer, expresses this point in pithy fashion when he comments, 'Paul presupposes, if he does not allude to the pre-existence of Christ'. See his 'Pauline Theology', *NJBC*, 1383. In view of Macquarrie's already mentioned indebtedness to Bultmann, we draw attention here to the fact that Macquarrie's scepticism as regards Paul and pre-existence constitutes a departure from Bultmann's beliefs on the question. The radical German exegete held that Paul taught Christ's pre-existence in the following texts: Phil 2:5ff; 2 Cor 8:9; and Rom 15:3. See Bultmann, *The Theology of the New Testament*, vol. 1 (London, 1952), 188.   117 Here we might note another comment from Fitzmyer when, in discussing the significance of the Pauline title *Kyrios* for Jesus, he states, among other things, that 'though in itself *Kyrios* does not mean "God" or assert the divinity of Christ, the fact that Paul (and early Jewish Christians before him) used of the risen Christ the title that Palestinian Jews had come to use of Yahweh, puts him on the same level with Yahweh and implies his transcendent status. He is in reality something more than human'. See his 'Pauline Theology', 1395.   118 Macquarrie's almost total reliance here on Dunn must be viewed as surprising in light of the extensive scholarly literature that has touched upon the question of pre-existence in Paul and come to conclusions at variance with Dunn's. Thus H.P. Owen has commented that he believes that Macquarrie 'invalidly follows Dunn in denying that Paul ascribed pre-existence to Paul'. See his review of *JCMT*, *New Blackfriars*, 72 (1991) 203-4. Charles C. Hefling (Jnr), has written that 'the chief warrant for the interpretation Macquarrie follows is a minority report filed by J.D.G. Dunn, whose discussion of the various issues is nothing if not thorough. But although Dunn's is not a solo voice, the supporting chorus is small'. See his 'Reviving Adamic Adoptionism: The Example of John Macquarrie', *Theological Studies*, 52 (1991) 482-3.   119 *JCMT*, 55.   120 The book is subtitled: *An Inquiry into the Origins of the*

incarnation was reached by the early Church. The Tübingen theologian, Karl-Josef Kuschel, has commented that, on account of this book, 'Dunn to some degree has a key role in ... [this] present debate in christology.'[121] Macquarrie notes that Dunn cautions strongly against the temptation to read later doctrines of the Church back into the New Testament and instead proposes that the christological enterprise should begin with the question:

> What would it have meant ... to their hearers when the first Christians called Jesus 'Son of God'? We must endeavour to attune our listening to hear with the ears of the first Christians' contemporaries. We must attempt the exceedingly difficult task of shutting out the voices of church fathers, councils and dogmaticians down the centuries, in case they drown the earlier voices, in case the earlier voices were saying something different, in case they intended their words to speak with different force to their hearers.[122]

When this is done, Macquarrie notes, with Dunn's exegesis in mind, then 'the idea of pre-existence which DuBose and a host of other scholars have confidently ascribed to Paul's understanding of Jesus Christ' will not seem so certain.[123] Macquarrie claims that they would be forced to concede that their assessment of whether Paul upheld Christ's pre-existence was 'demanded by logic rather than exegesis'. And as to the shape of this logic, he comments: 'if God sent forth his son, must not that son have already been in existence?' Macquarrie counsels extreme caution here and proposes that, since the language that is being dealt with here is metaphorical or even mythological, it must be faced that

> the language and logic of common sense may not be directly applicable. God's metaphorical 'sending' of his metaphorical 'son' can be understood in ways that do not imply pre-existence, once we accept that the language is metaphorical not literal. Here I come back to the views of James Dunn, who does in fact argue that passages in Paul which, at first sight, seem to entail a doctrine of the pre-existence of Jesus Christ, do not do so.[124]

Dunn comes to these conclusions after submitting those Pauline tests which are normally associated with the doctrine of pre-existence to his own exegetical

Doctrine of the Incarnation (London, 1980), 2nd ed., 1989. **121** K.-J. Kuschel, *Born before All Time? The Dispute over Christ's Origin* (London, 1992), 597, n. 6. **122** J.D.G. Dunn, *Christology in the Making*, 2nd ed. (London, 1989), 1, 13-4; quoted in *JCMT*, 55. **123** *JCMT*, 56. **124** Ibid. In saying this, Macquarrie has moved from the position he had enunciated some thirty-five years earlier when he commented: 'presumably St Paul too held a belief in the pre-existence of Christ'. See his 'The Pre-existence of Christ', 199.

scrutiny: Galatians 4:4, Romans 8:3, 2 Corinthians 8:9, and 'above all' Philippians 2:6-7.[125] Macquarrie confines his exposition of Dunn's exegesis of these
passages to that of the Philippians Christ-hymn since, in his own words, it is
'possibly the most important place in the Pauline epistles where pre-existence
is an issue'.[126] As Dunn's interpretation of this passage is of such importance
to Macquarrie's argument, our next task here will be to acquaint ourselves with
its broad thrust. In so doing, we shall see Macquarrie encountering the type of
christology that we saw him so heartily recommend above: Adam christology.

Dunn's interpretation of the Philippians Christ-hymn   At the heart of Dunn's
exegesis of the Philippians hymn rests an hypothesis about how Paul would
have understood this text. He claims that if we 'try to understand the words
against the background in which we may judge Paul understood them',[127] then
we would have to acknowledge that their roots are probably to be found in the
stories of the creation and fall in the early chapters of Genesis. Building his
theory upon this, Dunn goes on to propose, in Macquarrie's paraphrase, that

> Paul's christological teaching turns on a contrast between Adam and
> Christ, or between the sinful humanity of the fallen human race and the
> new humanity that came into being in Christ. Adam was made in the
> image or form of God (Dunn says that the words *eikon* and *morphe* are
> virtually synonymous) but grasped at something more – to take God's
> place, we may suppose, through this grasping he lost the likeness that
> was already within his reach. Jesus Christ, by contrast, 'faced the same
> archetypal choice that confronted Adam, but chose *not* as Adam had
> chosen (to grasp equality with God). Instead, he chose to empty himself
> of Adam's glory and to embrace Adam's lot'.[128]

125 *JCMT*, 56. Dunn's discussion of the question of Christ's pre-existence is to be found
primarily in *Christology in the Making*. Note the presence of the important 'Foreword', to the
second edition, xi-xxxix, (1989). Macquarrie characterises the book as 'Professor Dunn's
important work'. *JCMT*, 56. Dunn also returns to the theme of Christ's pre-existence in *The
Theology of Paul the Apostle* (Edinburgh, 1998), 266-93.   126 *JCMT.*, 56.   127 Ibid.
Macquarrie acknowledges that the hymn probably has a pre-Pauline origin but does not delay
on the point. Ibid., 47.   128 Ibid., 57. Although Macquarrie fails to allude to it, Dunn's theory
that Christ is being contrasted in this passage with Adam is a controversial one. Brendan Byrne
is unconvinced of the veracity of the claim. Thus in a comment on verse 6, he states: 'a contrast
with Adam at this point is difficult to prove'. In saying this, Byrne acknowledges that he is
distancing himself from the opinions of certain exegetes: P. Bonnard, O. Cullmann, J. Héring,
M.D. Hooker and J. Murphy-O'Connor and aligning himself with T.F. Glasson. In support of
his argument, Byrne refers to Glasson's article, 'Two Notes on the Philippians Hymn (2: 6-11)',
New Testament Studies, 21 (1974-75) 133-9. See Byrne, 'The Letter to the Philippians', *NJBC*,
794. Another scholar, the Evangelical Anglican exegete, N.T. Wright, has noted that while 'most

Macquarrie asserts emphatically at this point that 'the interpretation of the Christ-hymn offered by Professor Dunn is not reductionist',[129] because

> it still brings us to the point where Christ receives the 'name that is above every name'. But it is equally clear that the order of reasoning has been reversed. The conventional way of taking the Philippians hymn, as the story of a heavenly being who lays aside his pre-existent glory to become man is ... a 'christology from above' ... a 'catabatic' christology. The alternative interpretation represents the hymn as the story of a man who lays aside any desire to displace God, and who offers everything, even life itself, to God for the furtherance of God's purpose. This is what is popularly called 'christology from below' or 'anabatic christology'. This second type of interpretation not only fits well with the modern insistence on the full humanity of Christ ..., but also dispenses with the mythological idea of a personal pre-existence of Jesus Christ.[130]

It is amazing that Macquarrie, in relying so heavily in *Jesus Christ in Modern Thought* upon the work of one exegete, Dunn, shows no awareness of the strong criticisms that the latter's theories in *Christology in the Making* (published a decade earlier) have incurred. While such scholars as Donald M. MacKinnon, N.T. Wright and Brendan Byrne, for example, are prepared to acknowledge the presence of Adam christology in the Christ-hymn, they do not see that as ruling out the idea of pre-existence there as well.[131] Thus MacKinnon asks: 'is it absurd to

scholars are now happy to read' the Philippians Christ-hymn as an example of Paul's Adam christology 'doubts are still sometimes expressed on the subject, and there is certainly no agreement among those who do see Adam there as to what conclusions should be drawn from this supposition'. See Wright, *The Climax of the Covenant* (Edinburgh, 1991), 58.   **129** A charge levelled against it by the following reviewers of *Christology in the Making:* T. Weinandy, *Theological Studies*, 42 (1981) 96; D. Hagner, *Reformed Journal*, 32 (1982) 19-20; C. Stead, *Religious Studies*, 18 (1982) 96; L. Sabourin, *Religious Studies Bulletin*, 3 (1983) 113; R.G. Hamerton-Kelly, *Virginia Seminary Journal*, December (1983) 29-30. A.T. Hanson has spoken of it as pointing to 'a crude adoptionism', in his *The Image of the Invisible God* (London, 1982), 75.   **130** *JCMT*, 57. In contradistinction to Macquarrie's exegesis of this text, Raymond Brown, for example, has commented that 'most scholars ... would understand Phil 2:6-7 to mean that Jesus did not consider being equal to God something to be clung to. In this interpretation, unlike Adam who, as a creature was not equal to God but sought to be, Jesus was already equal to God but was willing to empty himself to accept the form of a servant by becoming a human being. Those who support this interpretation argue correctly that a more normal understanding of the Greek in Phil 2:7-8 would have the Son becoming a human being'. See his *An Introduction to New Testament Christology* (London, 1994), 135.   **131** In parenthesis, we can report that this was the position of Thornton when he stated that 1 Cor 15, Rom 5 and Phil 2 are 'passages which assign to our Lord the position of a second Adam who is also a heavenly pre-existent being'. See his *The Incarnate Lord* (London, 1928), 293.

find a parallel inter-weaving of the notion of pre-existence and authentic Adam in Philippians 2?'[132] Wright has written that the presence of Adam christology 'says nothing of itself against pre-existence. It may actually require it ...'[133] Byrne judges that 'finding pre-existence in the Philippians hymn in no sense excludes an allusion to Adam'.[134] C.F.D. Moule is also unconvinced by Dunn's thesis that Christ can be understood here purely in terms of Adam and that there would have been no difficulty for the first Christians in believing in the exaltation of Jesus without also believing in his pre-existence. This compels him to question radically Dunn's thesis: 'but is this so? Can a monotheist rank Jesus in a transcendental category (very different from that of a translated Moses or Elijah) and still manage not to perceive that this must imply eternal pre-existence? This point deserves discussion.'[135] Carl R. Holladay may have succeeded in summarising the general tone of these reviews when he characterises Dunn's thesis as one built upon 'a fair amount of special pleading, logically and exegetically'.[136]

132 He then goes on to comment that 'what Dr Dunn's book lacks is a deep theological engagement with what drove early Christian theologians to attribute nervously and uncertainly, but still with a genuine and mounting confidence, pre-existence to Christ, and with the way this attribution affected their whole understanding of the ultimate context of his mission and work'. See MacKinnon's review of *Christology in the Making, Scottish Journal of Theology*, 35 (1982) 364.   133 Wright inverts Dunn's use of Adam here by asserting that in this Philippians passage 'the temptation of Christ was not to snatch at a forbidden equality with God, but to cling to his rights and thereby opt out of the task allotted to him, that he should undo the results of Adam's snatching'. See his *The Climax of the Covenant*, 92. In saying this Wright acknowledges his agreement with E. Lohmeyer who has pointed out that only of a divine being can it be said that he was obedient unto death, since for all other human beings death comes as a mere necessity. See Lohmeyer, *Kyrios Jesus: Eine Untersuchung zu Phil.* 2:5-11 (Heidelberg, 1928).   134 B. Byrne, 'Christ's Pre-existence in Pauline Soteriology', *Theological Studies* 58 (1997) 318-9. 135 C.F.D. Moule, review of *Christology in the Making, Journal of Theological Studies*, 33 (1982) 262.   136 C.R. Holladay, review of *Christology in the Making, Journal of Biblical Literature*, 101 (1982) 611. In addition, we can note the following critical discussions: review by F.M Young, *Theology* 34 (1981) 303-5; and an article by B. Cranfield, 'Some Comments on Professor J.D.G. Dunn's Christology in the Making with Special Reference to the Evidence of the Epistle to the Romans', in L.D. Hurst & N.T. Wright (eds), *The Glory of Christ in the New Testament. Studies in memory of G.B. Caird* (Oxford, 1987), 267-80. A whole symposium written directly and indirectly against Dunn is to be found in H.H. Rowdon (ed.), *Christ the Lord: Studies in Christology presented to D. Guthrie* (Leicester, 1982). Further treatment of Dunn's christology is published in R. Jewett (ed.), *Christology and Exegesis: New Approaches* (Decatur, 1985): with contributions from C. Holladay, L. Hurtado, A.F. Segal, R.H. Fuller and D. Juel, and a response from Dunn himself; see the review of this volume by E. Schweizer, *Theologische Literaturzeitung*, 111 (1986) 741-4. In it Schweizer argues, against Dunn, that Paul does teach pre-existence: 'Richtig scheint mir (gegen Dunn) daß diese [Präexistenz] schon Phil 2:6-11 und Kol. 1:15-20, ja bei Paulus selbst vorausgesetzt ist ...'. Ibid., 743. Marcus Bockmuehl has noted that 'critics have pointed out that passages like 1 Cor 8:6; 2 Cor 8:9; Phil 2:6-11 appear to cast doubt on [Dunn's] argument'. See his *This Jesus* (Edinburgh, 1994), 194, n. 13. Elsewhere,

A clue to why Macquarrie feels able to pass over these criticisms of Dunn[137] is evident in a comment he makes in the course of a criticism of both DuBose and Knox. Both of these scholars accept that Paul believed that Christ pre-existed. Macquarrie comments that he sets aside their exegesis since what is at issue here is '[not] purely a question of exegesis' and he goes on:

> if it were purely a question of exegesis, I would hesitate when two eminent New Testament scholars differ. 'Who should decide when doctors disagree?' But it seems to me that economy favours Dunn, and makes us shy away from such a dubious notion as pre-existence. If we can make sense of Paul without it, that is in itself supportive of Dunn. I remember another New Testament scholar, William Barclay, saying to me that he was an adoptionist in christology because it was the only christology he could understand! An excellent reason![138]

Macquarrie does not delay much on Dunn's handling of the other Pauline texts traditionally interpreted as pointing to the personal pre-existence of Jesus Christ.[139] Yet Macquarrie does comment, *en passant*, that in his exegesis of these texts too, in his opinion, 'Dunn puts up a good case'. Thus for instance, Dunn's reading of 2 Corinthians 8:9 ('For you know the grace of our Lord Jesus Christ, that though he was rich, yet for our sake he became poor') is similarly seen as not advocating a kenotic christology. Macquarrie briefly quotes Dunn's summation:

> Adam's enjoyment of God's fellowship could readily be characterised as a 'being rich', just as his fall resulted in his 'becoming poor' ... Though he could have enjoyed the richness of an uninterrupted communion with God, Jesus freely choose to embrace the poverty of Adam's distance from God, in his ministry as a whole, but particularly in his death, in order that we might enter into the full inheritance intended for Adam in the first place.[140]

Bockmuehl has commented that 'Despite attracting a good deal of interest, Dunn's interpretation has failed to win the day'. See his ' "The Form of God" (Phil 2:6): Variations on a Theme of Jewish Mysticism,' *Journal of Theological Studies*, 48 (1977) 10. See further Hurst, 'Re-enter the Pre-existent Christ in Philippians 2:6-11?', *New Testament Studies* 32 (1986) 449-57; C.A. Wanamaker, 'Philippians 2:6-11: Son of God or Adamic Christology', *New Testament Studies* 33 (1987) 179-93.   137 Something which Dunn himself also does by virtue of his restatement of his interpretation of Christ's pre-existence in his recent *The Theology of Paul the Apostle*. Dunn finds that his own argument 'is still very persuasive'. Ibid., 282. See the following critical reviews: *Catholic Biblical Quarterly* 61 (1999) 153-5 [B. Byrne]; *The Tablet* (30 May, 1998), 709 [A.E. Harvey]; *Louvain Studies* 24 (1999) 377-9 [V. Koperski].   138 *JCMT*, 145. 139 He notes that the doctrine is also particularly associated with Gal 4:4, Rom 8:3 and 2 Cor 8:9. See ibid., 56.   140 J.D.G. Dunn, *Christology in the Making*, 122-3; quoted in *JCMT*, 58.

In a like manner, Macquarrie follows Dunn's interpretation of 1 Corinthians 10:4: 'they drank from the supernatural Rock which followed them, and the Rock was Christ'. Macquarrie comments that 'he offers us a perfectly sound and persuasive interpretation that does not entail that Paul had any thought of pre-existence in his mind. In Dunn's view, Paul is using the incident from Israel's history as a type of what is now happening in the church'.[141]

The significance of Dunn's exegesis   Dunn's exegesis is extremely attractive to Macquarrie because it serves to transform the meaning attached to those passages about 'self-emptying' and 'becoming poor' which hitherto seemed to point to a pre-existent heavenly being and which are now claimed to be about Christ as Adam.[142] To validate this approach, Macquarrie then proceeds to make two highly controversial claims about this Adam christology. Firstly, he asserts that it actually constitutes 'the mainstream of Paul's christological reflection',[143] and secondly, that it 'seems to have been current even before Paul so that it must be considered the most ancient christology of all'.[144] Whatever the truth of these claims, Mac-

---

141 *JCMT*, 389-90.   142 Interestingly, Dunn, some two years after Macquarrie published *JCMT*, acknowledged that most scholars would not accept his Adamic interpretation of the pre-existence texts. Thus he comments: 'the majority of scholars would question whether these ... verses are properly to be seen as expressions of Adam christology'. See his 'Christology (NT),' in D.N. Freedman (ed. in chief), *The Anchor Bible Dictionary*, vol. 1 (New York, 1992), 983.   143 *JCMT*, 59. It is extravagant of Macquarrie to claim that Adam christology constitutes the mainstream of Paul's christology. As we remarked in n. 128, there is no consensus about where it is to be found in Paul and, where it is found, what conclusions can be drawn about it. Far from being considered the mainstream of Paul's christology, most commentators on Paul are content to make more modest claims about Adam christology, often indeed only mentioning it in passing. Thus, for example, the highly respected Pauline scholar, Joseph A. Fitzmyer, in a relatively recent study of Paul, only gives passing mention to Adam, and at no stage hints that Adam christology occupies the importance in Paul that Dunn proposes. See his *According to Paul* (New York, 1993), 10, 15 and 26. (The book is sub-titled 'Studies in the Theology of the Apostle'). Evidence of recent Pauline scholarship in England which discusses Paul's Adam christology but does not ascribe to it the same importance is the work of C.K. Barrett (Dunn's predecessor as Professor of Divinity at Durham University, 1958-82). See his *Paul* (London, 1994), 109-12. As to what actually constitutes the mainstream in *Paul*, might Dunn not have been better advised to explore Paul's use of three certain titles for Jesus ('Messiah'; 'Lord' and 'Son of God') to describe Jesus? We can note that in his (authentic) letters the apostle used *Christos* 266 times; *Kyrios* 184 times, and *huios theou* 15 times. Thus to give an example of a different interpretation of what constitutes the mainstream in Paul, we can point to that proposed by Martin Hengel. He argues that the title, 'Son of God', though used rarely in Paul, 'is the real *content of his gospel* [italics his]'. Thus he can say that the title '"Son of God" has become an established, unalienable metaphor of Christian theology, expressing both the origin of Jesus Christ in God's being ... and his true humanity'. See his *The Son of God* (London, 1976), 7, 8 and 92-3.   144 Ibid., 59. It does not seem that there was an Adam christology developed by Christians prior to Paul. Rather the apostle seems to have drawn on

quarrie then goes on to affirm that this Adam christology is 'the most intelligible [christology]' in the New Testament since it is

> one that is relatively free from speculation and mythology, so that right at the beginning of Christian theology, in the earliest written witness to Jesus Christ, we find a theology of his person which can serve as a model for our post-Enlightenment mentality two thousand years later. For put at its simplest, the career of Jesus Christ is seen as a rerun of the programme that came to grief in Adam but has now achieved its purpose in Christ and with those who are joined with him in the Christ-event. The talk of 'rerunning a programme' (which I borrowed from Professor Dunn) may seem like an attempt to be up-to-date, but I do not think it expresses anything different from what Cardinal Newman expressed in his [famous] hymn ...'[145]

In conclusion, then, we note that Macquarrie, having argued that 'Paul's imagery leads to a christology that is "from below"', is 'careful to add quite explicitly that this is not a complete christology and obviously not a complete account of Paul's christology'.[146] Macquarrie states his reasons as follows:

> While I believe (in common with most Christian theologians who are writing about christology at the present time) that one has to begin at the human end, so to speak, I do not think one has to remain there. In 1 Corinthians, Paul puts Adam at the beginning, and acknowledges him as a 'living being', though 'a man of dust'. Only after the physical do we come to the spiritual, to the 'last Adam', the transfigured man whom he describes as a 'life giving Spirit'. The 'christology from below' is incomplete because it considers only the unfolding of the human, the exfoliation of the immense potentialities of the creature made in the image and likeness of God. The story needs to be completed by speaking of God's own action in all this. In

---

Jewish traditions and the Old Testament biblical accounts to develop in his own striking way the Adam christology which appears in 1 Corinthians and Romans. Joseph A. Fitzmyer produces evidence to show that 'the incorporation of all human beings in Adam' is an idea that 'seems to appear for the first time in 1 Cor 15:22'. See his *Romans, The Anchor Bible*, vol. 33, (New York, 1993), 412. Fitzmyer likewise produces evidence to qualify Paul's teaching about the way Adam's sin has had a 'maleficent influence' on all human beings as 'novel teaching'. Ibid., 136, 406. In short, the evidence points to Adam christology not being pre-Pauline, let alone the most ancient christology created by Jesus' followers.   **145** *JCMT*, 59. The hymn in question, from John Henry Newman's *Dream of Gerontius*, reads in part:/O loving wisdom of our God!/When all was sin and shame,/A second Adam to the fight/And to the rescue came./O wisest love! that flesh and blood,/Which did in Adam fail,/Should strive afresh against the foe,/Should strive and should prevail.   **146** Ibid., 63.

the words of Hans Urs von Balthasar, 'The raising of the man to the unique, the only-begotten, calls for a yet deeper descent of God himself, his humbling *kenosis*'. ... [A]ny mere adoptionist christology [Macquarrie goes on] must be completed by an incarnational christology. The rising of a man is made possible only by the condescension of God.[147]

In this section, we have travelled with Macquarrie as he, with the assistance of Dunn's theories, attempted to rescue those Pauline texts normally seen as pointing to Christ's pre-existence from being so understood. In this way the full humanity of Christ is preserved and docetism avoided. In doing this, however, Macquarrie has left himself very vulnerable to criticism, since he has based his exegesis of Paul on the controversial findings of Dunn.

It should be noted that Macquarrie is prepared to accept that the texts do uphold a vague notion that Jesus Christ somehow pre-existed in the mind and purpose of God, and comments 'I doubt if one should look for any other kind of pre-existence.'[148] This is, however, something that falls short of what the doctrine has traditionally been believed to uphold concerning the pre-existence of the *person* who became incarnate in Jesus the Christ: this is a question which we shall return to below. We now turn to Macquarrie's reading of John.

John

When Macquarrie examines John's Gospel, he sees there 'a clear doctrine of pre-existence'.[149] In saying this, however, we must be aware that what Macquarrie understands as pre-existence is something that does not match up to the orthodox understanding of a real personal pre-existence of God's Son. Rather, as we see below, it is a pre-existence conceived as more of an ideal and purpose in the mind of God. Since this contention is arguably even more controversial than his reading of Paul,[150] and, interestingly, one that is not shared by J.D.G.

---

147 Ibid. Macquarrie repeatedly states that the teaching that it is God himself who is present and at work in Jesus Christ is supremely encapsulated in the Second Letter to the Corinthians, where, having spoken of the creation of the new humanity in Christ, Paul exclaims, 'All this is from God, who through Christ reconciled us to himself ... that is, in Christ God was reconciling the world to himself' (5:17-19). See for instance, ibid., 64. The reference to Balthasar is taken from his *A Theology of History* (London, 1963), 11.   148 *JCMT*, 145.   149 Ibid., 388. Macquarrie claims that there is nothing in the synoptic Gospels that demands that pre-existence be recognised as being taught there, and comments that 'outside of the gospels, one could agree that some doctrine of pre-existence can probably be found in Hebrews, 1 Peter, Ephesians, and Revelation. So there is hardly a strong case for claiming that pre-existence is essential to christology. Pre-existence is certainly taught by some of the writers, yet there are very important parts of the New Testament where the idea seems to be absent'. Ibid.   150 Two exegetes who recognise a much more full-blooded doctrine of pre-existence in John are Rudolf Schnackenburg and Raymond Brown. Schnackenburg has asserted, for example, that 'John

Dunn,[151] it is appropriate to begin here by outlining the salient features of John's overall christology as seen through Macquarrie's eyes. We shall then be in a position to deal with his understanding of pre-existence in the Fourth Gospel.

John's overall christology   Macquarrie observes that 'with the composition of the Fourth Gospel, christology entered [a] new phase, and even today it is still argued whether the new development was a step forward or a step back'.[152] The change that arose was characterised by a shift from the *anabatic* type of christology found in Paul and the Synoptics, and so much favoured by Macquarrie, to a descending, *catabatic* christology which 'tells of a heavenly being who comes from the spiritual realm to dwell among human beings, yet perhaps we wonder if he is ever quite one of them ... [since] there has been a shift away from the humanity of Jesus in the direction of turning him into an otherworldly figure'.[153]

speaks unambiguously of Jesus' pre-existence' and has commented that 'the pre-existence of the Johannine Christ is affirmed in the prologue and in the testimony of the Baptist (1:30) ... , by Jesus himself in 6:62 ('where he was before'), 8:58 ('before Abraham was, I am'), in the high priestly prayer (17:5, 24) and indirectly in many other texts where his pre-existence is assumed (see 6:33, 58f; 7:28f.; 8:14, 23, 26, 42; 10:36; 16:28)'. See his *The Gospel according to St John*, vol. 1 (London, 1968), 511, 504. In addition, it should be noted that Schnackenburg is resolute in the belief that, whatever the seeming similarities between the Johannine treatment of Christ's pre-existence and the Gnostic notion of a pre-existent redeemer, 'the impression is illusory, as is apparent when one observes the real facts'. Ibid., 504. Brown has unambiguously stated his conviction that the theme of pre-existence is to be found in John's prologue; 8:58 and 17:5. Turning to a detailed exegesis of the prologue, he cautions: 'we find unacceptable the attempts to avoid an implication of pre-existence here'. See his *The Gospel according to John* (I-XII) (London, 1971), 63. Brown contends that the Fourth Gospel holds 'a uniquely high christology ... the highest in the New Testament' and that this was a product of the type of belief in Jesus that came to be accepted by the Johannine community. See his *The Community of the Beloved Disciple* (London, 1979), 45. He argues that 'a belief in the pre-existence of God's Son was the key to the Johannine contention that the true believer possessed God's own life; the Fourth Gospel had been written to bolster the faith of the Johannine community on that very point (20:31)'. Ibid., 109-10. This uniquely high Johannine christology of pre-existence, Brown's argument proceeds, was 'so high that Jesus can use the divine name "I AM" and the Jewish opponents accuse him of making himself God'. Ibid., 114. The baptism of Jesus administered by John the Baptist 'is no longer seen as a baptism of repentance for the forgiveness of sins (Mk 1:4); it now confirms the revelation of pre-existence found in the Prologue hymn'. Ibid., 117-8. Note that the content of this footnote overlaps largely with that of n. 179 and n. 180, chapter 4: the importance of this material for our present discussion calls for the repetition.   **151** Dunn succinctly summarises his view in the following words: 'for the first time in earliest Christianity we encounter in the Johannine writings the understanding of Jesus' divine sonship in terms of the personal pre-existence of a divine being who was sent into the world and whose ascension was simply the continuation of an intimate relationship with the Father which neither incarnation nor crucifixion interrupted or disturbed. See his *Christology in the Making*, 59.   **152** *JCMT*, 101.   **153** Ibid.

In view of what we have already seen of Macquarrie's implacable insistence on the need to uphold the full humanity of Christ, anything that would deviate from that end would be abhorrent to him.[154] Thus he is compelled to take cognisance of the fact that 'some eminent New Testament scholars have been finding in John evidences, as they believe, of a strong Gnostic influence', and that the question must thus be raised as to 'whether this brings John under suspicion, together with all the Christian theology that has drawn its inspiration from him'.[155] In his attempt to respond to this question, Macquarrie has recourse to the writings of his old mentor, Bultmann.[156] What struck Bultmann was the general dualistic similarity between the redemptive narrative circulating among the Gnostics and the story of Jesus as it is told by John. Macquarrie claims that we must give 'a cautious assent to Bultmann's thesis about the Gnostic affinities of John':[157] Gnosticism, he proceeds to argue, offered a language and conceptuality through which the Christian message was able to make contact with the needs of the time.[158] Nevertheless, Macquarrie is clear on the limits of this relationship and counsels that 'we must recognise ... that John has been critical and selective in his use of Gnostic or proto-

---

154 Macquarrie notes that Ernst Käsemann's reading of John as being fundamentally docetic compelled him to disqualify the Fourth Gospel as a credible witness to Jesus Christ and the Christ-event since the Johannine Christ is 'God striding over the earth'. See his *The Testament of Jesus* (London, 1968), 9; quoted *JCMT*, 104.   155 *JCMT*, 102. This suspicion arises from the fact that Christian Gnostics denied Christ's real incarnation and the *salus carnis* (Latin 'salvation of the flesh') he effected. See 'Gnosticism' in G. O'Collins, & E.G. Farrugia, *A Concise Dictionary of Theology* (New York, 1991), 84.   156 Macquarrie comments that 'the scholar who has made the major contribution to this question of Gnostic influences in John was Rudolf Bultmann, and he was writing on these questions long before he produced his magnificent commentary, *The Gospel of John*'. *JCMT*, 102.   157 Ibid., 103. Macquarrie's aligning himself with Bultmann's contention that Johannine dualism arises because the Gospel is a christianisation of early Greek schemes is highly controversial. Francis J. Moloney has noted that there are indications that the form of dualism found in John was not foreign to first-century Jewish thinking. Thus he points to the studies of the Qumran texts that have been discovering that this body of literature has affinities with John's Gospel. He draws attention in particular to the following collection of essays: J.H. Charlesworth (ed.), *John and Qumran* (London, 1972). See Moloney, 'Johannine Theology', in *NJBC*, 1422. Martin Hengel has professed himself tired of suggestions that the New Testament shows evidence of a pre-Christian docetism. He states emphatically that 'in reality there is no gnostic redeemer myth in the sources which can be demonstrated chronologically to be pre-Christian. This state of affairs should not be confused with the real problem of a late Gnosticism standing apart from Christianity, as we find, e.g. in the Hermetica and in some of the Nag Hammadi writings'. See his *The Son of God*, 33-4.   158 *JCMT*, 103. Macquarrie notes that 'perhaps we could say that John's attitude to Gnosticism was something like Bultmann's own attitude to existentialism, because both Gnosticism and existentialism expressed the alienation of an age together with its longing for spiritual satisfaction, and so these movements offered a language and conceptuality through which the Christian message might make contact with the needs of the time'. Ibid.

Gnostic ideas'. There is nothing in John corresponding to the central tenet of Gnosticism: i.e. the 'belief that the material world is inherently evil and that it is the creation not of the one true God but of demonic powers of one sort or another'.[159] Rather, Macquarrie goes on,

> John makes it clear in his prologue that everything derives its being from the Father, acting through the agency of the Logos: 'all things were made through him, and without him was not anything made that was made' (1:3). This carefully constructed sentence seems to be explicitly designed to affirm that everything that is in existence has been created by God through the Logos, and at the same time to deny that anything has been brought into existence through any other creative agency. Once this crucial point has been established, then the human bodily, historical existence of Jesus is made secure. This is quite compatible with the knowledge that John, like Mark before him, may sometimes ascribe to Jesus' supernatural powers and that modern criticism will call into question the veracity of reports of such powers ... But while this feature of the gospel calls for critical treatment, it certainly does not amount to full-blown docetism.[160]

Having seen how Macquarrie is satisfied that John presents no insuperable obstacles to the recognition of Jesus Christ's full humanity, we now briefly indicate the approach he adopts to the prologue. Macquarrie devotes some sixteen pages of *Jesus Christ in Modern Thought* to an exegesis of the prologue. Three points seem to be of particular interest to our explorations here. The first is his reading of verse 11: 'He came to his own home but his own would not receive him'. Macquarrie interprets this as a strongly anti-docetic statement, emphasising that 'he comes not as a stranger of an alien race (that would be Gnosticism!) but truly as one of the human race – as the true man, shall we say, the man who has not forgotten his origin but stands in intimate relation to the Father?'[161] And that being so, Macquarrie admits that, in spite of the 'massive shift' that he has already spoken of as occurring between John's christology and that of the earlier New Testament witness, the

159 Ibid., 104. 160 Ibid., 105. Macquarrie is aware of the challenge that the first Christians faced in finding an appropriate vocabulary with which to speak of the Christ-event. He remarks that 'those first-century Christians had undergone a revelatory experience that had "thrown them to the ground" and in the years after it, they were searching for words to express it. Inevitably they made mistakes as they tried to give their witness, but one can only admire the extraordinary inventiveness that they showed. John was the most inventive of all, perhaps especially by his use of paradox, a way of speaking which employed two contradictory statements, neither of which is cancelled out by the other but which together point to a state of affairs that cannot be itself directly expressed. We meet an example of this in the very first verse of John's Gospel, the opening of the prologue, possibly the most celebrated passage in the whole of the New Testament.' Ibid. 161 Ibid., 114.

essential christology of Paul and the Synoptics has not been abandoned by John. Thus he comments that 'in John, Jesus remains, in the words of Charles H. Dodd, "the *alethinos anthropos*, the real or archetypal Man", and this expression is perfectly adequate to embrace both the solidarity of Jesus with the human race ("his own") and his distinctness from fallen or sinful humanity'.[162]

The second point of particular interest emerging from Macquarrie's exegesis of the prologue that deserves mention here is his determination to underline the paradoxical character of its assertion of identity in difference between the Logos and God. Thus, for example, writing of verse 1: 'In the beginning was the Word, and the Word was with God, and the Word was God', Macquarrie counsels that

> even if we are correct in speaking of the 'identification' of Jesus with the Word, we could not go on to infer an identification of Jesus with God'. Here, I think, we have to take note of the many subtle variations of meaning in the little word 'is'. Sentences in which the word 'is' asserts identity are convertible, that is to say they can be turned around. An illustration would be, 'George Bush is the President of the United States', which entails the assertion, 'The President of the United States is George Bush". But it is still not at all clear that by conversion we can assert that 'God is the Word', or, still less, 'God is Jesus'. In fact, the logic of Christian theology positively forbids us to say any such things. We can say that 'The Word is/was God' or that 'Jesus is/was God', but when we make God the subject of the sentence, we have to allow that God is 'more' than the 'Word' or Jesus, God is also the Father from whom the Word proceeds or the Son is begotten ..[163]

The third and final point of special interest to us which arises from Macquarrie's reading of the prologue is his claim that the language John uses in speaking of the incarnation is figurative. Thus in relation to verse 14: 'And the Word became flesh and dwelt among us, full of grace and truth; we have beheld his glory, glory as the only Son from the Father',[164] Macquarrie asks how are we to understand the utterance 'the Word was made flesh'? He claims that 'if we try to understand it literally, it is nonsense. The Word is Meaning, and Meaning cannot be transformed into the biological tissue we call flesh. The word "flesh" is to be understood in a figurative sense for the realm of the human, the empirical, the historical.'[165]

---

162 Ibid.   163 Ibid., 109-10.   164 He begins his exegesis of this text by claiming that this verse 'must rank with verse 1 as the very essence of the prologue or even of the entire Johannine teaching. And, as between these two crucial verses the weight seems to lie with verse 14. As Augustine said in his Confessions, the teaching that there is a Word and what has been said on this subject in the prologue so far is something he could have learned from Plato and his followers. But that the Word was made flesh is the distinctively new teaching that he has learned from Christianity.' Ibid., 116.   165 Ibid. Macquarrie goes on: 'it is true, of course, that John says quite simply, "The Word became flesh" (*ho Logos sarx egeneto*), and that we have traditionally spoken of this

Macquarrie is touching here upon the difficulties that inevitably arise when one attempts to speak of the divine and he acknowledges that this question was to assume great prominence in the nineteenth century and give rise to various kenotic christologies. He also suggests, interestingly, that 'perhaps he [John] already believed, as Justin did so many years after, that all human beings participate in the divine Word and so have the potentiality for manifesting the Word'.[166] It must be said, however, *apropos* of the Johannine language of the 'Word becoming flesh' that Macquarrie does not seem to be aware of the fact that the Fathers of the Church long ago saw the problem and distinguished between 'becoming' in the sense of water ceasing to be water and changing into wine and 'becoming' in the sense of 'taking on' or 'assuming'. In his *Quod unus sit Christus* St. Cyril of Alexandria, for example, pointed out that John 1:14 did not mean a change as if the Word turned into 'flesh'. He introduced analogous examples from the psalms (e.g. Ps 89: 1; 93:22) where the Lord 'becomes' a refuge for me/us, taking on a protective role for the people and not changing into something like a rocky fortress. Along these lines, Cyril explained the 'becoming' of John 1:14 as the Word taking on 'flesh' – that is to say, uniting a humanity to himself for the sake of our salvation (717c-719a; 727c-729e).[167]

To conclude: Macquarrie has articulated an interpretation of the Johannine Christ in line with the directions for christology that we saw him indicate earlier in this chapter. Christ is fully human, the true Man.[168] Having seen the broad outline of Macquarrie's overall approach to the christology of John, we shall now see how he presents the evangelist's treatment of the pre-existence of Christ.

John and Christ's pre-existence We recall Macquarrie's assertion about the identity in difference between the Logos and God in John.[169] He acknowledges that in

---

event as the "incarnation", derived from the Latin word *caro*, "flesh", and signifying, "becoming flesh". Unfortunately the language does all too easily conduce to a literal and crudely mythological way of thinking, as if the Logos were animating, or enclosed in, a framework of flesh and bones and blood. Some such view is alleged to have been taught by Apollinarius, and was condemned by the Council of Constantinople in 381. In opposition to that, the church taught that in Jesus Christ the Logos assumed a complete humanity. It might have been better therefore if the church had not used the word "incarnation" but had devised a term corresponding to the Greek *enanthropesis*, "becoming human". But clearly whatever term may be used, one has to move away from any supposedly literal meaning and to recognise the figurative character of the language. If it is nonsense to say that Meaning can be transformed into flesh in a literal way, there are still very formidable difficulties in the way of understanding what could be meant by God becoming man. For God is infinite, eternal, immortal and so on while a human being is finite, temporal, mortal, and has a good many other characteristics that are apparently the opposites of those that belong to God.' Ibid., 116-7. 166 Ibid., 117. 167 See G.M. de Durand (ed. and trans.), *Sources Chrétiennes*, 97 (Paris, 1964), 313-7, 343-53. 168 Macquarrie's treatment of the miracles in John sees them as signs that point beyond themselves to the one true miracle, the new life from God that Jesus shares with those who believe in him. Ibid., 120. 169 Macquarrie notes

this Gospel the Wisdom or Logos is considered a distinct hypostasis and that it 'is so close in being to God that it must share in the eternity of God. Thus John can say, "In the beginning was the Word". The Word pre-existed everything that has been created, for everything has been created through the Word. If then we are prepared to speak of God, then there seems to be every reason for saying that God's Word is pre-existent.'[170]

Problems arise for Macquarrie, however, when he is faced with the Church's traditional teaching that the *person* of Jesus Christ has eternally pre-existed. Interpreting the doctrine as implying that the humanity of Christ pre-existed the incarnation, he comments: 'we would be undermining his humanity if we thought of his pre-existence in any way that would make artificial his birth and fleshy existence in Palestine'.[171] And again, in the midst of his Johannine exegesis: 'What would threaten the genuineness of his humanity would be the belief that Jesus consciously pre-existed in "heaven", almost, if one may say so, like an actor in the wings waiting for the moment when he must go on to the stage of history.'[172] Macquarrie admits that at first glance 'some such idea does seem to be present in John, when Jesus prays to the Father: "Glorify thou me in thy own presence with the glory that I had with thee before the world was made" (17:5).' But in keeping with the anti-supernatural hermeneutic that we have seen him consistently articulate, he counsels that the language being employed here is mythological, and 'if allowance is not made for this, then it does seem hard to reconcile with a true humanity in Jesus'. If allowance is made, however, Macquarrie goes on, then it becomes clear that John intended by this language 'neither more nor less than he has said more soberly in the prologue concerning the Word that has been from the beginning and that becomes flesh in Jesus Christ'. And that being so, 'then the humanity of Christ is not impugned'.[173]

In speaking of pre-existence, Macquarrie wants to draw a sharp distinction between the Logos and Jesus. He notes that 'strictly speaking, Jesus is the Word *incarnate*' and asks:

that talk of the Logos arose since 'we think of God as both perfectly self-contained and yet at the same time as related as Creator to those beings which are not God. So, to begin with at any rate, we think of God's being in two modes – his being in himself and his being in relation to that which is other than himself.' He goes on to comment that 'we already see this recognition of two modes in the divine Being in the Old Testament, especially in the Wisdom-hymn of Proverbs'. He realises that although Wisdom is spoken of as if she were a person in the hymn from Proverbs, 'it is likely that the language is metaphorical and she has not yet been considered as a distinct hypostasis. But already by John's time that hypostatisation has taken place. The logos ... is understood to hover between identity and distinctness in relation to God.' Ibid., 388-9. **170** Ibid., 389. **171** 'Some Problems of Modern Christology', *The Indian Journal of Theology*, 23 (1974) 172. **172** *JCMT*, 121. See also Macquarrie, *Christology Revisited* (London, 1998), 114. **173** *JCMT*, 121.

must we not say that prior to the incarnation, the Word pre-existed Jesus? Perhaps even during the life of Jesus, the Word was *more* than Jesus, for although the question is a highly speculative one, there are surely some reasons for assenting to the so called *extra-Calvinisticum*. So when Jesus says in John's gospel, 'Before Abraham was, I am' (8:52) or when he speaks of 'the glory I had with [the Father] before the world was made' (17:5), perhaps we are to understand that in John's intention it is the Word who is speaking in and through Jesus, and that although the Word pre-existed not only before Abraham but the whole creation, this is not the case with Jesus, as the Word incarnate.[174]

To draw the threads of this discussion together, we can say that while Macquarrie has accepted that the Fourth Gospel teaches a doctrine of pre-existence, he envisages it as pointing to an understanding very different from what traditional christology understood by it. His estimation of the importance of post-Enlightenment thought to modern religious consciousness has led him to adopt an anti-supernaturalistic *modus operandi* which cannot countenance the thought that the *person* of Christ pre-existed. Thus he interprets pre-existence as referring only to the Logos who pre-existed the historical incarnation in Jesus. (This prompts the question: is the Logos one and Jesus another? If so, has Macquarrie not departed from his stated intention of being faithful to Chalcedon?)[175]

This exposition of Macquarrie's exegesis of Paul and John has clearly indicated his case against the doctrine of personal pre-existence. We shall suspend comment on the quality of his exegesis and the strengths and weaknesses of his philosophical and theological arguments, except to observe that the reader could have expected more philosophical stringency from one who has written so much on the history of ideas. One may ask whether it is really credible for him to align

---

174 Ibid., 389. **175** The force of this criticism is heightened if one has recourse to the christology section of Macquarrie's generally well received volume in fundamental theology where he offered a more balanced theological perspective on this issue in the following words: 'it seems hardly adequate to say that Christ pre-existed as the divine Logos, while in his humanity, as Jesus of Nazareth, he was a being of time and history. The inadequacy of such an interpretation of the paradox lies in its separation of the divine and human in Christ, whereas the tradition is that in some sense that the whole Christ [an odd term for his pre-existent person!] pre-existed. On the other hand, there is little attraction in the elaborate speculation of Origen that the soul of Jesus (like all rational souls in Platonist philosophy) had existed from the beginning and was joined to the Logos. But would it make sense to say that from the beginning of creation, the Logos has been coming to expression in Jesus Christ, so that Christ has been present in creation from the beginning as its aim? He has been prefigured at every age. This is to take the view that the universe is not only a "vale of soul-making" but has christhood as its goal. Or, alternatively, this is the extension of the idea of sacred history to the whole cosmic process'. See his *Principles of Christian Theology*, revised edition, (London, 1977), 308-9.

himself so much with post-Enlightenment thought that he does not engage with those current thinkers who are struggling with the issues involved in the concepts of person, natures, eternity and related issues.[176] Consequently, one may ask whether it can be said of Macquarrie that his work shows that 'it is much easier to cultivate a knowing apologetic style than to attempt the sort of detachment without which the question of truth and falsity cannot be raised'.[177]

In parenthesis, it can be noted here that Macquarrie's treatment of the resurrection, another central doctrine of the Christian faith, runs along lines broadly similar to those pursued in relation to pre-existence. He asserts that 'for the post-Enlightenment mentality, resurrection is a very difficult idea to accept' (although he admits that it has always been a stumbling block [1 Cor 15:1ff.]).[178] But for those who find it too much, Macquarrie proposes 'an alternative scenario' (what he terms 'The Austere Ending'), where he omits 'the 'joyful mysteries' that traditionally come after the cross'. In this alternative scenario, the account of the career of Jesus ends with the cross. Macquarrie claims that this approach would not 'destroy the whole fabric of faith in Christ', since 'the two great distinctive affirmations would remain untouched – God is love, and God is revealed in Jesus Christ'.[179] In allowing such a reduced ending to this utterly central Christian belief, Macquarrie is disregarding the fact that the Church down the Christian centuries has pinned its central faith on the personal passage of Christ from death to a transformed, definitive life. Gerald O'Collins puts the traditional understanding succinctly: 'the risen Christ was/is personally identical with the earthly Jesus'.[180] William P. Loewe has characterised Macquarrie's interpretation of the resurrection as manifesting an 'apparent willingness to sacrifice the resurrection to modernity'.[181]

ALTERNATIVE UNDERSTANDINGS OF PRE-EXISTENCE

Having argued that the Fourth Gospel implies a pre-existence of the Logos and not a personal pre-existence of Jesus Christ, Macquarrie acknowledges that his approach raises two fundamental questions. Firstly, he asks whether it

---

176 We mention here once again scholars already referred to in n. 62 above: Richard Swinburne, Stephen Davis, Thomas V. Morris, Brian Hebblethwaite and William Alston. 177 This is a criticism of Macquarrie penned by Donald M. MacKinnon more than three decades ago in the course of a review of the former's *Studies in Christian Existentialism*, in the *Journal of Theological Studies*, 18 (1967) 297. 178 *JCMT*, 406. 179 Ibid., 412. Macquarrie claims to find scriptural warrant for this approach in Jn 12: 32-33 ('I when I am lifted up from the earth, will draw all men to myself'. He said this to show by what death he was to die'). Ibid., 413. 180 G. O'Collins, 'Paschal Mystery II: The Resurrection', in R. Latourelle, & R. Fisichella (eds), *Dictionary of Fundamental Theology* (New York, 1994), 772. 181 W.P. Loewe, review of JCMT, *Horizons*, 19 (1992) 141.

runs the risk of separating Jesus from the Logos or Wisdom, and secondly, whether it implies that Jesus just came along by accident, as it were, and turned out to be a suitable candidate in whom the Logos could become incarnate. To help answer these questions, Macquarrie advocates moving on to a second way of understanding pre-existence, one that considers 'the whole Christ, not only the Logos but [also] the human Jesus' as pre-existent.[182] We shall now examine that approach, and then press on to consider a third and final way of understanding the doctrine that Macquarrie offers. It is a view made possible by the modern evolutionary understanding of the world.

'Definite plan and foreknowledge of God' (Acts 2:23)
A second way of understanding pre-existence suggested by Macquarrie 'is a way which includes the whole Christ, not only the Logos but the human Jesus, but not in any literal conception of pre-existence that would have to be judged mytholog- ical or a denial of Jesus' true humanity'.[183] It takes its origin from the primitive preaching recorded in Acts 2:23 which speaks of the 'definite plan and fore- knowledge of God' in the event of Jesus Christ. Its significance for our discussion is, so Macquarrie suggests, that 'if one accepts this idea of a providential plan, of a purpose or intention of God, then one must say that from the beginning Jesus too had existed in the mind and purpose of God. This is not literal or personal pre-existence, but it may be the only pre-existence we can begin to understand and the only kind that is compatible with Jesus' true humanity'.[184]

Macquarrie notes that these ideas have been worked out most fully by Karl Barth when he spoke of the election of Jesus Christ as 'the beginning of all God's works and ways'.[185] Macquarrie uses (or misuses?) Barth to argue that

> the notion of election does give an intelligible and non-mythological sense
> to belief in the pre-existence of Jesus Christ, understood not simply as the
> Logos but as the Logos united to the man Jesus of Nazareth. If someone
> objects that on such a view Jesus Christ pre-existed 'only' in the mind of

182 *JCMT*, 390.   183 Ibid.   184 Ibid., 390-1. A variation on this theme has been published elsewhere by Macquarrie: 'we can say that Christ pre-existed in the sense that the Christ-event did not begin with the conception of the individual Jesus in the womb of Mary, but was already taking shape in the history of Israel, with its covenants and promises and expectations and images. Some theologians (and this would seem to be true of Bultmann) would similarly under- stand the post-existence (or risen life) of Jesus in the persistence of the kerygma and the unfolding of the new humanity in the life of the Christian community. I do not say that this is an adequate understanding of the risen Christ, but it does make some worthwhile contribution to the question.' See his 'The Concept of the Christ-Event' in A.E. Harvey (ed.), *God Incar- nate: Story and Belief* (London, 1981), 78. See also Macquarrie, 'Current Trends in Anglican Christology', *Anglican Theological Review* 79 (1997) 569.   185 See K. Barth, *Church Dogmatics*, vol. II/2, (Edindurgh, 1957), 350; 94-194.

God, I think that one would have to reply that to be conceived and affirmed in the intention of God is to enjoy a very high degree of reality, even if it is different from the reality of existing in space and time.[186]

The claim for 'a very high degree of reality' in this conception of a merely intentional pre-existence of Christ is little less than disingenuous. Surely we too pre-exist in precisely the same way in the mind of God?[187] In making this claim, Macquarrie has neglected to address adequately the primitive Christians' experience of the resurrection. As the distinguished New Testament Scholar, C.F.D. Moule, has written, 'the primitive Christians experienced [the risen] Jesus himself as in a dimension transcending the human and the temporal. It is not just that, owing (somehow) to Jesus, they found new life; it is that they discovered in Jesus himself, alive and present, a divine dimension such that he must always and eternally have existed in it'.[188] Christians thus come to *define* God in terms of the risen Christ. Paul, on a number of occasions, refers to a formula from the early tradition that identified God as 'having raised Jesus from the dead' (e.g. Gal 1:1, Rom 10:9, 1 Cor 6:14). Consequently, Gerald O'Collins has said that 'St Paul saw clearly that *to be wrong about the resurrection was to be wrong about God.*'[189] The first Christians thus came to believe that the person, cause and fate of Jesus Christ belong definitively to a determination of the eternal being of God. By this, then, they meant more than the statement that Jesus (like all men and women) existed from all eternity 'in God's thoughts', or in 'God's plan' (intentional pre-existence). We shall now examine the third and final way of understanding pre-existence that Macquarrie proposes.

Pre-existence and the modern evolutionary understanding of the world
Macquarrie argues that the evolutionary understanding of the world that is so influential in contemporary cosmology can be of assistance in understanding the pre-existence of Christ, 'and once again [as with the "definite plan and foreknowledge of God"] it would include the human and material aspects of Jesus Christ'.[190] Macquarrie begins by stating that

186 *JCMT*, 391. Elsewhere Macquarrie writes: 'I myself am inclined to think that we may equate pre-existence in the mind of God with real pre-existence, and that we do not need to carry speculation on this point any further.' *Christology Revisited*, 64.   187 It is clear that the New Testament does recognise a connection between talk of Christ's pre-existence and that of human beings. W. Thüsing has stated that in the New Testament, 'the pre-existence of Jesus is related to the pre-existence of those to whom God wishes to save through Jesus, that is, those whom he chose in Christ before the beginning of the world and who were pre-destined according to his will (see Eph 1:4ff.; Rom 8:28)'. See K. Rahner & W. Thüsing, *A New Christology* (London, 1980), 172.   188 C.F.D. Moule, *The Origin of Christology* (Cambridge, 1977), 138.   189 G. O'Collins, *Interpreting Jesus* (London, 1983), 108; italics his.   190 *JCMT.*, 391.

according to contemporary cosmologists (and, of course, we all know that scientific theories may change considerably in the course of time) the universe had its origin in a great burst of energy some fifteen or twenty billion years ago. From that initial event the world as we know it has gradually taken shape – galaxies and stars have been formed, the chemical elements have been built up, planetary systems have been formed, on some planets, perhaps many, perhaps very few, life has appeared and on earth at least, there have come into being creatures possessing rationality and personality. Some writers tell us that all this was already determined within minutes of the beginning. There was, so to speak, a 'fine tuning' and if the values of the natural constants had varied just a little one way or the other, the present universe would not have come about, there would not be intelligent beings on earth, there would be no cosmological theories for these could only arrive in an 'anthropic' or quasi-anthropic universe that has produced its own possibilities for understanding. I am not being so naive as to suppose that an argument from design could be easily based on modern cosmology, and in any case I have consistently argued that if there is some *nisus* or goal-seeking striving in the evolutionary process, it is better understood in immanental terms than as imposed from outside by a transcendent 'watchmaker' But I am saying that, (however one may interpret the matter), this earth, the human race, yes, Jesus Christ himself were already latent, already predestined, in the primaeval swirling cloud of particles.[191]

Macquarrie claims that Schleiermacher was saying much the same when he wrote that 'Christ, *even as a human person*, was ever coming to be simultaneously with the world itself'.[192] Macquarrie also refers to Teilhard de Chardin and says that he too was saying much the same when he wrote that 'the prodigious expanse of time which preceded the first Christmas was not empty of Christ'.[193] This evolutionary understanding ties in well with the approach to christology that Macquarrie has been advocating. Thus Macquarrie comments: 'If I were to offer a definition of "incarnation", I would say that it is the progressive presencing and self-manifestation of the Logos in the physical and historical world.' Macquarrie then proceeds to argue that, for the Christian,

this process reaches its climax in Jesus Christ, but the Christ-event is not isolated from the whole series of events. That is why we can say that

191 Ibid., 391-2.   192 F.D.E. Schleiermacher, *The Christian Faith* (Edinburgh, 1928), 402; quoted in *JCMT*, 392.   193 P. Teilhard de Chardin, *Hymn of the Universe* (London, 1970), 70; quoted in *JCMT*, 392. For Macquarrie, then, 'the incarnation was not a sudden once-for-all event which happened on 25 March of the year in which the archangel Gabriel made his annunciation to the Blessed Virgin, but is a process which began with the creation'. Ibid.

the difference between Christ and other agents of the Logos is one of degree, not of kind. In particular the evolution of the cosmos resolves itself eventually into the history of the human race, and within that history a special significance belongs to Israel and the prophetic tradition, and out of that in the fullness of time is born Jesus Christ. It is in some such way, I believe, that the mystery of pre-existence is to be understood.[194]

To conclude our exploration of Macquarrie, it is enough to say that his rejection of the notion of personal pre-existence, his scriptural exegesis, and his attempt to rework the concept into a more general idea that the divine Son (like us) merely pre-existed in a plan of preparation of God's mind, raise a number of critical issues which will be dealt with in the concluding chapter.

194 Ibid.

6

Critical issues

INTRODUCTION

In this study we have been attempting to come to terms with the interpretations of Christ's pre-existence advanced by four Anglican scholars. We have found that these authors can be separated into two camps. On the one hand, Thornton and Mascall are similarly convinced of the truthfulness and appropriateness of the classical interpretation of the doctrine as pointing to Christ's personal pre-existence. On the other, Robinson and Macquarrie deny the validity of talk of Christ's personal pre-existence and regard the concept as a relic from an outmoded supernaturalistic world view that is out of place in our modern world. The task that now faces us in this chapter is to offer some critical reflections on their treatments of the doctrine.

PRE-EXISTENCE AND POST-EXISTENCE

We have seen that our four authors' interpretations of Christ's pre-existence parallel their reading of the doctrine of Christ's resurrection. We have also noted, *en passant,* their individual approaches to the resurrection. A word, then, is called for to explain how one's understanding of the resurrection is relevant to one's interpretation of pre-existence.

What lies at the heart of the doctrine of Christ's personal pre-existence is the belief of the Church, across the Christian centuries, that Christ's personal existence and identity is that of the eternal Son of God and that his personal being did not originate when his earthly human history began. What constitutes the intimate connection between this doctrine (which points to Christ's personal identity as that of a divine, eternal being) and that of the resurrection is that it was with his resurrection from the dead that Christians began to recognise first the personal identity and saving function of Jesus as the Son of God (1 Thes 1:10, Rom 1:3-4, Gal 4:4-7) and as their exalted and divine Lord (1 Cor 12:13, Rom 10:9, Phil 2:9-11). Both these titles, 'Son of God' and 'Lord', so favoured by Paul, and indeed by the pre-Pauline tradition, indicate that the risen, exalted Christ has a life, power and authority after death (a 'post-existence') on a divine level.[1] There then followed a progressive deepening of this recognition of Christ's identity. The Gospel of Mark includes a 'baptism christology': at the commencement of his ministry Jesus is proclaimed by God to be 'my beloved Son' (1:11). Matthew and Luke carry matters further back to add a 'conception christology': the unique divine intervention in the conception of Jesus revealed that there was never a moment in history when Jesus was not Son of God. Finally, other New Testament authors went even further back to add a 'pre-existence christology' (although as we have seen above scholars are not always in agreement as to where it is to be found, and when it is, what is to be understood by it). By means of this pre-existence christology, as Gerald O'Collins points out, 'without saying anything about the manner of Jesus' conception, they [these biblical authors] acknowledged in his coming the incarnation of the One who was previously "with God" and now was made flesh'.[2]

It is thus clear that the recognition of Jesus' personal identity that began with his resurrection deepened through the Christian community's on-going experience of the presence and power of the post-existent Christ. There is thus, so to speak, a continuum between the doctrines of pre-existence and resurrection.[3] The recognition of Jesus as the Son of God and Lord which began at the resurrection was pushed back under the impetus of the Christian community's experience of the presence and power of the post-existent Lord so that it was recognised that he must always and eternally have existed as the Son of God. If Jesus is really the Son of God, then he belongs to the eternal nature of God.[4] C.F.D. Moule encapsulates this point succinctly when he comments that primitive Christians, in the wake of Christ's resurrection 'discovered in Jesus himself, alive and present, a divine dimension such that he must always and eternally have existed in it'.[5] We also recall a comment of O'Collins mentioned above: 'the progressive recognition of Jesus Christ's identity and destiny ... began at the end with his post-existence and finished at the beginning with his eternal pre-existence'.[6]

1 G. O'Collins, 'Jesus', in M. Eliade (ed. in chief), *The Encyclopedia of Religion*, vol. 8 (New York, 1987), 19. 2 G. O'Collins, *Interpreting Jesus* (London, 1983), 198. 3 Certain scholars are keen to underline the priority of the resurrection in relation to pre–existence. Thus we note, for example, W. Thüsing's assertion that statements about pre–existence in the New Testament are to be viewed as 'secondary in comparison with the Christology of resurrection or exaltation'. See his *Die neutestamentlichen Theologien und Jesus Christus*, Band 1 (Düsseldorf, 1981), 264. 4 Walter Kasper makes a useful distinction when he comments that 'the pre–existence theme does not arise from a speculative interest, but serves as a basis for soteriological concern'. See his *Jesus the Christ* (London, 1976), 173. 5 C.F.D. Moule, *The Origin of Christology* (Cambridge, 1977), 53. 6 O'Collins, *Interpreting Jesus*, 198. Jacques Dupuis thinks along similar lines when he writes that, in the wake of Easter, 'the early Christians deepened their faith reflection in Jesus who is the Christ': thus 'starting with the glorified state and the "divine condition" of the Risen one, Jesus' personal identity and divine Sonship will be gradually deepened through a process of "retro–projection", first through the "mysteries" of his life down to his human birth, and

We can now return to our four authors and recall that both Thornton and Mascall held firmly to an orthodox reading of the doctrine of the resurrection, insisting on the reality of the bodily resurrection and on the personal existence and divine identity of the risen One. Robinson[7] and Macquarrie, on the other hand, displayed a curious ambivalence towards the reality of the resurrection. Robinson suggested as one explanation of the empty tomb that it came about through a total molecular transformation of the body of the dead Christ, and said that he wanted 'to argue for retaining the possibility of ambiguity and openness, and therefore for agnosticism rather than dogmatism' on the issue. Macquarrie in his discussion of the resurrection proposed 'an alternative scenario', where the account of the career of Jesus ended with the cross so that post-Enlightenment sensibilities would not be offended by talk of 'the joyful mysteries that tradition-ally come after the cross'. It was thus clear to us that Robinson and Macquarrie (in contradistinction to Thornton and Mascall) were unclear as to the personal exis-tence and identity of the risen One.

Since there is such a close relationship between the doctrines of resurrection and pre-existence, it comes as no surprise that those who are clear (or unclear) on the personal existence and identity of the post-existent One are similarly clear (or unclear) on the personal identity and existence of the pre-existent One.

PRE-EXISTENCE AND DIVINE IDENTITY

For Thornton and Mascall, then, the personal identity of the risen Christ is identical with that of the Jesus who lived and died, who at the resurrection was recognised as the Son of God and Lord, and who was thus seen to have a divine identity. For them, the primitive Christian community came to realise that the divine condition of Jesus, which the Father caused to shine forth through the glorified state of his human existence, was but, and could only be, a reflection, in his humanity, of the divine identity that was his in his eternal pre-existence with God.

In what will follow here, we shall contend that the positions maintained by Robinson and Macquarrie on resurrection and pre-existence arise as a con-sequence of a certain theological presupposition which they share, and which we have alluded to many times above: namely, contemporary christology, in the wake of the Enlightenment, must unambiguously uphold the full humanity of Christ. In holding to this approach, it must be acknowledged that they have the honourable intention of overcoming the kind of practical monophysitism that

then beyond this to the "preexistence" in the mystery of God'. See his *Who Do You Say I Am?* (Maryknoll, New York, 1994), 57.   7 We recall that the earlier Robinson held a more orthodox interpretation of Christ's resurrection.

had been apparent for so long in much 'high christology', whereby the reality of Christ's humanity was undermined by the excessive emphasis placed on his divinity.[8] This led them, however, to have recourse, as we have reported, to 'degree christologies'. In doing this, they followed in the tradition of the German theologian, Friedrich Schleiermacher, who, in his desire to uphold the full humanity of Christ, spoke of him as an ordinary man in whom God was present in an extraordinary degree.[9] It is characteristic of a 'degree christology' that supernaturalistic interpretations of Christ are set aside, in favour of a more *functional* approach altogether more in keeping with the contemporary *Weltanschauung*. Thus we can recall Robinson's insistence noted above that Christ is not a divine or semi-divine being who comes from the other side. He is a human figure raised up from among his brothers and sisters to be an instrument of God's decisive work and to stand in relationship to him in a way to which no other human being is called. And along similar lines, we recall Macquarrie's claims that Christ differs in degree and not in kind from us and that a contemporary christology must give priority to the raising of a human being towards God, since it is necessary to maintain the full and utter humanity of Christ against all the docetic tendencies that would turn him into a supernatural being.

We have already recognised that Robinson and Macquarrie's goal of upholding the full humanity is indeed a highly laudable one, and one that is in line with conciliar orthodoxy – not least the teachings of the Councils of Constantinople I and Chalcedon. When all is said and done, however, it is clear that, in their eagerness to expunge any hint of a docetic Christ, they have failed to deal adequately with that other essential component of a balanced christology, the question of Christ's divine identity. In common with all 'degree christologies', those outlined by Robinson and Macquarrie, in putting so much emphasis on the need to assert unambiguously Christ's full humanity, end up finding that any assertion of Jesus' divine personal identity is impossible, since it is claimed that to do so would be to threaten the fulness of the humanity. This leaves both of their christologies open, as they acknowledge, to the charge of adoptionism. Macquarrie is arguably more sensitive to this criticism than Robinson and tries to resolve the issue by laying much emphasis on a transcendental approach to christology and its talk of the raising of a human being to God. Nevertheless, the impression remains that

8 We can recall here the injunction proffered by the International Theological Commission when it commented: 'The untold riches of Jesus' humanity need to be brought to light more effectively than was done by the Christologies of the past'. See 'Select Questions in Christology', in M. Sharkey (ed.), *International Theological Commission: Texts and Documents, 1964–1985* (San Francisco, 1989), 188.   9 We note here that Schleiermacher had a similarly reductionist interpretation of the resurrection. He portrays Jesus as recovering from a death-like trance after he was taken down from the cross. See his *The Life of Jesus*, ed. by J.C. Verheyden, (Philadelphia, 1975), 431–81.

Macquarrie and, even more so, Robinson, in their determination to uphold the full humanity have not been successful in maintaining the integrity of the christological mystery, since they have failed to hold together both poles, the divine and the human, beyond any form of reductionism.

To conclude here, we can say that if a christology falls short of affirming the divine identity of Christ lest it be seen to compromise the humanity, then it follows that the doctrine of Christ's personal pre-existence, which takes its rise from the need to affirm the eternal dimensions of this divine identity, will be even more problematic. Such a christology also raises serious questions for other key elements of the Christian faith like incarnation and redemption.

WHAT IS MEANT BY PRE-EXISTENCE?

Hitherto we have seen that our four authors divide into two opposing camps on the interpretation of the doctrine of Christ's personal pre-existence. Thornton and Mascall hold to it: Robinson and Macquarrie reject it. We have also seen that their interpretations of pre-existence parallel their readings of Christ's post-existence and divine identity. Robinson and Macquarrie claim that talk of a personally pre-existent Christ is an outmoded supernaturalistic construction which serves to threaten the genuineness of his humanity. The burden of their arguments against such pre-existence is that it implies that the humanity of Christ eternally pre-existed the incarnation. If this were true, it would be an illusion to speak of Jesus' humanity as being consubstantial with ours (as Chalcedon taught; *DS* 301), since it would have an origin altogether different from ours. Here both Robinson and Macquarrie are confused as to what is meant by the term personal pre-existence and as to what the Council of Chalcedon has actually taught. Our first task now will be to set out to clarify what is intended by talk of Christ's personal pre-existence. We shall then suggest how light can be shed on the doctrine by recourse to current discussions, increasingly influential in the Anglo-American world and especially in the United States, among philosophers of religion. This school of thought has been reflecting on the question of God, eternity and the nature of time, and has been coming up with ideas that would seem to have important consequences for christology and not least for the doctrine of Christ's personal pre-existence.

For classical christology, as we have mentioned above, the doctrine of Christ's personal pre-existence teaches that Christ's personal existence is that of an eternal Subject within the oneness of God. He is not derived from this world and the human beings who inhabit it. His personal being did not originate when his earthly human history began. There is no suggestion, despite what Robinson and Macquarrie have claimed to the contrary, that the humanity of

Christ is believed to have pre-existed the incarnation: it first came into existence around 5 BC. Classical christology holds that the person of Jesus Christ
who is an eternal Subject within the oneness of God shares in the divine
attribute of eternity. He thus exists timelessly, since eternity is itself timeless.
Thus talk about Christ's pre-existence is concerned with the actual existence of
the eternal Word/Son before the conception of Jesus and the historical growth
of his humanity. It must be admitted, as Gerald O'Collins has acknowledged,
that there is a certain ambiguity in the language that classical christology has
used to express this belief.[10] It uses the categories of space and time to speak of
what was before the creation of the world and before God's revelation in Christ.
Thus the tensed language employed by Nicea I ('there never was a time when
he was not' [*DS* 126]) could easily be misleading.[11] Even the classical definition
of eternity left by Boethius, '*interminabilis vitae tota simul et perfecta possessio*
(the all-at-once, complete, and perfect possession of endless life)',[12] could
misrepresent matters. The phrase 'all-at-once (*simul*)' in a positive way, and the
word 'endless (*interminabilis*)' in a negative way, point us towards time and temporal duration. Eternity and eternal life, however, are not to be reduced to any
such temporal duration. If it were possible to reduce them to temporal duration, it would mean that talk about Christ as pre-existing his incarnation and
even the very creation of the world (when time began) could be (erroneously)
interpreted as implying a 'before' and 'after' for his personal, divine existence.
It must be pointed out here that an addition made at Constantinople I to the
Nicene Creed, 'Begotten from the Father *before all ages*',[13] might lead the reader
to mistakenly conclude that what is meant here is temporal succession as though
Christ merely anteceded or 'antedated' everything that later began in or with
time.[14] To clarify the situation, Gerald O'Collins reminds us that 'pre-existence
means, rather, that Christ personally belongs to an order of being other than the
created, temporal one', and to help reduce the risk of such confusion in the
future, he goes on to propose that since 'his personal, divine existence transcends

10 G. O'Collins, *Christology* (Oxford, 1995), 237–8.   11 Jacques Dupuis also notes that 'the
concept of "pre-existence" and all the expressions where this concept is implied are misleading'.
See his *Jesus Christ and His Spirit* (Bangalore, 1977), 124. Elsewhere Dupuis writes: 'It is true that
the concept of preexistence ... [is] open to misunderstanding. Preexistence is not existence in a
fictitious time before time'. See his *Towards a Christian Theology of Religious Pluralism*
(Maryknoll, New York, 1997), 296.   12 Boethius, *Consolatio Philosophiae*, Book V, Prose 6. For
text see E.K. Rand (ed.), in H.F Stewart, E.K. Rand, & S.J. Tester, (eds), *Boethius: The
Theological Tractates and the Consolation of Philosophy* (London, 1973).   13 *DS* 150; addition
italicised.   14 This consideration leads Karl-Josef Kuschel to comment that 'this word "pre-
existence" is a[n] [sic] unfortunate theological coinage. It almost certainly leads to the misunderstanding that the person of Jesus Christ can be split into two phases (first the "eternal Son" and
then the "temporal Son" ...'. See his *Born Before All Time? The Dispute over Christ's Origin*
(London, 1992), 496.

temporal (and spatial) categories; it might be better expressed as trans-existence, meta-existence, or, quite simply eternal existence'.[15]

In what follows now, we shall explore the potential offered towards a better elucidation of the doctrine of pre-existence by a current debate concerning the eternity of God among philosophers of religion in the Anglo–American world.[16] This is of significance to christology because it suggests lines along which it would be intellectually acceptable for them as philosophers to speak of an eternal divine being assuming a temporal existence. If this were to be true, it would raise serious questions for the dismissive interpretation of pre-existence held by Robinson and Macquarrie. It is beyond the scope of this study to get immersed in the detail of the wider debate on eternity: we shall be content to confine our attentions to those features which would seem to be of significance for our discussion on Christ's personal pre-existence.

15 O'Collins, *Christology*, 238. By way of clarification, it should be noted that O'Collins, in using the term 'meta–existence', presupposes that the term 'meta' belongs to a higher language: it is thus not to be so confused as to be interpreted as pointing to a temporal priority. **16** By way of introduction to this debate, we shall note with T.V. Morris, Professor of Philosophy at the University of Notre Dame, that 'the past twenty years have been a remarkable time for the philosophy of religion [in the Anglo–American world]. The sheer number of prominent philosophers who recently have devoted their energies to a careful examination of traditional religious topics is in itself quite noteworthy, given the rather inhospitable climate for matters of religion prevailing among leading members of the profession throughout most of this century. What is of real importance, however, is the degree of disciplined creativity, the novel perspectives and rigorous analysis which have been brought to bear on a whole range of time–honoured religious issues during these two decades. Much of the recent work has been broadly epistemological in scope, dealing with traditional arguments for and against the existence of God, as well as with related issues concerning the rationality of religious belief; and a great deal of progress has been made on these issues'. Morris also states that 'in recent years, numerous philosophers have talked about God with a degree of confidence which, interestingly, is not to be found among many professional theologians'. See T.V. Morris (ed.), *The Concept of God* (Oxford, 1987), 1, 10. Elsewhere Morris has drawn attention to 'tremendous changes within the world of philosophy over the last couple of decades'. He goes on to claim that, in that short time, 'we have seen a dramatic and unexpected resurgence in religious belief and commitment taking place among the ranks of some of the most active practitioners and teachers of philosophy on college and university campuses all over America ...'. See his 'Introduction' to T.V. Morris (ed.), *God and the Philosophers* (Oxford, 1994), 5. Similarly, Richard Swinburne, the Nolloth Professor of the Philosophy of the Christian Religion at the University of Oxford, has written: 'For the last twenty or thirty years there has been a revival of serious debate among philosophers in Britain and the United States about the existence of God, conducted at a high level of intellectual rigour. It has been recognized that the subject is not only of the highest importance, but also of great intellectual interest. Christian thinkers have been to the fore in this debate, and the debate has led to a considerable growth in numbers of philosophy students taking courses on the philosophy of religion. Little of this, however, has reached the general public, who have been led by journalists and broadcasters to believe that the existence of God is,

THE CONCEPT OF ETERNITY

Belief that God is eternal was a prominent theme for Thomas Aquinas,[17] and one which has deep roots in the early Christian tradition and before. It has, however, been largely misunderstood or dismissed as incoherent in the wake of the new mathematical spirit of the metaphysics of the seventeenth century.[18] The concept of eternity finds its *locus classicus* in Boethius (*c.*480–*c.*524) and his already quoted definition of eternity as 'the all-at-once, complete, and perfect possession of endless life'.[19] The concept has, however, reappeared in scholarly literature in recent times in the wake of an article by Eleonore Stump and Norman Kretzmann published in 1981.[20] Before discussing this article, we shall acquaint ourselves with what is meant by the concept of eternity.

The debate about eternity turns on the significance of the claim for absolute divine eternity. Peter Manchester defines eternity as 'the condition or attribute of divine life by which it relates with equal immediacy and potency to all times'.[21] When we examine Stump and Kretzmann's article, we find them retrieving and adapting the concept of eternity to elucidate the claim that a timeless God[22] can act in, and know of, the temporal world. Adopting their own terminology, and favouring the Boethian conception of eternity, they set out four features of what they term 'eternality – the condition of having

intellectually, a lost cause and that religious faith is an entirely non–rational matter'. See his *Is There a God?* (Oxford, 1996), 1.   **17** For Thomas Aquinas God is simple, and thus immutable and eternal. Since God does not change or move, God is not in time. Further, all of time is present to God 'at once' in eternity. St Thomas appeals to the image of a circle: the centre of a circle is outside the circumference, but all of the circumference is present to the centre. God's eternity is like the centre of the circle: he is outside of time, yet all of time is present to him. See *Summa contra Gentiles*, I, 66. For a recent treatment of St Thomas on eternity, see B. Davies, *The Thought of Thomas Aquinas* (Oxford, 1992), 103–14.   **18** P. Manchester, 'Eternity', *The Encyclopedia of Religion*, vol. 5, 170.   **19** It can be traced back to Parmenides, Plato and Plotinus. See R. Amerio, 'Probabile fonte della nozione boeziana di eternità', *Filosofia*, 1 (1950) 365–73.   **20** E. Stump & N. Kretzmann, 'Eternity', *The Journal of Philosophy*, 78 (1981) 429–58; reprinted in T.V. Morris (ed.), *The Concept of God*, 219–52. One scholar, Alan G. Padgett, in the course of a criticism of their argument, has written: 'Among the defenders of divine timelessness in modern times, Stump and Kretzmann are increasingly becoming influential'. See Padgett, *God, Eternity and the Nature of Time* (New York, 1992), 66. Another commentator, Paul Fitzgerald, while similarly critical of the detail of Stump and Kretzmann's argument, has stated that the authors 'deserve our thanks for their imaginative and historically informed attempt' to make the idea that God is eternal intelligible. See Fitzgerald, 'Stump and Kretzmann on Time and Eternity', *The Journal of Philosophy*, 82 (1985), 260. See also the critical comments of Richard Swinburne in his *The Christian God* (Oxford, 1994), 39–40; 248–9.   **21** Manchester, 'Eternity', 167.   **22** Manchester has noted that 'the single feature most vividly affirmed of eternity by its classical expositors is that it is life, and not just life but divine life, 'a god manifesting himself as he is' as the third–century CE Neoplatonist mystic Plotinus says in one place'. Ibid., 168.

eternity as one's mode of existence'.[23] First, whatever has eternality has 'life': not mere biological life, but presumably a life of consciousness. Thus we cannot say that a number, a truth, or the world is eternal.[24] Second, on the basis of the word 'illimitable' (*interminabilis*) in the Boethian definition, Stump and Kretzmann state that eternality involves 'infinite duration, beginningless as well as endless'.[25] Third, eternality involves *duration*, and four, it is *atemporal*: 'The life that is the mode of an eternal entity's existence is thus characterized not only by duration but also by atemporality'.[26]

Stump and Kretzmann also point out that two other things need to be said if we are to grasp the Boethian understanding of eternality and the eternal being. First, everything temporal is present *all at once* to an eternal being[27] and second, each eternal particular or feature of an eternal entity is in some sense simultaneous with every other. These considerations lead them to contend that there is a simultaneity between God's eternity and all of human time – what they term 'ET' (i.e. eternal-simultaneity).[28] The implications of this ET-simultaneity, they go on, are that if anything exists eternally [i.e. God],

> its existence, although infinitely extended, is fully realized, all present at once. Thus the entire life of any eternal entity is co-existent with any temporal entity at any time at which that temporal entity exists. From a temporal standpoint, the present is ET-simultaneous with the whole infinite extent of an eternal entity's life. From the standpoint of eternity, every time is present, co-occurrent with the whole of infinite atemporal duration.[29]

Stump and Kretzmann illustrate this argument by means of an example which considers the relationship between an eternal entity and a future contingent event. The example concerns the death of a person who we are told is to die on a certain date in 1991 (ten years after they published their article). Stump and Kretzmann say that the death of this individual some years from now *will be* present to those who will be at his deathbed, but it *is* present to an eternal entity.[30] In this way, they maintain that the concept of eternity implies that in this 'one objective reality [*i.e.* the person's death]' there is contained 'two modes of real existence in which two different sorts of duration are measured

23 Stump and Kretzmann, 'Eternity', 430.   24 Ibid., 432–3.   25 Ibid., 433.   26 Ibid., 433–4.
27 Ibid., 431.   28 Stump and Kretzmann define ET-simultaneous in the following terms: For every x and for every y, x and y are ET-simultaneous if: i) either x is eternal and y is temporal, or vice versa; and ii) for some observer, A, in the unique eternal reference frame, x and y are both present – i.e., either x is eternally present and y is observed as temporally present, or vice versa; and iii) for some observer, B, in one of the infinitively many temporal frames, x and y are both present – i.e., either x is observed as eternally present, or vice versa. See their 'Eternity', 439.
29 Ibid., 441.   30 Ibid., 442.

by two irreducibly different sorts of measurement: time and eternity'.[31] The person's death is ET-simultaneous to the life of an eternal entity, while for us, given our location on the temporal continuum, it is future. At all events it is clear to Stump and Kretzmann that there is 'the possibility of interaction between eternal and temporal entities'.[32] We must turn to that aspect of Stump and Kretzmann's argument that is of particular interest here: the insight it may offer into a better elucidation of the mystery of the incarnation.

In their brief treatment of the incarnation, Stump and Kretzmann aim to show that God's sending of his Son (see Gal 4:4) is compatible with God's eternality.[33] To begin with, they acknowledge the distinctiveness of the incarnation in that it implies that an eternal entity itself enters time. Thus in this case, they state, 'an eternal entity is also a *component* of the temporal effect – an effect which is, to put it simplistically, an eternal entity's having become temporal without having ceased (*per impossibile*) to exist eternally'.[34] Stump and Kretzmann argue that this difference does not invalidate the approach that they have hitherto outlined concerning God's eternality. They maintain that 'the doctrine of the Incarnation is not incompatible with the doctrine of God's eternality', since the doctrine of Christ's dual natures 'provides *prima facie* grounds for denying the incompatibility of God's eternality and God's becoming man'.[35] They spell out what they intend by proposing 'a Boethian account of the compatibility of divine eternality and the Incarnation'. It runs as follows:

> The divine nature of the second person of the Trinity, like the divine nature of either of the other persons of the Trinity, cannot become temporal; nor could the second person at some time acquire a human nature he does not eternally have. Instead, the second person eternally has two natures; and at some temporal instance, all of which are ET-simultaneous with both these natures in their entirety, the human nature of the second person has been temporally actual. At those times and only in that nature the second person directly participates in temporal events.[36]

By these means Stump and Kretzmann are confident that they have demonstrated that

---

31 Ibid., 443. 32 Ibid., 447. They also comment: 'we can see no reason for thinking it absurd to claim that a divine action resulting in the existence of a temporal entity is an atemporal action'. Ibid., 450. 33 They comment: 'A full treatment of those philosophically intricate [trinitarian and christological] doctrines lies outside the scope of this paper, but we will consider them very briefly on the basis of our limited understanding of them in order to suggest some reasons for supposing that the doctrine of the Incarnation is not incompatible with the doctrine of God's eternality'. Ibid., 452. 34 Ibid., 451. 35 Ibid. 452. 36 Ibid., 452–3.

the doctrine of the Incarnation cannot be reduced to the belief that God became temporal and that, if it is understood as including the doctrine of the dual natures, it can be seen to have been constructed in just such a way as to avoid being reduced to that simple belief. And those observations are just enough for now in order to allay the suspicion that eternality must be incompatible with the central doctrine of orthodox Christianity.[37]

They conclude by asserting that the concept of eternity is coherent and that there is no logical impossibility in the notion of an eternal being acting in time.[38]

As we have said, Stump and Kretzmann's article has stimulated a renewal of interest in the idea of God's eternality. Arguably the most significant treatment of the issue is a book by an assistant professor of philosophy at Fordham University, Brian Leftow. He published his well-received *Time and Eternity*,[39] a work of almost four hundred pages, a decade after the Stump and Kretzmann article and it may be characterised as an extended philosophical commentary on their paper.[40] We may note that he finds no contradiction between the claim that God is timeless and the Christian claim that God was incarnate in Jesus Christ. He comments that his Christian readers might ask whether

the claim that God is timeless is compatible with the claim that God was incarnate in Jesus Christ. Reading below that whatever is timeless is necessarily so, they may ask whether a timeless God who is necessarily timeless became a temporal man is neither harder nor easier to understand than the claim that a God who is necessarily omniscient became a fallible, humanly ignorant man or the claim that a God who is necessarily omnipotent and everlasting became a man of limited power who died. If so the Incarnation is no more and no less an objection to the doctrine of divine timelessness than it is to the doctrines of divine omnipotence and omniscience. So too, if (as I agree) the doctrine of divine timelessness is not intrinsically prob-

---

37 Ibid., 453.   38 Ibid.   39 London, 1991. One reviewer, William Hasker, who is quoted on the dustjacket, claims that the volume 'will become the key text around which further discussions of divine timelessness will revolve. It will be required reading for philosophers and theologians concerned with classical theism'.   40 After some preliminaries, the first half of *Time and Eternity* studies the views of Augustine, Boethius and Anselm from which Leftow draws a critique of Stump and Kretzmann and develops his own view, that a timeless God is durationless, and that the whole of his temporal creation is *with* God in eternity, a view which he derives from Anselm. He then proceeds to reject the duration concept of timelessness which is to be found in Boethius, and in Stump and Kretzmann. He comments in the preface: 'This book seeks to defend the claim that God is timeless, that is, exists, but exists at no time'. See Leftow, *Time and Eternity*, xi. Eleonore Stump is quoted on the dustjacket: 'This book is among the most interesting and original of recent works on the doctrine [of eternity], and no subsequent discussion will be able to neglect it'.

lematic, it does not add to the burden a defender of the Incarnation must bear.[41]

The Significance of the Concept of Eternity for the Doctrine of Christ's Pre-existence
This Anglo-American debate among philosophers of religion on the concept of eternity is of the highest significance to our discussion of Christ's pre-existence. If the arguments of Stump, Kretzmann and Leftow, among others, are persuasive, then key christological doctrines of the Church, and in particular Christ's personal pre-existence, are not to be branded and dismissed as philosophically incoherent. The metaphysical distinctions that we have seen these philosophers of religion use show, on the contrary, that it is possible to maintain, in line with classical christology, that the One who is eternal in basic metaphysical status takes on the status of a fully human being, Jesus of Nazareth, at a specific point in time.

It is not our task here to judge between the different nuances, and at times sharply debated arguments, of these philosophers of religion on the concept of eternity; what is of interest, however, is to underline the fact that these authors, through the retrieval of a line of thought that was prominent with Thomas Aquinas, and which has roots in Boethius and earlier, have been able to show that the doctrine of the incarnation of the Eternal Son of God is not inherently impossible and self-contradictory. Given that Stump and Kretzmann initiated this debate on eternity in 1981, and that their arguments and those of other philosophers of religion who have entered into this theatre of debate since have enjoyed a certain prominence in America and Britain, not least in the pages of the journal, *Religious Studies*, it is surprising that Macquarrie has never even alluded to them in his subsequent publications.[42] (In Robinson's case death was to intervene all too quickly in 1983). It seems fair to say that Macquarrie's christology in general, and his treatment of Christ's pre-existence in particular, would have profited greatly from an exposure to such issues.[43] As it stands, his *Jesus Christ in Modern Thought* has confined itself to an extended, if controversial, perusal of the scriptures and to an in-depth treatment of post-Enlightenment christology. In the constructive section of the book, Macquarrie clearly aligns himself with certain

---

41 Ibid., 19.   42 We have in mind here, in particular, his *Jesus Christ in Modern Thought* (London, 1990). Macquarrie has touched on the question of time and eternity in his *Christian Hope* (London, 1980), 122–7, but not in relation to christology.   43 On this point, we can observe that Karl–Joseph Kuschel's massive study of the doctrine of Christ's pre-existence, *Born Before All Time?*, shares this weakness. It wrestles with the scriptures and a wide range of religious writings for some six hundred and sixty pages, but for all that, it lacks any serious philosophical dialogue with the questions of time and eternity. See G. O'Collins' review of it in *The Tablet*, (August, 14 1993) 1045, and his comments in the volume of essays he co-authors with D. Kendall: *Focus on Jesus* (Leominster, 1996), 2.

post-Enlightenment presuppositions. Boethius is only referred to once (concerning the concept of person) and Thomas Aquinas is dealt with in less than a page. Since Macquarrie's treatment of pre-existence involves the drastic step of jettisoning this important tenet of classical christology, it seems all the more surprising that he, surely aware that the burden of proving such a thesis should lie with those who propose it, passes over the deliberations of these philosophers of religion. This omission constitutes a *lacuna* in his christology.

Mascall, moreover, never attempted to explore more fully in his christological writings the potential offered by the concept of eternity to the task of rebutting the reductionist christological ideas that so troubled him during the 1960s and afterwards. Admittedly, he had a very clear idea, as one would expect of a Thomist, that God is *timeless* and that talk of the pre-existence of the Eternal Word is a temporal metaphor.[44] Nevertheless, he failed to draw out at length the significance of this point. Bearing in mind his knowledge of Thomism and the fact that he was in open debate with certain detractors of the doctrine of pre-existence, it must be considered a matter of surprise and regret that he did not explore the concept of God's timelessness and eternity.[45] This oversight is probably explained by the fact that his writings on christology in general (during the later part of his career), and on pre-existence in particular, were never intended to be systematic treatments. They were, instead, written as responses to, and rejoinders of, various liberal ideas that were increasingly in vogue in Church of England circles from the 1960s. It should also be acknowledged that when the Stump and Kretzmann article which revived interest in eternity appeared in 1981, Mascall was already in his seventy-sixth year. He had retired eight years earlier from his chair at King's College and had completed his major writings.[46] It must also be said that Thornton, despite the importance he attaches to the concept of 'the eternal order',[47] as we saw above, does not dwell on the issue of God, eternity and time in his christology. Indeed, two classical Christian authors who are closely associated with the question receive little, if any attention, from him. Thus in *The Incarnate Lord* Boethius is not mentioned at all and Thomas Aquinas receives perfunctory attention (there are only four entries under his name in the index).

---

44 E.L Mascall, *Whatever Happened to the Human Mind?* (London, 1980), 94.   45 For an example of where Mascall touches on the question of God and timelessness, see his *Christ, the Christian and the Church* (London, 1946), 99.   46 His main christological publication that followed on the Stump and Kretzmann article was *Jesus* (1985). A slim-volume of some fifty six pages, it makes no claims to comprehensiveness, preferring instead to concentrate on the consequences for christology of the new scientific mentality that has emerged in the wake of the collapse of Newtonian physics.   47 Which, we recall, is that 'order of reality whose significance in no way depends upon the conditions of change and development characterising the series of events in space–time'. See his *The Incarnate Lord* (London, 1928), 56.

ANGLICAN THEOLOGY

It is time to raise the question of whether there exists a distinctively Anglican approach to christology in general, or to the doctrine of Christ's pre-existence in particular? As we have said often before, Thornton and Mascall, on the one hand, exhibit a steadfast commitment to doctrinal orthodoxy. Robinson and Macquarrie, on the other, are extremely sensitive to the post-Enlightenment *Weltanschauung* and are only too prepared to submit the tenets of christological orthodoxy to Ockham's razor.

Michael Ramsey has claimed that the marked characteristics of Anglican divinity, 'seldom absent from divinity in any age', are 'the appeal to Scripture and the Fathers, the fondness for Nicene categories, the union of doctrine and liturgy, the isolation from continental influences'.[48] Judged along these lines, the writings of the High Churchman, Thornton, are probably the most characteristically Anglican of the four christologies studied here. This is because they combine a firm grounding in the Scriptures, in the Fathers and in the early Councils with the striving after synthesis between theology and contemporary culture in the shape of Whitehead's philosophy of organism.

Mascall is a conspicuous figure among Anglicans: his constant espousal of Chalcedonian orthodoxy situates him very firmly within the ranks of the High Church,[49] while his intimacy with Thomism and contemporary, Continental Catholic thought sets him apart. He also departs from Ramsey's schema by virtue of his tendency not to concern himself with exegetical matters.

Robinson, as we have noted, was born into the very heart of the Anglican establishment, a world more open to Protestant currents of thought from both within and without the Church of England than those inhabited by either Thornton or Mascall. While primarily an exegete, Robinson's interpretation of the biblical witness concerning Christ and his christological constructions were deeply influenced by the ideas of such prominent contemporary, Continental Protestant scholars as Bultmann, Tillich and Bonhoeffer. Robinson stands very much in the tradition of Anglican modernism by virtue of his readiness to reinterpret drastically, and sometimes reject flatly, certain tenets of scriptural and early conciliar christological orthodoxy. He occupies, therefore, a position very much at variance with those held by Thornton and Mascall.

That the Church of England has felt itself able to tolerate such striking differences on matters pertaining to core issues of Christian belief is due to what it terms its 'comprehensiveness'. Thus the Church of England is comprised of three sub-sections: the Low Church, the Broad Church, and the High Church.[50]

---

48 A.M. Ramsey, *From Gore to Temple* (London, 1960), viii.   49 It must be acknowledged here that the Evangelicals are similarly attached to Chalcedon.   50 George L. Carey, currently Archbishop of Canterbury, has delineated the differences between the three sub-sections thus:

Each of these sections has its own peculiar approach to theology.[51] Characteristics of the High Church approach have emerged in our examinations of Thornton and Mascall. The Broad Church is more open to Protestant ideas, and on the whole it objects to positive definition in theology and endeavours to interpret the Anglican formularies and rubrics in a broad and liberal sense. The Low Church approximates in its beliefs to those of evangelical Protestantism. Robinson is best designated as a Broad Churchman.

Macquarrie's christology is evidently closer to that of Robinson than to that of either Thornton or Mascall. Despite the fact that Macquarrie himself tends to the view that he stands in the High Church, Catholic tradition,[52] the detail of his christological investigations and constructions shows that it is not self-evident that this claim can be corroborated.[53] First, one is struck by the brevity of his treatment of the early Councils and the Fathers: a mere twenty eight pages compared with over one hundred and sixty devoted to christology in the wake of the Enlightenment. Like Robinson, Macquarrie claims that the New Testament does not uphold the doctrine of Christ's personal pre-existence; and he has no com-

'Evangelical Anglicans, generally "low church", emphasize preaching. The middle of the way, or broad church, is noted for the affirmation of the mind. The Anglo-Catholic wing, deeply influenced by Cardinal John Henry Newman and the Oxford movement, is strikingly similar to Roman Catholicism'. See Carey, 'Anglicanism' in Richard P. McBrien (general ed.), *The HarperCollins Encyclopedia of Catholicism* (New York, 1995), 49. For further information see, L. Klein, 'Anglikanische Theologie im 20. Jahrhundert', in H. Vorgrimler & R.V. Gucht (eds), *Bilanz der Theologie Im 20. Jahrhundert*, vol. 2 (Freiburg etc., 1969), 124–53. 51 By way of clarification here, we should note that the Anglican Church has never had a single theological orthodoxy. As Aidan Nichols writes: 'Although it has promulgated confessional statements, and above all the Thirty Nine Articles of Religion of 1571, it has never committed itself to a single theological elucidation of those statements. There is no one theologian, in other words, who plays anything like the rôle of Calvin in the Reformed churches, or even of Luther in Lutheranism'. See his *The Panther and the Hind* (Edinburgh, 1993), xvi–xvii. For a criticism of the dominance of scepticism in English academic theology in recent decades, especially during the 1970s, see R. Hannaford, 'The Legacy of Liberal Anglican Theology, *Theology*, 103 (2000) 89–96. 52 *TCM*, 5. 53 His writings on such themes as mariology, liturgy and sacraments suggest that he is strongly attracted towards the Catholic intuition on these matters – not least in one of his most recent books *A Guide to the Sacraments* (Oxford, 1997) which aims to be a guide to a clearer understanding of the sacraments and their place in the Church. (see 'Preface', vii). Nonetheless, the impression remains, notwithstanding his own claims to the contrary, that this is not true of his christology (see *JCMT*, 383). That being so, we are forced to doubt the veracity of Louis Bouyer's judgement (admittedly, written a decade before the publication of *JCMT*) that Macquarrie's Anglicanism is very Catholic ('un anglicanisme trés catholicisant'). See Bouyer, *Le métier de théologien* (Paris, 1979), 157. Similarly problematic is Aidan Nichols' assessment that Macquarrie is perhaps numbered among a small band of Anglican writers in whom 'the orthodox Roman Catholic can recognise with but little effort "separated doctors" of the Catholic Church'. See Nichols, *The Panther and the Hind*, 128.

punction in dispensing with a doctrine clearly implied by the Council of Nicea, taught by subsequent classical theology and firmly upheld by many luminaries of the High Church.[54] It would seem, then, that Macquarrie's christology is more influenced by his critical predilection for certain categories of liberal Protestant thought, such as those proposed by Schleiermacher. These would have been well known to him long before he converted to Anglicanism: we can recall that his doctorate had explored Heidegger's influence on the thought of the radical biblical scholar, Bultmann.

The diversity of approach displayed by our four twentieth-century Anglican authors implies, if they may in any way be regarded as representative of opinions within the Church of England during this period, that we cannot speak of a single, *distinctive* Anglican approach to christology in general, or to the doctrine of Christ's pre-existence in particular. It need come as no surprise to us, however, that this is the case. The characteristic insistence on the 'comprehensiveness' of the Church of England, whereby High, Broad and Low Church schools of theology co-exist under the one Anglican umbrella, has meant in practice that conflicting theological opinions over a wide spectrum of beliefs have been accommodated under it.[55] It should be noted here that the Anglican Church has no equivalent of the Roman Catholic Church's Congregation for the Doctrine of the Faith, one of whose functions is to act as an agency of theological correction by investigating and reproving writings that seem contrary or dangerous to the faith.[56]

To return to the notion of 'comprehensiveness', it is interesting to note, *en passant*, that the Anglican theologian and bishop, Stephen W. Sykes,[57] has traced its origins back to a mid-Victorian theologian, F.D. Maurice. While we cannot delay on the detail of his careful analysis and critique of 'comprehensiveness', we

---

54 For example, Henry Parr Liddon (1829–90) in his *The Divinity of Our Lord* (1867). 55 Nichols says that Anglican 'comprehensiveness' is variously interpreted. It can be understood as either i) pointing to a Church that is 'committed to the Bible and the creeds of the early councils, episcopal in structure, a single eucharistic communion, yet tolerating a wide range of theological interpretation of the common faith within its peace', or on the contrary ii) 'as a euphemism for the self-contradictions of a national church, brought into existence for political ends and preserved as a unity by historical nostalgia ... On this view, one might prefer to see the collapse of Anglicanism into its constituent parties, Evangelical, Catholic, Philo–Orthodox, Liberal and so on ...'. Ibid., xviii.   56 The question of authority in Anglicanism is a moot point: Stephen W. Sykes has commented that within Anglicanism: 'the problem of authority has become a central theological issue, especially in ecumenical dialogues and within these dialogues especially with the Roman Catholics'. See his *Unashamed Anglicanism* (London, 1995), 140. See also the volume he has edited: *Authority in the Anglican Communion* (Toronto, 1987). In addition, see R. Runcie, *Authority in Crisis: An Anglican Response* (London, 1988); G.R. Evans (ed.), *Christian Authority* (Oxford, 1988) and H. St John, 'Authority in the Anglican Mind', *Blackfriars*, 39 (1958) 242–60.   57 Sykes is currently the principal of St John's College, Durham. He was formerly bishop of Ely, 1990–99.

can note that he holds that it has had 'disastrous' consequences for Anglican theology, since, in one way or another,

> the failure to be frank about the issues between the parties in the Church of England has led to an ultimately illusory self-projection as a Church without any specific doctrinal or confessional position ... And it is greatly to be feared that generations of Anglicans, learning their theories from Maurice and his disciples, have substituted for the form of catholicism or protestantism which any convinced believer of those respective forms of Christian discipleship would recognise a tame and Anglicanised *tertium quid*.[58]

It is also worth suggesting here that the Church of England is not as well equipped as other Christian communions to get to grips with such wide variations in approach because of the almost total absence of systematic theological reflection in England. Thus Sykes, writing in the 1970s, has lamented the fact that 'for seventy years at least', in Oxford and Cambridge,

> no systematic or dogmatic theology has been taught ... [And] the neglect of systematic theology in the universities partly accounts for its neglect in the seminary training of Anglican ordinands. For the teachers themselves, never having been taught the discipline, found neither the impetus nor the time to devote themselves to the proper cultivation of systematics outside the university ... The result is as we see it today. Not merely is there no tradition of systematic theology in the Church of England, there is no recognition of the part it could play in fostering a critical self-understanding without which no church is truly alive.[59]

From what we have seen in this study, it is clear that Thornton and Mascall pose no problem to Roman Catholic theological orthodoxy: indeed it is quite apparent in the case of Mascall, owing to his attachment to Thomism and to such thinkers as Bouyer and Galot, that his position is rigorously orthodox. Thornton, too, for all his interest in Whitehead and neglect of Thomas Aquinas, is orthodox (though some critics of process thought might choose to differ on this judgement).[60] Also, it must be pointed out that their firm commitment to christological

---

58 S.W. Sykes, *The Integrity of Anglicanism* (London, 1978), 19–20.   59 Ibid., 80–2.   60 See, for example, Thomas G. Weinandy's (who, incidentally, is a former doctoral student of Mascall) highly critical estimation of process thought in general in his *The Father's Spirit of Sonship* (Edinburgh, 1995), 116, n. 7. He claims that process theology's understanding of God is 'in almost complete identity with Neo-Platonism'. See also his critique of the philosophical and theological adequacy of process christology in his *Does God Change? The Word's Becoming in the Incarnation* (Petersham, MA, 1985), 124–53.

orthodoxy, especially that taught by Chalcedon, reminds us of the perennial, ecumenical significance of that Council of AD 451,[61] and of the classical status and authority which its teachings enjoy among many, though of course not all Anglicans.[62]

Robinson and Macquarrie, however, are a different matter. Both of them have rejected the doctrine of Christ's personal pre-existence: firstly, on the basis of extremely controversial exegesis and, secondly, by aligning themselves with the presuppositions of post-Enlightenment thought so that they are driven to reject the categories of classical christology on the grounds of incoherence. As regards the question of controversial exegesis, it can be recalled that Robinson has been heavily criticised in the literature for relying on very questionable exegesis. Macquarrie has been similarly taken to task for his reliance on Dunn's disputed reading of Paul. Surely the christologist would be on firmer ground if his constructions were based on more widely accepted results coming from mainline exegetes? As regards their rejection of the categories of classical christology, we have seen that Robinson and Macquarrie have been too hasty in accepting the presupposition that classical christology is incoherent. The current debate concerning the concept of eternity among certain Anglo-American philosophers of religion shows that the doctrine of the incarnation in time of the Eternal Son of God has been shown to be *not* inherently impossible. Since these philosophers undermine the closed assertions of Robinson and Macquarrie, we noted above our surprise that Macquarrie (Robinson died too early) has failed to take account of the work carried on by Stump, Kretzmann and their colleagues.

For all Macquarrie's intimacy with the contours of modern thought, it is clear that he has hitherto chosen to avoid the challenges that these philosophers of religion pose for his post-Enlightenment theological constructions.[63] In this oversight

---

61 This ecumenical significance is the shared heritage of not only Roman Catholics and Anglicans, but also of the Orthodox and those from the main traditions of Reformation theology. 62 As evidence that not all Anglicans are similarly convinced of the merits of Chalcedon, we need only allude to the radical opinions voiced at 'The Myth of God Incarnate' symposium in 1976, by such Anglican scholars as, among others, Denis Nineham and Maurice Wiles: see J. Hick (ed.), *The Myth of God Incarnate* (London, 1977). (It must be acknowledged that there are radical voices from within the Roman Catholic tradition similarly critical of certain tenets of christological orthodoxy – such as Edward Schillebeeckx and Piet Schoonenberg). For a discussion of the status and authority of Chalcedon among Anglicans, see J. Robert Wright, 'The Authority of Chalcedon for Anglicans' in G.R. Evans (ed.), *Christian Authority: Essays in Honour of Henry Chadwick* (Oxford, 1988), 224–50. In order to avoid the danger of misunderstanding here and the impression being given that Chalcedon was the last word in christology, it is good to recall Karl Rahner's axiom that the definition of Chalcedon and other such classic formulae 'derive their life from the fact that they are not end but beginning, not goal but means, truths which open the way to the – ever greater – Truth'. See Rahner, 'Current Problems in Christology', *Theological Investigations*, vol. 4 (London, 1966), 149. 63 In parenthesis, it can be

by Macquarrie, it seems fair to say, we can observe in microcosm that tendency of Anglican theology to be less than rigorous in terms of philosophy. Unlike its Continental counterpart, 'Anglo-Saxon' theology has had a long history of *not* seeing philosophy as an indispensable and stimulating conversation-partner.[64] Yet, if we are really to get to grips with the doctrine of pre-existence, whether to accept or reject it, then we must never confine our attentions to the particular philosophical presuppositions of the day, or to the findings of certain exegetes; we must also be prepared to face the *full* philosophical debate on time and eternity. Anglican christology, then, can only be enriched by engaging in a broader and deeper dialogue with philosophy. And when that is done, it may become clear, that the doctrine of Christ's pre-existence, a doctrine which has figured so conspicuously in the scriptural testimony and classical christology, is more solidly based than its detractors may have imagined.

reported that Anglican (Episcopalian) and Protestant theological circles in the United States have been more disposed towards dialogue with these philosophers of religion than their counterparts in England. American publications like Thomas V. Morris, *The Logic of God Incarnate* (Ithaca, New York, 1986) and Steven Davis, (who is a Presbyterian) *Risen Indeed: Making Sense of the Resurrection* (London, 1993) indicate the assistance that theologically and biblically well–informed philosophers of religion can offer towards a rationally coherent articulation of doctrinal orthodoxy. And it is worth noting that this school of thought in the United States, (in the tradition of Mascall), is finding the Thomist tradition very helpful in the challenge of articulating a Christian theology which is at once orthodox and accessible to contemporary religious consciousness.   64 So judges Sykes in his 'Theology through History', in D. Ford (ed.), *The Modern Theologian*, 2nd ed. (Oxford: Basil Blackwell, 1997), 229.

Bibliography

WORKS BY LIONEL S. THORNTON

Books

Richard Hooker: A Study of His Life (London: SPCK, 1924)

The Incarnate Lord: An Essay concerning the Doctrine of the Incarnation and Its Relation to Organic Conceptions (London: Longmans, Green & Co., 1928)

The Doctrine of the Atonement (London: Unicorn Press, 1937)

The Common Life in the Body of Christ, 1st ed. (London: Dacre Press, 1942). 2nd ed. (London: Dacre Press, 1944). 3rd ed., with corrections (London: Dacre Press, 1950). 4th ed. (London: Dacre Press, 1963)

Revelation and the Modern World (London: Dacre Press, 1952)

Articles

'The Christian Conception of God', in Selwyn, E.G. (ed.), *Essays Catholic and Critical by Members of the Anglican Communion* (London: SPCK, 1926), 121-50

'St Irenaeus and Contemporary Theology', in Aland, K. & Cross, F.L. (eds), *Studia Patristica*, vol. 2, Papers presented to the Second International Conference on Patristic Studies held at Christ Church, Oxford, 1955, Part II (Berlin: Akademie-Verlag, 1957), 317-27

WORKS ON THORNTON

Books and articles

Anon. 'Lionel Thornton, CR: A Distinguished Theologian', *Church Times*, 148 (1960) 11

Cooper, R.M. 'A Note on L.S. Thornton: An Early Process Theologian', *Anglican Theological Review*, 55 (1973) 182-8

Culp, J. 'Modern Thought Challenges Christian Theology: Process Theology and Anglican Theologian Lionel Thornton', *Anglican Theological Review*, 76 (1994) 329-51

Ford, L.S. 'Response: Lionel S. Thornton and Process Christology', *Anglican Theological Review*, 55 (1973) 479-83

Ramsey, A.M. 'Lionel Thornton: Theologian' in Thornton, L.S., *The Common Life in the Body of Christ*, 4th ed. (London: Dacre Press, 1963), vii-xi

Shen, P.S.Y. *The Christology of L.S. Thornton* (Chicago: University of Chicago Press, 1969)

Selected reviews of books by Thornton

The Incarnate Lord, 1928: *Anglican Theological Review*, 12 (1929-30) 93 [Hall, F.J.]; *Journal of Theological Studies*, 30 (1928-29) 325-8 [Boys-Smith, J.S.]; *Modern Churchman*, 19 (1929) 220-3 [Bezzant, J.S.]; *Theology* 28 (1929) 289-90 [Brabant, B.]; *Revelation in the Modern World*, 1951: *Theology*, 54 (1951) 442-8 [Ramsey, A. M.].

Research through the appropriate periodicals has failed to turn up any German, French, Spanish or Italian reviews of Thornton's works. More surprising is the lack of such reviews of those writings of Mascall, Robinson and Macquarrie that are of significance to this study.

WORKS BY ERIC L. MASCALL

Books
He Who Is: A Study in Traditional Theism (London: Longmans, Green & Co., 1943). Revised ed. (London: Libra Books, published by Darton, Longman & Todd, 1966)
Christ, the Christian and the Church: A Study of the Incarnation and Its Consequences (London: Longmans, Green & Co., 1946)
Christian Theology and Natural Science. Some Questions in Their Relations, The Bampton Lectures of 1956 (London: Longmans, Green & Co., 1956)
Via Media (London: Longmans, Green & Co., 1956)
The Importance of Being Human (Oxford: OUP, 1959)
Theology and History (London: Faith Press, 1962)
Up and Down in Adria: Some Considerations of the Volume entitled Soundings (London: Faith Press, 1963)
The Secularisation of Christianity: An Analysis and a Critique (London: Darton, Longman & Todd, 1965)
The Christian Universe (London: Darton, Longman & Todd, 1966)
Existence and Analogy: A Sequel to 'He Who Is' (London: Darton, Longman & Todd, 1966)
Theology and the Future (London: Darton, Longman & Todd, 1968)
The Openness of Being (London: Darton, Longman & Todd, 1972)
Theology and the Gospel of Christ: An Essay in Reorientation (London: SPCK, 1977)
Whatever Happened to the Human Mind? (London: SPCK, 1980)
Jesus: He Who Is And How We Know Him (London: Darton, Longman & Todd, 1985)
Saraband: The Memoirs of E.L. Mascall (Leominster: Gracewing, 1992)

Articles
'Contemporary Scientific Thought and Divine Personality', *Theology* 19 (1929) 139-46
'The Incarnation and Space-Time', *Theology*, 19 (1929) 312-19
'The Divine Logos and the Universe', *Theology*, 20 (1930) 146-51
'The Nature of the Resurrection', *Theology*, 21 (1931) 203-13
'Some Axioms of Catholic Christology', *Theology*, 39 (1939) 406-12
'The Future of Anglican Theology', *Theology*, 39 (1939) 496-512
'The Dogmatic Theology of the Mother of God', in Mascall, E.L. (ed.), *The Mother of God* (London: Dacre Press, 1949), 37-59
'Theism and Thomism: Some Answers to Professor Emmet', *Theology*, 53 (1950) 129-137
'Is the Incarnation Unique?', *Theology*, 56 (1953) 288-94
'Anglican Dogmatic Theology: 1939-1960', *Theology*, 63 (1960) 1-7
'Secularism and Theology', in Shook, L.K. (ed.), *Renewal of Religious Thought* (New York: Herder & Herder, 1968), 193-207
Review of G.W.H. Lampe's *God as Spirit*, *Journal of Theological Studies*, 29 (1978) 617-21
'The Relevance of Chalcedon Today', in Marcheselli, C.C. (ed.), *Parola e Spirito. Studi in Onore di Settimio Cipriani*, vol. 2 (Brescia: Paideia, 1982), 1043-50
'Whither Anglican Theology?', in Kilmister, A. (ed.), *When Will Ye Be Wise?* (London: Blond & Briggs, 1983), 30-49

WORKS ON MASCALL

Books and articles
Anon. 'Dr E.L. Mascall [Obituary]', *The Times* (17 February, 1993), 17
Kallunkamakal, J. *The Problem of the Supernatural in the Theological Anthropology of Eric Lionel Mascall* (Rome: P.U.G., 1989)
Macquarrie, J. 'Obituaries: Canon E.L. Mascall', *The Independent* (17 February, 1993), 25
Piotrowski, E.L. *The Christology of E.L. Mascall* (Rome: PUG, 1987)
Smythe, H. 'Obituary: Eric Mascall', *The Tablet* (20 February, 1993), 256-7

Selected reviews of books by Mascall
Via Media, 1956: *Journal of Theological Studies*, 8 (1957) 382-5 [Stead, G.C.]; *Secularization of Christianity*, 1965: *Expository Times*, 77 (1966) 58-9 [Roberts, H.]; *Religious Studies*, 1 (1966) 241-8 [Roberts, T.A.]; *Theology Today*, 24 (1967-68) 513-5 [Fennell, W.O.]; *The Thomist*, 30 (1966) 435-43 [Jelly, F.]; *Theology and the Future*, 1968: *Downside Review*, 87 (1969) 229-30 [Trethowan, I.]; *Expository Times*, 80 (1969) 174 [Greeves, F.]; *Theology and the Gospel of Christ*, 1977: *Theological Studies*, 39 (1978) 342-3 [O'Donnell, J.]; *Theology*, 81 (1978) 214-6 [Ward, K.]; *Whatever Happened to the Human Mind?*, 1980: *Expository Times*, 92 (1981) 153 [McIntyre, J.]

WORKS BY JOHN A.T. ROBINSON

Books
Honest to God (London: SCM Press, 1963)
(With Edwards, D.L.), *Honest to God and the Honest to God Debate in One Volume* (London: SCM Press, 1964)
The Human Face of God (London: SCM Press, 1973)
The Use of the Fourth Gospel for Christology Today: Christ and Spirit in the New Testament (Cambridge: CUP, 1973)
Redating the New Testament (London: SCM Press, 1976)
Can We Trust the New Testament? (London & Oxford: Mowbrays, 1977)
The Roots of a Radical (London: SCM Press, 1980)
Twelve More New Testament Studies (London: SCM Press, 1984)
The Priority of John (London: SCM Press, 1985)

Articles
'The Most Primitive Christology of All?', *Journal of Theological Studies*, 7 (1956) 177-89
'The New Look of the Fourth Gospel', *Studia Evangelica* 73 (1959) 338-50
'The Destination and Purpose of John's Gospel', *New Testament Studies*, 6 (1960) 117-31
'Resurrection in the New Testament', in Buttrick, G.A. (ed.), *The Interpreter's Dictionary of the Bible*, vol. 4 (New York: Abingdon Press, 1962), 43-53
'Need Jesus have been Perfect?', in Sykes, S.W. & Clayton, J.P. (eds), *Christ, Faith and History* (Cambridge: CUP, 1972), 39-52
'The Use of the Fourth Gospel for Christology Today', in Lindars, B. & Smalley, S.S. (eds), *Christ and Spirit in the New Testament: Studies in honour of C.F.D. Moule* (Cambridge: CUP, 1973), 61-78
'Dunn on John', *Theology*, 85 (1982) 332-8
'Rudolf Bultmann: A View from England', in Jaspert, B. (ed.), *Rudolf Bultmanns Werk und Wirkung* (Darmstadt: Wissenschaftliche Buchgesellschaft, 1984), 149-54
'His Witness Is True': A Test of the Johannine Claim' in Bammel, E. & Moule, C.F.D. (eds), *Jesus and the Politics of His Day* (New York: CUP, 1984), 453-761

WORKS ON ROBINSON

Books and Articles

Butler, B.C. 'Notes and Comments: Bishop Robinson's Christ', *Heythrop Journal*, 14 (1973) 425-30

Butterworth, R. 'Bishop Robinson and Christology', *Religious Studies*, 11 (1975) 73-86

James, E. *A Life of Bishop John A.T. Robinson: Scholar, Pastor, Prophet* (London: Collins, 1987)

—— *God's Truth: Essays to Mark the Twenty-Fifth Anniversary of the Publication of 'Honest to God'* (London: SCM Press, 1988)

Kee, A. *The Roots of Christian Freedom: The Theology of John A.T. Robinson* (London: SPCK, 1988)

Knox, J. 'J.A.T Robinson and the Meaning of New Testament Scholarship', *Theology*, 92 (1989) 251-68

McBrien, R.P. *The Nature and Mission of the Church according to Bishop Robinson* (Rome: P.U.G., 1966)

Moloney, F.J. 'The Fourth Gospel's Presentation of Jesus as "The Christ" and John A.T. Robinson's Redating', *Downside Review*, 95 (1977) 239-53

Owen H.P. 'The Later Theology of Dr. J.A.T. Robinson', *Theology*, 73 (1970) 449-53

Tihon, P. 'J.A.T. Robinson et la recherche d'un Style, theologique pour notre temps', *Nouvelle Revue Theologie*, 91 (1968) 149-68

Wiles, M. 'John Robinson [on his death]', *Theology*, 37 (1984) 84-6

Selected reviews of books by Robinson

The Human Face of God, 1973: *Downside Review*, 91 (1973) 232-6 [Trethowan, I.]; *Gregorianum*, 56 (1975) 384-5 [O'Collins, G.]; *Journal of Biblical Literature*, 93 (1974) 137-9 [Fuller, R.H.]; *Journal of Religion*, 55 (1975) 483-5 [Braaten, C.E.]; *Journal of Theological Studies*, 25 (1974) 236-9 [Baelz, P.]; *Theology* , 76 (1973) 486-7 [Gunton, C.] *Redating the New Testament*, 1976: *Interpretation*, 32 (1978) 309-13 [Fitzmyer, J.A.]; *The Priority of John*, 1985: *The Journal of Theological Studies*, 39 (1988) 200-4; [Bammel, E.]; *Times Literary Supplement*, 4 October 1985; quoted by James, E., *A Life of Bishop John A.T Robinson*, 323, [Houlden, L.]

WORKS BY JOHN MACQUARRIE

Books

Twentieth-Century Religious Thought: The Frontiers of Philosophy and Theology, 1900-1960 (London: SCM Press; New York: Harper & Row, 1963). 2nd ed. with additional chapter, 1960-1970 (London: SCM Press, 1971). 3rd ed. with Postscript, 1960-1980 (London: SCM Press; New York: Charles Scribner's Sons, 1981). 4th ed. reworked to 1988 (London: SCM Press, 1988)

Principles of Christian Theology (New York: Charles Scribner's Sons, 1966). 2nd ed. revised and enlarged (New York: Charles Scribner's Sons; London: SCM Press, 1977)

Studies in Christian Existentialism (SCM Press, 1966)

Thinking about God (London: SCM Press, 1975)

The Humility of God (London: SCM Press, 1978)

In Search of Humanity (London: SCM Press; New York: Crossroad, 1982)

In Search of Deity: An Essay in Dialectical Theism, The Gifford Lectures delivered at the University of Saint Andrews in session 1983-8 (London: SCM Press, 1984)

Theology, Church and Ministry (London: SCM Press, 1986)

Jesus Christ in Modern Thought (London: SCM Press, Philadelphia: Trinity Press International, 1990)

Mary for All Christians (London: William Collins & Co., 1991)
Heidegger and Christianity (London: SCM Press, 1994)
The Mediators: Nine Stars in the Human Sky (London: SCM Press, 1995); published in the United States as *Mediators Between Human and Divine: From Moses to Muhammad* (New York: Continuum, 1996)
A Guide to the Sacraments (London: SCM Press, 1997)
Christology Revisited (London: SCM Press, 1998)
On Being a Theologian: Reflections at Eighty (London: SCM Press, 1999)

Articles

'A Dilemma in Christology', *Expository Times*, 76 (1965) 207-10
'The Pre-existence of Jesus Christ', *Expository Times*, 77 (1966) 109-202
'Schleiermacher Reconsidered', *Expository Times*, 80 (1968) 196-200
'Friedrich Daniel Ernst Scheiermacher', in Richardson, A. (ed.), *A Dictionary of Christian Theology* (London: SCM Press, 1969), 306-7
'The Nature of Theological Language', in Ramsey, A.M. (ed.), *Lambeth Essays on Faith* (London: SPCK, 1969), 1-10
'The Humanity of Christ', *Theology*, 74 (1971) 243-50
'Kenoticism Reconsidered', *Theology*, 77 (1974) 115-24
'Some Problems of Modern Christology', *Indian Journal of Theology*, 23 (1974) 155-75
'Whither Theology?', in Martin, C. (ed.), *Great Christian Centuries to Come* (London & Oxford: Mowbrays, 1974), 152-68
'Recent Thinking on Christian Beliefs: Christology', *Expository Times*, 88 (1976) 36-9
'Christianity without Incarnation? Some Critical Comments', in Green, M. (ed.), *The Truth of God Incarnate* (London: Hodder & Stoughton, 1977), 140-4. This article is a book review of Hick, J. (ed.), *The Myth of God Incarnate* (London: SCM Press, 1977), reprinted with alterations from *Theology* 80 (1977) 370-2
'Existentialism and Theological Method', *Communio*, 6 (1979) 5-15
'Foundation Documents of the Faith: III. The Chalcedon Definition', *Expository Times* 91 (1979-80) 68-72
'Tradition, Truth, and Christology', *Heythrop Journal*, 21 (1980) 365-75
'Truth in Christology', in Harvey, A.E. (ed.), *God-Incarnate: Story and Belief* (London: SPCK, 1981), 24-33
'The Concept of a Christ-Event', ibid., 69-80
'Existentialist Christology', in Berkley, R.E., & Edwards, R.A. (ed.), *Christological Perspectives* (New York: Pilgrim Press, 1982), 269-81
'Jesus Christus VI' and 'Jesus Christus VII', in Bael, H.R., et al. (eds), *Theologische Realenzyklopädie*, Band 17 (Berlin: Walter de Gruyter, 1988), 16-42 & 42-64
'Pluralism in Christology', in Jeanrond, W.G. & Rike, J.L. (eds), *Radical Pluralism and Truth. David Tracy and the Hermeneutics of Religion* (New York: Crossroad, 1991), 176-86
'Doctrinal Development: Searching for Criteria' in Coakley, S. & Palin, D. (eds), *The Making and Remaking of Christian Doctrine: Essays in Honour of Maurice Wiles* (Oxford: Clarendon Press, 1993), 161-76
'Current Trends in Anglican Christology', *Anglican Theological Review*, 79 (1997) 563-70

WORKS ON MACQUARRIE

Books and articles
Connell, P.J. *The Theology of John Macquarrie: Becoming as a Hermeneutical Principle* (Rome: PUG, 1989)

Hefling, C.C. (Jnr), 'Reviving Adamic Adoptionism: The Example of John Macquarrie' *Theological Studies*, 52 (1991) 476–94

Jenkins, D. *The Scope and Limits of John Macquarrie's Existentialist Theology* (Uppsala: Uppsala UP, 1987)

Kee, A. & Long, E.T. (eds), *Being and Truth. Essays in honour of John Macquarrie* (London: SCM Press, 1986)

Pratt, D. 'The Imago Dei in the Thought of John Macquarrie: A Reflection on John 10:10', *Asian Journal of Theology*, 3 (1989) 79–83

Selected reviews of books by Macquarrie

Studies in Christian Existentialism, 1966: *Journal of Theological Studies*, 18 (1967) 292–7 [MacKinnon, D.M.]; *Principles of Christian Theology*, 2nd ed., 1977: *Journal of Theological Studies*, 29 (1978) 617 [Kelly, J.N.D.]; *In Search of Humanity*, 1982; *Heythrop Journal*, 25 (1984) 373 [O'Donnell, J.]; *Jesus Christ in Modern Thought*, 1990: *Gregorianum*, 72 (1991) 582–3 [O'Donnell, J.]; *Horizons*, 19 (1929) 139–41 [Loewe, W.P.]; *Journal of Religion*, 73 (1992) 271–2 [Wilson, C.A]; *Journal of Theological Studies*, 42 (1991) 793–7 [Bauckham, R.B.]; *New Blackfriars*, 72 (1991) 203 [Owen, H.]; *Scottish Journal of Theology*, 44 (1991) 533–4 [Thatcher, A.]; *Theology*, 94 (1991) 211 [Logan, A.H.B.]

FURTHER WORKS

Books

Alston, W. *Divine Nature and Human Language* (Ithaca, New York: Cornell UP., 1989)

Andrewes, L. *Opuscula Quadem Posthuma* (Oxford: Library of Anglo-Catholic Theology, 1852).

Attridge, H.W. *The Epistle to the Hebrews* (Philadelphia: Fortress Press, 1989)

Baillie, D.M. *God Was in Christ*, 3rd ed. (London: Faber & Faber, 1961)

Balthasar, H.U. von *A Theology of History* (London: Sheed & Ward, 1963)

—— *Theo-Drama: Theological Dramatic Theory*, vols. 1–3 (San Francisco: Ignatius Press, 1988–1992)

Barrett, C.K. *Paul* (London: Geoffrey Chapman, 1994)

Barth, K. *Church Dogmatics*, vol. II/2 & vol IV/2 (Edinburgh: T. & T. Clark, 1957 & 1958)

—— *Protestant Theology in the Nineteenth Century* (London: SCM Press, 1972)

Bockmuehl, M. *This Jesus* (Edinburgh: T. & T. Clark, 1994)

Boethius Consolatio *Philosophiae*, Book V, Prose 6. For text see Rand, E.K. (ed.), in Stewart, H.F., Rand, E.K., & Tester, S.J. (eds), *Boethius: The Theological Tractates and the Consolation of Philosophy* (London: Heinemann, 1973)

Bonhoeffer, D. *Christology* (London: Fontana Books, 1971)

Bouyer, L. *Le Fils éternel* (Paris: Cerf, 1974)

—— *Le métier de théologien* (Paris: Editions France-Empire, 1979)

Brown, R. *The Gospel according to John* (I-XII) (London: Geoffrey Chapman, 1971)

—— *The Community of the Beloved Disciple* (London: Geoffrey Chapman, 1979)

—— *An Introduction to New Testament Christology* (London: Geoffrey Chapman, 1994)

—— *An Introduction to the New Testament* (New York: Doubleday, 1997)

Bultmann, R. *The Theology of the New Testament*, vol. 1 (London: SCM Press, 1952)

Chadwick, O. *Michael Ramsey: A Life* (Oxford: OUP, 1990)

Carnley, P. *The Structure of Resurrection Belief* (Oxford: Clarendon Press, 1987)

Conzelmann, H. *I Corinthians* (Philadelphia: Fortress Press, 1975)

Craddock, F.B. *The Pre-existence of Christ in the New Testament* (Nashville: Abingdon Press, 1968)

Creed, E.J. *The Divinity of Christ: A Study in the History of Christian Doctrine since Kant* (Cambridge: CUP, 1938)

Cross, F.L. & Livingstone, E.A. (eds), *The Oxford Dictionary of the Christian Church*, 3rd ed. (Oxford: OUP, 1997)

Cullmann, O. *The Christology of the New Testament* (London: SCM Press, 1959)

Darwin, C. *On the Origin of the Species by Means of Natural Selection* (London: Murraay, 1859)

Davies, B. *The Thought of Thomas Aquinas* (Oxford: Clarendon Press, 1992)

Davis, S (ed.), *Encountering Jesus* (Atlanta: John Knox Press, 1988)

—— *Risen Indeed: Making Sense of the Resurrection* (London: SPCK, 1993)

Denzinger, H. & Schönmetzer, A. (eds), *Enchiridion Symbolorum, definitionum et declarationum de rebus fidei et morum*, 25th ed. (Freiburg: Herder, 1973).

de Wulf, M. *Scholasticism Old and New: An Introduction to Scholastic Philosophy, Medieval and Modern* (Dublin: M.H. Gill & Son, 1907)

DuBose, W.P. *The Gospel according to Paul* (London: Longmans, Green & Co., 1907), reprinted in Armentraut, D.S., *A DuBose Reader* (Sewanee: University of the South, 1984)

Dunn, J.D.G. *Christology in the Making: An Inquiry into the Origins of the Doctrine of the Incarnation* (London: SCM Press, 1980). Revised 2nd ed. (London: SCM Press,1989); see the following reviews: *Journal of Biblical Literature*, 101 (1982) 609-12 [Holladay, C.R]; *Journal of Theological Studies*, 33 (1982) 258-63 [Moule, C.F.D.]; *Reformed Journal*, 32 (1982) 19-20 [Hagner, D.]; *Religious Studies Bulletin*, 3 (1983) 113 [Stead, C.]; *Scottish Journal of Theology*, 35 (1982) 362-4 [MacKinnon, D.M.]; *Theological Studies*, 42 (1981) 96 [Weinandy, T.]; *Virginia Seminary Bulletin*, December (1983) 29-39 [Hammerton-Kelly, R.G.]

—— *The Theology of Paul the Apostle* (Edinburgh: T. & T. Clark, Edinburgh, 1998); see the following reviews: *Catholic Biblical Quarterly* 61 (1999) 153-5 [Byrne, B]; *Louvain Studies* 24 (1999) 377-9 [Koperski, V.]; *The Tablet* (30 May, 1998) 709 [Harvey, A.E].

Dupuis, J. *Jesus Christ and His Spirit* (Bangalore: Theological Publications in India, 1977)

—— *Who Do You Say I am?* (Maryknoll, New York: Orbis Books, 1994)

—— *Towards a Christian Theology of Religious Pluralism* (Maryknoll, New York: Orbis Books, 1997)

Durand, G.M. (ed. and trans.), *Sources Chrétiennes*, 97 (Paris: Éditions du Cerf, 1964)

Edwards, D., *Leaders of the Church of England*, 1828-1978 (London: Hodder, 1978)

Emmet, D.M. *Whitehead's Philosophy of Organism* (London: Macmillan, 1932)

Evans, G.R. (ed.), *Christian Authority: Essays in honour of Henry Chadwick* (Oxford: Clarendon Press, 1988)

Fitzmyer, J.A. Romans, *The Anchor Bible* (New York: Doubleday, 1993)

—— *According to Paul* (New York, Paulist Press, 1993)

Furnish, V.P. *II Corinthians, The Anchor Bible* (Garden City, New York: 1984)

Galot, J. *La Personne du Christ* (Gembloux: Duculot; Paris: Lethielleux, 1969)

—— *Vers une nouvelle christologie* (Gembloux: Duculot; Paris: Lethielleux, 1971)

Gill, R. & Kendall, L. (eds), *Michael Ramsey as Theologian* (London: Darton, Longman & Todd, 1995)

Gore, C. *Lux Mundi* (London: John Murray, 1890)

Goulder, M. (ed.), *Incarnation and Myth: The Debate Continued* (London: SCM Press, 1979)

Green, M. (ed.), *The Truth of God Incarnate* (London: Hodder & Stoughton, 1977)

Grillmeier, A. *Christ in the Christian Tradition*, Part 1 (Atlanta: John Knox Press, 1987)

Hahn, F. *The Titles of Jesus in Christology* (London: Lutterworth Press, 1969)

Haight, R. *Jesus Symbol of God* (Maryknoll, New York: Orbis Books, 1999)

Hall, F.J., *The Incarnation* (London: Longmans, Green & Co., 1915)

Hammerton-Kelly, R.G. *Pre-Existence, Wisdom, and the Son of Man: A Study of the Idea of Pre-existence in the New Testament* (Cambridge: CUP, 1973)

Hanson, A.T. *Christ in the Old Testament* (London: SPCK, 1965)

—— *Grace and Truth. A Study of the Doctrine of the Incarnation* (London: SPCK, 1975)

—— *The Image of the Invisible God* (London: SCM Press, 1982)

—— *The Prophetic Gospel* (Edinburgh: T. & T. Clark, 1991).

Harvey, A.E. (ed.), *God Incarnate: Story and Belief* (London: SPCK, 1981)

—— *The Incarnation. Collected Essays in Christology* (Cambridge: C.U.P., 1987)

Hastings, A. *A History of English Christianity, 1920-1985* (London: Collins, 1986)

—— *Robert Runcie* (London: Mowbray, 1991)

Hebblethwaite, B.A. *The Incarnation* (Cambridge: CUP, 1987)

Hengel, M. *The Son of God* (London: SCM Press, 1976)

—— *The Johannine Question* (London: SCM Press, 1989)

Hick, J. (ed.), *The Myth of God Incarnate* (London: SCM Press, 1977)

Hodgson, L. *The Doctrine of the Trinity* (Digswell Place, Herts: Nisbet, 1943)

Hurst, L.D. & Wright, N.T (eds), *The Glory of Christ in the New Testamen: Studies in memory of G.B. Caird* (Oxford: Clarendon Press, 1987

Hylson–Smith, K. High *Churchmanship in the Church of England* (Edinburgh: T. & T. Clark, 1993)

Jewett, R. *Christology and Exegesis* (Decatur: Scholars Press, 1985); see review by Schweizer, E., *Theologische Literaturzeitung*, 111 (1986) 741-4

Käsemann, E. *The Testament of Jesus* (London: SCM Press, 1968)

Kasper, W. *Jesus the Christ* (London: Burns & Oates, 1976)

—— *The God of Jesus Christ* (London: SCM Press, 1984)

Kaufman, G.D. *Systematic Theology: A Historical Perspective* (New York: Scribner, 1968)

Knox, J. *The Humanity and the Divinity of Christ* (Cambridge: CUP., 1967)

Küng, H. *The Incarnation of God: An Introduction to Hegel's Theological Thought as Prolegomena to a Future Christology* (Edinburgh: T. & T. Clark, 1989)

Kuschel, K-J. *Born before All Time? The Dispute over Christ's Origin* (London: SCM Press, 1992); see review by O'Collins, G., *The Tablet* (August 14, 1993) 1045

Lampe, G.W.H. *God as Spirit* (Oxford: Clarendon Press, 1977)

Lawrence, N. *Alfred North Whitehead: A Primer of His Philosophy* (New York: Twayne Publishers, 1974)

Leftow, B. *Time and Eternity* (London: Cornell University Press, 1991).

Lofthouse, W.F. *The Father and the Son: A Study in Johannine Thought* (London: Student Christian Movement, 1934).

Lohmeyer, E. *Kyrios Jesus: Eine Untersuchung zu Phil. 2: 5-11* (Heidelberg: Carl Winter, 1928)

McAdoo, H.R., *The Spirit of Anglicanism: A Survey of Anglican Theological Method in the Seventeenth Century* (London: Adam & Charles Black, 1965)

—— *Anglican Heritage: Theology and Spirituality* (Norwich: Canterbury Press, Norwich, 1991)

McGrath, A.E. *The Making of Modern German Christology* (Oxford: Blackwell, 1986)

—— *The Renewal of Anglicanism* (London: SPCK, 1993)

Mackey, J. *The Problem of Religious Faith* (Dublin: Helicon, 1972)

Martin, R.P. *Carmen Christi: Philippians 2:5-11 in Recent Interpretation and in the Setting of Early Christian Worship* (Cambridge: CUP., 1967)

Morris, T.V. *The Logic of God Incarnate* (Ithaca, New York: Cornell UP, 1986)

—— (ed.), *The Concept of God* (Oxford: OUP., 1987)

—— *God and the Philosophers* (Oxford: OUP., 1994)

Morgan, R. (ed.), *The Religion of the Incarnation. Anglican Essays in commemoration of Lux Mundi* (Bristol: Bristol Classical Press, 1989)

Moule, C.F.D. *The Origin of Christology* (Cambridge: CUP., 1977)

Neufeld, K. *Adolf von Harnack – Theologie als Suche nach der Kirche* (Paderborn: Verlag Bonifacius-Druckerei, 1977)

Neuner, J. & Dupuis, J. (eds), *The Christian Faith in the Doctrinal Documents of the Catholic Church* (London: Collins, 1983)

Nichols, A. *A Grammar of Consent* (Edinburgh: T. & T. Clark, 1991)

—— *The Panther and the Hind* (Edinburgh: T. & T. Clark, 1993)

O'Collins, G. *Fundamental Theology* (London: Darton, Longman, & Todd, 1981)

—— *Interpreting Jesus* (London: Geoffrey Chapman, 1983)

—— *What Are They Saying about Jesus?* (New York/Ramsey, New Jersey: Paulist Press, 1977). Revised 2nd ed. (New York/Ramsey, New Jersey: Paulist Press, 1983)

—— *Christology* (Oxford: O.U.P, 1995)

—— *Focus on Jesus* (Leominster: Gracewing, 1996)

O'Collins, G. & Farrugia, E.J. *A Concise Dictionary of Theology* (New York, 1991)

O'Donnell, J. *The Mystery of the Triune God* (London: Sheed & Ward, 1988)

—— *Hans Urs von Balthasar* (London: Geoffrey Chapman, 1992)

—— *Introduction to Dogmatic Theology* (Casale Monferrato: Piemme, 1994)

Oppenheimer, H. *Incarnation and Immanence* (London: Hodder, 1973)

Padgett, A.G. *God, Eternity and the Nature of Time* (New York: St. Martin's Press, 1992)

Pittenger, W.N. *The Word Incarnate: A Study of the Doctrine of the Person of Christ* (London: Nisbet, 1959)

—— *Christology Reconsidered* (London: SCM Press, 1970)

Rahner, K. & Thüsing, W. *A New Christology* (London: Burns & Oates, 1980)

Rahner, K. & Vorgrimler, H. *A Dictionary of Theology* (New York: Crossroad, 1981)

Ramsey, A.M. *From Gore to Temple* (London: Longmans, 1960)

Raven, C.E. *Natural Religion and Christian Theology*, The Gifford Lectures, 1952, vol. 2 (Cambridge: CUP., 1952)

Relton, H.M. *Study in Christology* (London: SPCK, 1917)

Richard, L. *Christ the Self-Emptying of God* (New York, 1997)

Rowdon, H.H. (ed.), *Christ the Lord: Studies in Christology presented to D. Guthrie* (Leicester: Intervarsity Press, 1982)

Runcie, R *Authority in Crisis: An Anglican Response* (London: SCM Press, 1988)

Sanders, E.P. *Jesus and Judaism* (London: SCM Press, 1985)

Schoonenberg, P. *The Christ* (London: Sheed & Ward, 1972)

Schackenburg, R. *The Gospel according to John*, vols. 1 & 2 (London: Burns & Oates, 1968)

Scheeeben, M.J. *Nature and Grace* (Saint Louis: Herder & Co., 1954).

Schleiermacher, F.D.E. *The Christian Faith*, 2nd ed. (Edinburgh: T. & T. Clark, 1928)

—— *On Religion: Speeches to Its Cultured Despisers* (London: Harper & Row, 1958)

—— *The Life of Jesus*, ed. by Verheyden, J.C. (Philadelphia: Fortress Press, 1975)

Sellers, R.V. *The Council of Chalcedon* (London: SPCK, 1953)

Smedes, L.B. *The Incarnation: Trends in Modern Anglican Thought* (Amsterdam: Kok, 1953)

Strauss, D.F. *The Christ of Faith and the Jesus of History* (Philadelphia: Fortress Press, 1977)

Swinburne, R. *Revelation* (Oxford: Clarendon Press, 1991)

—— *The Christian God* (Oxford: Clarendon Press, 1994)

—— *Is There a God?* (Oxford: OUP, 1996)

Sykes, S.W. *The Integrity of Anglicanism* (London: Mowbrays, 1978)

—— (ed.), *Authority in the Anglican Communion* (Toronto: Anglican Book Centre, 1987)

—— *Unashamed Anglicanism* (Darton, Longman & Todd, 1995)

Sykes, S.W. & Clayton, I.P. (eds)., *Christ, Faith and History* (Cambridge: CUP, 1972)

Teilhard de Chardin, P. *Hymn of the Universe* (London: Collins, 1970)

Thüsing, W. *Die neutestamentlichen Theologien und Jesus Christus*, Band 1 (Düsseldorf: Patmos, 1981)

Torrance, T.F. Space, *Time and Resurrection* (Edinburgh: Hansel Press, 1976)

van Buren, P. *Theological Explorations* (London: SCM Press, 1968)

—— *The Secular Meaning of the Gospel* (London, 1963)

Vidler, A. (ed.), *Soundings: Essays Concerning Christian Understanding* (Cambridge: CUP., 1962)

Weinandy, T. *Does God Change? The Word's Becoming in the Incarnation* (Petersham, MA: St Bede's Publications, 1985)

—— *The Father's Spirit of Sonship* (Edinburgh: T.& T. Clark, 1995)

Welch, P.A. *Protestant Theology in the Nineteenth Century* (New Haven: Yale UP, 1985)

Welsby, P.A. *A History of the Church of England, 1945-1980* (Oxford: O.U.P., 1984)

Wilkinson, A. *The Community of the Resurrection. A Centenary History* (London: SCM Press, 1992)

Wright, N.T. *The Climax of the Covenant* (Edinburgh: T. & T. Clark, 1991)

Articles

Amerio, R. 'Probabile fonte della nozione boeziana di eternitè, *Filosofia*, 1 (1950) 365-73

Attridge, H.W. 'Hebrews, Epistle to the, in Freedman, D.N. (ed. in chief), *The Anchor Bible Dictionary*, vol. 3 (New York: Doubleday, 1992), 97-105

Basevi, C. 'La Cristologia de G.W.H. Lampe o una cristologia en disolución', *Scripta Theologica*, 12 (1980) 483-96

Betz, H.D. 'Hellenism', *ABD*, vol. 3, 127-35

Bockmuehl, M. '"The Form of God" (Phil 2:6): Variations on a Theme of Jewish Mysticism', *Journal of Theological Studies*, 48 (1997) 1-23

Brinkman, B.R. 'Notes and Comments on Christ and the Church: Macquarrie, Schillebeeckx and Moltmann', *Heythrop Journal*, 32 (1991) 539-43

Bultmann, R. 'Foreword' to Macquarrie, J., *An Existentialist Theology*, vii-viii

Byrne, B. 'The Letter to the Philippians', in Brown, R., et al. (eds), *The New Jerome Biblical Commentary* (Englewood Cliffs, New Jersey: Prentice Hall, 1990), 791-7

—— 'Christ's Pre-Existence in Pauline Soteriology', *Theological Studies*, 58 (1997) 308-30

Carey, G.L. 'Anglicanism' in McBrien, Richard P. (general ed.), *The HarperCollins Encyclopedia of Catholicism* (New York: HarperCollins, 1995), 49.

Caird, G.B. 'The Development of the Doctrine of Christ in the New Testament' in Pittenger, N. (ed.), *Christ for Us Today* (London: SCM Press, 1968), 66-81

Cranfield, B. 'Some Comments on Professor J.D.G. Dunn's Christology in the Making with Special Reference to the Evidence of the Epistle to the Romans' in Hurst, L.D. & Wright, N.T. (eds), *The Glory of God in the New Testament* (Oxford: Clarendon Press, 1987), 267-80

Dunn, J.D.G. 'Christology', *ABD*, vol. 1, 979-1

Dupuis, J. 'On Some Recent Christological Literature', *Gregorianum*, 69 (1988) 713-40

Fitzgerald, J.T. 'Philippians, Epistle to the', *ABD*, vol. 5, 318-26

Fitzgerald, P. Stump and Kretzmann on Time', *Journal of Philosophy*, 82 (1985) 260-9

Fitzmyer, J.A. 'Two Views of New Testament Interpretation: Popular and Technical', *Interpretation*, 32 (1978) 309-13

—— 'Paul', *NJBC*, 1329-37

—— 'Pauline Theology', *NJBC*, 1382-416

Flesseman-van Leer, E. 'Christologische Discussie in Engeland', *Nederlands Theologisch Tijdschrift*, 33 (1979) 125-38

Galvin, J.P. 'Jesus Christ', in Fiorenza, F.S. & Galvin, J.P. (eds), *Systematic Theology: Roman Catholic Perspectives* (Minneapolis: Fortress Press, 1991), 251-324

Gill, R. 'Michael Ramsey: A Theological Speculation', in Gill, R. & Kendall, L. (eds), *Michael Ramsey as Theologian* (London: Darton, Longman & Todd, 1995)

Glasson, T.F. 'Two Notes on the Philippians Hymn', *New Testament Studies*, 21 (1974-1975) 133-39

Hannaford, R., 'The Legacy of Liberal Anglican Theology', *Theology*, 103 (2000) 89-96

Hardy, D.W 'Theology through Philosophy' in Ford, D. (ed.), *The Modern Theologians*, vol. 2, 1st ed. (Oxford: Basil Blackwell, 1989), 30-71; and the new revised article in the single volume 2nd ed. (Oxford: Basil Blackwell, 1997), 252-85

Klein, L. 'Anglikanische Theologie im 20. Jahrhundert', in Vorgrimler, H. & Gucht, R.V. (eds), *Bilanz der Theologie Im 20. Jahrhundert*, vol. 2 (Freiburg, Basel, Wien: Herder, 1969), 124-53

Leeming, B. 'Reflections on English Christology', in Grillmeier, A. & Bacht, H. (eds), *Das Konzil von Chalkedon*, vol. 3 (Würzburg: Echter Verlag, 1954), 696–718

Manchester, P. 'Eternity', in Eliade, M. (ed. in chief), *The Encyclopedia of Religion*, vol. 5 (London: Collier Macmillan Publishers, 1987), 167–71

Moule, C.F.D. 'The Manhood of Jesus in the New Testament', in Sykes, S.W. & Clayton, J.P. (eds), *Christ, Faith and History* (Cambridge: CUP., 1972)

Moloney, F.J. 'Johannine Theology', *NJBC*, 1417–26

O'Collins, G. 'Fundamental Theology' in Richardson, A. & Bowden, J. (eds), *A New Dictionary of Christian Theology* (London: SCM Press, 1983), 224

—— 'Jesus', in *The Encyclopedia of Religion*, vol. 8, 15–28

—— 'Christ, Pre-existence of', in *The New Catholic Encyclopedia, vol. 18, Supplement, 1977–1988* (Washington, DC: Catholic University Press of America), 92–3

—— 'Paschal Mystery II: The Resurrection', in Latourelle, R. & Fisichella, R. (eds), *Dictionary of Fundamental Theology* (New York: Crossroad, 1994), 769–76

Quinton, A. 'British Philosophy', in Edwards, P. (ed. in chief), *The Encyclopedia of Philosophy*, vol. 1 (London: Collier Publishers, 1967), 369–96

Rahner, K. 'Current Problems in Christology', *Theological Investigations*, vol. 1 (London: Darton, Longman & Todd, 1961), 149–200

—— 'On the Theology of the Incarnation', *Theological Investigations*, vol. 4 (London: Darton, Longman & Todd, 1966), 105–20

—— 'Christology Within an Evolutionary View of the World', *Theological Investigations*, vol. 5 (London: Darton, Longman & Todd, 1966), 157–92

—— 'Dogmatic Reflections on the Knowledge and Selfconsciousness of Christ', ibid., 193–215

—— 'The Two Basic Types of Christology', *Theological Investigations*, vol. 17 (London: Darton, Longman & Todd, 1981), 213–3

Sabourin, L. 'Christ's Pre-existence', *Religious Studies Bulletin*, 4 (1984) 22–9

Schilson, A, 'Christologie', *Lexikon für Theologie und Kirche*, vol 2, 3rd ed (Freiburg etc.: Herder, 1994), 1164–74

Sharkey, M. (ed.), 'Selected Questions in Christology' & 'Theology, Christology, Anthropology', in *International Theological Commission. Texts and Documents*, 1964–1985 (San Francisco: Ignatius Press, 1989), 185–206; 207–24

Shaw, D.W.D., 'Personality, Personal and Person', in Kee, A. & Long, E.T. (eds), *Being and Truth: Essays in honour of John Macquarrie* (London: SCM Press, 1986), 155–67

St John, H., 'Authority in the Anglican Mind', *Blackfriars*, 39 (1958) 242–60.

Stump, E. & Kretzmann, N. 'Eternity', *Journal of Philosophy*, 78 (1981) 429–58

Sykes, S.W. 'The Strange Persistence of Kenotic Christology', in Kee, A., & Long, E.T. (eds), *Being and Truth. Essays in honour of John Macquarrie* (London: SCM Press, 1986), 349–75

—— 'Theology through History', in Ford, D. (ed.), *The Modern Theologians*, 2nd ed. (Oxford: Basil Blackwell, 1997), 229–51

Trethowan, I. 'Christology Again', *Downside Review*, 95 (1977) 1–10

Uullrich, L. 'Preexistence of Christ', in Beinert, W. & Fiorenza, F.S. (eds), *Handbook of Catholic Theology* (New York: Crossroad, 1995) 543–5

van Peursen, C. 'Man and Reality – The History of Human Thought', *Student World*, 56 (1963) 13–21; reprinted in J. Bowden & J. Richmond (eds), *A Reader in Contemporary Thought* (London: SCM Press, 1971), 115–26.

Wanamaker, C.A., 'Philippians 2:6–11: Son of God or Adamic Christology', *New Testament Studies*, 33 (1987) 179–93

Index